MW00768779

30 DAYS TO THE SAT

Rajiv N. Rimal, Ph.D.
and
Peter Z Orton, Ph.D.

Macmillan • USA

First Edition

Macmillan General Reference
A Simon & Schuster Macmillan Company
1633 Broadway
New York, NY 10019-6785

An Arco Book

Manufactured in the United States of America

10 9 8 7 6 5 4 3 2

ISBN: 0–02–861262–0

Introduction

This book is designed to help you master the SAT in just 30 days. You will learn about important general test strategies. And you will be introduced to dozens of specific verbal and math strategies designed to make you a smart test taker. You will also find two full-length tests in this book—tests that have been modeled after the real thing. To get the most out of this book, we suggest that you follow the 30-Day program closely. Depending upon your schedule and how quickly you work, you will need to set aside 30 to 60 minutes each day. Here is the program.

THE 30-DAY PROGRAM

About the Authors

Rajiv N. Rimal, Ph.D., and Peter Z Orton, Ph.D., have a combined twenty years experience teaching SAT preparation programs for the California State Universities. Together they wrote and produced "TEAM SAT," a multimedia, interactive CD-ROM program (Zelos Digital Learning) which was awarded the "Best of Show" prize at the International Interactive Computer Society's 1995 Summit Awards and the Gold Prize in Interactive Education at the 1995 CINDY Awards.

Dr. Rimal is an Assistant Professor of Speech Communication at Texas A&M University, where he writes, teaches, and conducts research on health and communication.

Dr. Orton is a producer of new media at Harvard Business School Publishing and co-author of fourteen test-preparation textbooks.

Test Structure and Strategies

Day 1

Get to Know the SAT

Assignments for Today:

1. Learn the structure of the SAT.
2. Learn how the SAT is scored.
3. Call schools you want to apply to.

THE STRUCTURE OF THE SAT

Sections of the Test

The SAT consists of six sections that count toward your score and one "equating section" that does not count toward your score. The seven sections are as follows:

1.	Math	—	30 minutes
2.	Math	—	30 minutes
3.	Math	—	15 minutes
4.	Verbal	—	30 minutes
5.	Verbal	—	30 minutes
6.	Verbal	—	15 minutes
7.	Equating section	—	30 minutes

Note: These seven sections can be in any order, not necessarily in the order shown above.

The "equating section" can be either a math section or a verbal section. It is 30 minutes long and it can come at any point in the test. The "equating section" is used by the testmakers to check their own test questions. The points earned in this section do not count toward your final score. However, you will *not* know which 30-minute section is the one that doesn't count.

During the time allotted for a section, you can work only in that section. You are not permitted to move from section to section, even if you finish a section before time is called. You can go to the next section only when told to do so, and you can never return to a previous section. But you can move around within the one section you are working in.

TYPES OF QUESTIONS ON THE TEST

Verbal (approximately 78 questions)

There are three types of verbal questions:

1. Reading: Read a passage, and answer questions.

   Total questions – 40

2. Sentence Completion: Read a sentence that has one or more blanks, and choose the word or words that fit the meaning of the sentence.

   Total questions = 19

3. Analogy: Figure out the relationship between two words, and select the choice that has the same relationship.

   Total questions = 19

Math (approximately 60 questions)

There are three types of math questions:

1. Problem Solving: Standard multiple-choice math questions, with five answer choices.

   Total questions = 35

2. Quantitative Comparison: Compare two quantities and determine which is greater, or if they are equal, or if there's no way to determine the relationship. Quantitative Comparison questions have only four answer choices.

   Total questions = 15

3. Grid-in: Typical math questions. No answer choices are provided. You have to come up with the right answer.

   Total questions = 10

Scoring of the SAT

You will get two scores, one for math and one for verbal. Each score ranges from 200 (no questions answered correctly) to 800 (all, or nearly all, questions answered correctly). The "median" score is 500, meaning that about half the students taking the test score higher than 500, and half score lower than 500.

You'll get your scores in the mail four to six weeks after you take the test.

Call Your Schools

You probably have a number of schools that you are interested in attending. Call them today, and find out how much you need to score on the SAT. Schools can often give you the average SAT scores of their incoming students. You can use this information to set your own personal SAT goals.

Day 2

Test Strategies

Assignment for Today:

Learn seven important test-taking strategies.

TEST STRATEGY 1.

Don't Get Stuck

The most important thing to know for your test is this: Don't get stuck. You're not expected to get all the questions right on the test. In fact, if you can answer just *half* the questions right, you'll get an above-average score! That means when you hit a question that's a killer, just guess and move on.

Find the questions that you can do or have a shot at. For the others, just guess and move on. So remember:

If a question's do-able, work it. Circle the answer in your test booklet and then darken the proper space on your answer sheet.

As soon as you realize a question's a killer, put a question mark beside it, and fill in a guess answer.

If a question will take a lot of time, even if you can do it, mark it, take a guess at the answer, and come back to it later if you have time.

TEST STRATEGY 2.

Zap the Losers

Do you know what the directions on your test say? They ask you to choose not the *right* answer, but the *best* answer.

Why "best"? Because the "right" answer may not even be in the choices. So sometimes you've got to settle for the best of what they offer, and the best may not be great.

Suppose you read a passage, and it's all about how to improve your social life in high school. One question might go something like this:

> Which of the following is the most appropriate title for this passage?

Now you're thinking the title ought to be something like "How to improve a high school social life," or "How high school students can improve their social life," or "How a high school social life can be improved," or some arrangement of those words.

But on the SAT, there's a good chance that none of these will be in the choices.

Let's look at the choices:

(A) Improving your college social life
(B) Improving your social life in school
(C) Improving your test scores in high school
(D) Improving the quality of life in high school
(E) How to get backstage concert passes

Choice (A) has one key word wrong: college. The passage was about the social life of high school students, so the word "college" makes this choice off-topic and wrong. At this point take your pencil and "zap (A)"—cross it off in your test booklet.

Now to choice (B). This says, "Improving your social life in school." To be perfect, it should read "Improving your social life in high school." Just the word "school," by itself, is too general. But so far it's better than choice (A), and it might be the best answer of all. So quickly draw a question mark and keep going.

Choice (C) is highly commendable, but off topic. Knock it out.

Choice (D), "Improving the quality of life in high school," is also not perfect. You'd like it to read "Improving the quality of social life in high school." Here you have "high school," but you don't have social life. So what do you do? It's too general, but it's possible, so consider it. Put a question mark beside it.

Choice (E) would certainly improve your high school social life, but it's off-topic. Zap it!

So now you're down to two possible answers.

Compare choice (B) against choice (D) to find the better one. But even if you can't find the one winner, you've narrowed five choices down to just two, so take your best guess and move on.

Zapping wrong choices not only saves time, but helps you get more questions right.

So remember: Zap the losers and come out a winner.

Test Strategy 3.

Always Guess

What if you can't do a problem? Should you leave it blank, or should you take a guess? The SAT people say that there's a "penalty" for guessing. This simply means that if you get a question wrong, they'll deduct a fraction from your score. However, you should know that if you guess an answer, even if you have no idea what the question was about, the probability of your losing a point is the same as the probability of your gaining a point.

So, our suggestion is that you always guess. If you take a guess, you have a chance of getting it right. But if you leave a blank, you get nothing.

And, if you can knock out even one answer choice and guess from the other choices, you'll have a better chance of getting it right. So at least take a guess. Never leave a blank.

Here's another reason why you should not leave a question unanswered. If you skip questions and leave blanks on your answer sheet, there's a chance that you'll darken the wrong spaces. Keeping track of where the answers go is a headache. And it's confusing. But if you fill in an answer for every question, even with guess answers, you won't make this serious error. And you can always erase an answer if you need to.

Test Strategy 4.

Answer What's Asked

One way people lose points on the test is that they know how to work a problem, but they don't read the question correctly. This should *never* happen to you. Take a look at this question.

If $3n - 7 = 2$, what is $5n$?

(A) 3
(B) 6
(C) 9
(D) 12
(E) 15

You might answer this question this way:

$$
\begin{aligned}
3n &= 2 + 7 \\
3n &= 9 \\
n &= \frac{9}{3} \\
n &= 3
\end{aligned}
$$

At this point, you might think (A) is your answer, because n equals 3. But the answer is *not* 3, because the question asks for the value of $5n$, not n. You have to take the value of n (3) and multiply by 5 to get choice (E), 15.

This might look simple enough, but imagine you're taking your test. You're under time pressure, you've been working for several hours under severe stress, your concentration's starting to flag, and the person sitting behind you is tapping his pencil and sniffling.

Under such conditions it's easy to misread the question and answer the wrong thing. So what can you do?

Here's something that can help.

As you read a problem, identify what you finally have to solve for, and circle it! Circling helps you focus on your final goal. And it helps you avoid the common misreading errors that are built into the test.

You should also use this circling strategy on the reading questions of your test. What would you circle in this typical reading question:

> "With which of the following would the author disagree?"

"Disagree" or "author disagree" is really the heart of the question. You're looking for an answer that's the opposite of the author's point of view. If you circle "author disagree" you will avoid misreading the question.

Circling your "goal" is a super strategy to make sure you answer what's asked. The worst thing that can happen on your test is knowing how to work a problem, spending time working it, and yet getting it wrong because you answered the wrong thing. Circling your "goal" helps you get those questions right.

TEST STRATEGY 5.

Know Where the Question Lives

Most question sets on the test start easy and get harder. Why is this important to know? And how can it help you?

The first few questions in each set are very easy, almost obvious. The rest are of medium difficulty, except for the last two or three which are very difficult, if not downright tricky.

So what do you do? On the first few questions, you're probably safe choosing the obvious answer. But on a question near the end, you should be wary of the fast answer because it is probably wrong.

Here's how this works. Suppose the last math question in a section goes like this:

> On a thermometer, R is 7 degrees away from P, and P is at 5 degrees. What is the reading at R?
>
> (A) 12°
>
> (B) 7°
>
> (C) –2°
>
> (D) –2° or 12°
>
> (E) None of these

Remember, this is a question at the end of the math section. So what is the correct answer?

The fast answer here is (A), 12°. But (A) is only partially correct. Yes, R could be at 12°, since 12 is 7 degrees higher than 5. But what if R is 7 degrees lower than P? R could be at either 12° or –2°. So the more thoughtful—and correct—answer is (D).

Use this strategy on all math questions and on the sentence completion and analogy questions. The first few of each will be easy, and the last few will be very tricky.

Don't use this strategy for the critical reading questions, as these are scrambled in order of difficulty.

Remember, knowing where questions live can be important to you when you take the test.

TEST STRATEGY 6.

Know the I–II–III Strategy

A few questions on your test may use Roman numerals. These questions look something like this:

XXXXXXXXXXXX XXXXXXXXXXXXXXX XXXXX XXXXXXX XXXXXXXX XXXXXXXX XXXXXX XXXXXXXXXXX XXXXXXXXX?

I. XXXXXX
II. XXXXXX
III. XXXXXX

(A) I only
(B) II only
(C) III only
(D) I and II only
(E) I, II, and III

Believe it or not, these questions are easier than the regular questions—the ones without Roman numerals. Let's look at an example.

Sal, Pat, and Chris run in a race with ten other people. Sal finished somewhere ahead of Chris. Which of the following must be true?

I. Sal did not finish in last place.
II. Chris finished in first place.
III. Pat finished in second place.

(A) I only
(B) II only
(C) III only
(D) I and II only
(E) I, II, and III

Which do you think is the right answer? The question asks, "What is true?" We know that Sal finished somewhere ahead of Chris. So let's see which of the Roman numerals are true.

Since Sal finished ahead of Chris, Roman numeral I is true: Sal did *not* finish in last place. This tells you that the correct answer must include numeral I. At this point, you can knock out choices (B) and (C) because they do not include numeral I. With your pencil strike out (B) and (C).

Now look at numeral II: Chris finished in first place. Since Sal finished ahead of Chris, we know Chris could not have finished first. This Roman numeral is false. So you should take your pencil and strike out all remaining answer choices that include numeral II. This means you can knock out choices (D) and (E).

Immediately you can see that only one choice remains—choice (A)—and so that has to be the right answer. Notice that you didn't even have to try the third Roman numeral. You will not always be this lucky, but you can see how this strategy helps you beat the test.

TEST STRATEGY 7.

Don't Read the Directions

Here's a quick tip that will save you time, and because it saves you time it will help you get a few more questions right: **Do not waste time reading directions on your test.** The more time you spend reading the directions, the less time you have to answer questions. So what should you do? Work through this program. By the time you finish, you'll know the directions for every question type inside and out. And you'll also know which strategies and tips to use for which questions.

So when your test day comes and the proctor tells you to open your test booklet and begin section one, you can go directly to the questions because you will already know the directions.

Here's a quick list of question types for your review:

Verbal Section

1. Critical reading: Read the passage and answer questions based on what's stated or implied in the passage.
2. Sentence completions: Select the word or words that best complete the sentence from the list of choices.
3. Analogies: Find the relationship between the two words in the question and look for the answer choice that has the same relationship.

Math Section

1. Problem solving: Solve the problem and find the answer from among the five choices given.
2. Quantitative comparison: Compare the two quantities given in Column A and Column B and choose

   (A) if Column A is greater than Column B
   (B) if Column B is greater than Column A
   (C) if Column A is equal to Column B
   (D) if the relationship cannot be determined based on the information given.

Do not choose (E). There is no such choice in this question type.

3. Grid-ins: Work the problem and supply your own answer.

Instant Replay: Test Strategies

1. Don't get stuck.
2. Zap the losers.
3. Always guess.
4. Answer what's asked.
5. Know where the problem lives.
6. Know the I–II–III Strategy.
7. Don't read the directions.

Day 3

Verbal Strategies: Critical Reading

Assignment for Today:

Learn Critical Reading strategies and question types.

The reading part of the verbal section takes a lot of time. You've got to read some long passages and answer questions based on them. In the 30-minute verbal sections it's best to do the reading questions last.

What else should you know about the critical reading parts? Here are some good tips.

Reading Strategy 1.

Read the Interesting Passages First

One passage may be more interesting to you than another. If so, start with the one you find more interesting. You will have a better chance of getting more questions right. But if you read passages out of order, be sure to put your answers in the right places on your answer sheet.

Reading Strategy 2.

Use Only What You Read

The reading questions test only what's *in* the passage, so don't bring in any outside information. Use *only* what's stated or implied *in* the passage, even if you know a lot about the topic.

Reading Strategy 3.

Let the Paragraphs Help

A reading passage can seem really long. But the author has already broken it down for you into manageable pieces—the paragraphs. Don't try to rush through from the first word to the last word. Instead, read paragraph by paragraph. After reading the first paragraph, take a quick mental breath, and think to yourself, "What, briefly, was *that* paragraph about?" Then read the next paragraph and do that again. And then the one after that. When you finish the passage, what have you done? You've summarized all the important ideas in the passage.

Reading Strategy 4.

Read and Mark

Use your pencil and mark the passage as you read. If you think something's important, circle it. If something's unusual or troublesome, mark that too. But don't mark so much that you can't find anything. And don't let your marking slow you down. Keep moving ahead, like a shark.

READING STRATEGY 5.
Make a Movie in Your Head

What if you're reading a passage and nothing is sinking in? The clock's ticking and you have no idea of what you just read. This happens to all of us. If it happens to you, the best thing to do is to "make a movie" in your head. Believe it or not, you understand better if you visualize what you read. Don't memorize, just visualize. As you read the passage, form interesting pictures in your head.

READING STRATEGY 6.
Know the Different Types of Reading Questions

Here are the most common types of reading questions. Familiarize yourself with these questions so that when you see them on the test, you'll know what they are asking you to do.

Type 1. Main Idea

For each passage you'll be asked to determine the main idea. Sometimes the question says just that: "What is the main idea of the passage?" Or it can use other words, such as, "What is the most appropriate title for this passage?" or "What is the author's central argument?" or "The passage is primarily concerned with the subject of . . ." Each of these questions asks the same thing—what is the main theme of the passage? The correct answer to a "main idea" question isn't necessarily found in the first sentence or the last. These may, or may not, express the "main idea." But the main idea is always a theme that runs through most, if not all, of the paragraphs.

Type 2. Vocabulary

Some questions ask you to define words or phrases from the passage. To do this, you'll have to look back to where the word was used and see what it means as it's used in that particular sentence. For example, the question might say, "The word "estate" in line 46 most nearly means . . ." Depending on the sentence, "estate" could mean someone's property, someone's status, a piece of land, or even an inheritance. To figure out which sense of the word is meant, start from a little before line 46, and read through that line and past it. You'll then have a handle on what the author meant by that term. Then answer the question.

Type 3. Specific Information

Some questions ask about specific information from the passage. For example, "The passage mentions which of the following as important to the success of a feature film?" Or, "The author discusses the hobbies of which Presidents?" Or, "The incident in lines 21–35 resulted in which of the following?" If you can answer these from what you remember having read in the passage, great! Otherwise, simply go back to the paragraph, find that part, and re-read enough to find the answer.

Type 4. Author's Point-of-View

Another type of question asks you to determine the author's tone or point of view. For example, "The author's attitude toward large dogs is . . ." Or, "The author believes strongly that . . ." Or, "The author would most likely agree with which of the following?" As you read, small details should help you become aware of how the author of the passage feels about the topic presented. Is the author in favor . . .? or opposed . . .? or neutral . . .? or sarcastic . . .? or doubtful . . .? or excited . . .? And so on.

Type 5. Reasoning

And finally, questions also ask you to apply or interpret what you just read. For example, "The author most likely describes the traffic on the highway in order to . . ." Or, "The reference to loud chewing is inappropriate as an argument for gum control because . . ." Or, "The description of George Washington's cow serves to . . ." Reasoning questions are usually the toughest because the answers won't be stated directly in the passage. You have to read beneath the surface. But you still can't bring in your own information. Use only what the author implies. It's tough, but with practice you can do it.

Instant Replay: Critical Reading

1. Read the interesting passages first.
2. Use only what you read.
3. Let the paragraphs help.
4. Read and mark.
5. Make a movie in your head.
6. Know the different types of reading questions.

Day 4

Verbal Strategies: Analogies

Assignment for Today:

Learn analogy strategies and question types.

One of the sections on your test is called analogies. They look something like this:

STEM:WORDS::
(A) first pair
(B) second pair
(C) third pair
(D) fourth pair
(E) fifth pair

ANALOGY STRATEGY 1.
Figure Out the Relationship Between the Stem Words

The analogy questions follow a simple rule. Find the relationship between the stem words, then find that same relationship in one of the choices. Let's try one.

SKYSCRAPER:SHACK::
(A) elevator:escalator
(B) house:building
(C) village:town
(D) jetliner:biplane
(E) chimney:fireplace

The stem words are skyscraper and shack. What's the relationship between skyscraper and shack? A *skyscraper* is a large, modern structure. A *shack* is a small structure. So the relationship is: The first word is a large, modern version of the second word.

ANALOGY STRATEGY 2.
Find the Same Relationship Between the Words in One of the Answer Choices

Once you know how the stem words are related, your next job is to find the one answer choice that best matches this relationship. Let's try the answer choices above one at a time.

Choice (A): Is the first word, *elevator*, a large, modern version of the second word, *escalator*? Obviously not. So knock this choice out.

Choice (B): Is a *house* a large, modern version of a *building*? Not at all. So cross out this choice.

Choice (C): Is a *village* a large, modern version of a *town*? Of course not. So eliminate this choice.

Choice (D): Is a *jetliner* a large, modern version of a *biplane*? Yes. A jetliner is a large, modern aircraft.

A biplane is one of those small double-wing planes with two seats. So the relationship in this choice matches the relationship of the stem words. The first word is a large, modern version of the second word. Looks like you have a winner. Mark it, but let's look at the remaining choice, just in case.

Choice (E): Is a *chimney* a large, modern version of a *fireplace*? Well, a chimney is a part of a fireplace, not a modern version of it. Even though this choice has something to do with buildings, its relationship doesn't match, so knock it out.

Did you notice something? The stem words are about buildings, but the correct answer has nothing to do with buildings. You're looking for same relationships, not same categories. The first word was a-modern-and-big "whatever the second word was."

ANALOGY STRATEGY 3.

Consider Starting with the Second Stem Word

Sometimes it's easier to define the relationship between the stem words if you start with the second word in the pair instead of the first one. Let's look at another analogy question to see how this strategy works.

SPORT:SOCCER::

(A) fish:river

(B) volleyball:net

(C) field:fun

(D) stadium:game

(E) literature:sonnet

Here it's easier to say, "Soccer is a kind of sport." The second word is a specific type of the first word. Can you find the choice where the second word is a specific type of the first word?

The correct answer is choice (E): A sonnet is a type of literature. ***Remember:*** Whatever order you choose to use in the stem words must be *the same order* that you use in the choices.

ANALOGY STRATEGY 4.

Use the Answer Choices to Help You Determine the Part of Speech of the Stem Words

Sometimes you need to know the part of speech of the stem words in order to determine their meaning and figure out how they are related. For example, suppose you have this question.

SPRING:RAIN::

(A) suitor:gifts

(B) pollen:bee

(C) farm:tractor

(D) automobile:traffic

(E) requirement:limitation

The stem words are puzzling. Is *spring* the action-verb meaning *jump* or *bounce*? Or is *spring* a thing, the noun that means the season? Or the noun that means the coiled piece of metal that you find in mattresses and watches? One way to find out is to look at the answer choices. Are the first words in the answer choices verbs or nouns?

Farm can be either a verb or a noun, but the other first words are nouns. So from that you know that all the first words are nouns, including *spring* and *farm*. We don't know what the second words are yet. But now that you know the stem word *spring* is a noun—not the verb that means *to jump*—can you find the answer to this question?

Choice (A) is the right answer. Spring, the season, brings rain, in the same way that a suitor brings gifts.

Questions like that one can be tricky if a word has more than one meaning. If you try one meaning and have no luck, then try another meaning and see if that one works. But once you know a word is, say, a noun, try only different noun meanings, not meanings of verbs or adjectives.

Analogy Strategy 5.
Make Sure You Know the Most Common Analogy Relationships

Here are the eleven most common SAT analogy relationships:

1. Type of.

SOCCER:SPORT:: You saw one like this before, remember? *Soccer* is a type of sport. Here's another example: JAYWALK:MISDEMEANOR:: *Jaywalk* is a type of misdemeanor, or minor crime.

2. Definition.

PROCRASTINATOR:DELAY:: A *procrastinator* is someone who delays. Or you could say, *delay* is what a procrastinator does. Whatever order you use for the stem words is the order you must use for each of the choices.

3. Opposites.

STARVATION:BINGEING:: *Starvation* is the opposite of *bingeing*.

4. Lack of.

PAUPER:MONEY:: A *pauper* lacks *money*. The first word lacks the second word.

5. Same.

PERSUASIVE:CONVINCING:: Someone who is *persuasive* is also *convincing*; the two words are synonyms.

6. Extremes.

HOT:SCALDING:: The second word is the *extreme* of the first word.

7. Part to whole.

PLATOON:SOLDIER:: The second word is *part* of the first word.

8. Use.

GILLS:BREATHING:: *Gills* are used for *breathing*. The first word is used for the purpose of the second word.

9. Place.

DESERT:OASIS:: The second word is located *in* the first word.

10. Sign of.

SNARL:ANGER:: The first word is a *sign* of the second word.

11. Job-related pairs.

Analogies that have to do with jobs or work also appear on your test. For example:

a) SURGERY:INCISION:: An *incision* is performed in *surgery*. The second word is something that is done during the first word.

b) SCALPEL:SURGERY:: A *scalpel*—which is a doctor's cutting tool—is used in *surgery*. The first word is a tool used for doing the second word.

c) CONSTRUCTION:CARPENTER:: The second word is someone who performs the first word.

Analogy Strategy 6.
Practice With Lots of Analogy Questions

The best thing you can do to improve your analogy score is to practice answering analogy questions. That way, you can learn the many types of analogies, practice using the strategies, and learn meanings of new words. There are many analogy questions in this book. Make sure you do them all.

Instant Replay: Analogy Strategies

1. Figure out the relationship between the stem words.
2. Find the same relationship in one of the answer pairs.
3. Consider starting with the second stem word.
4. Use the answer choices to help you determine the part of speech of the stem word.
5. Make sure you know the most common analogy relationships.
6. Practice with lots of analogy questions.

Day 5

Verbal Strategies: Sentence Completion

Assignment for Today:

Learn Sentence Completion strategies.

In this section of your test, all you do is fill in the blanks. But, you've got to find the choice that makes the most sense. Here's a sample question:

> Although my uncle is usually a generous person, yesterday he gave —— to a woman soliciting for a popular charity.
>
> (A) money
>
> (B) advice
>
> (C) thanks
>
> (D) nothing
>
> (E) food

SENTENCE COMPLETION STRATEGY 1.

Use Your Own Word

What word best fits the blank in the sentence above? The correct answer is choice (D): nothing. Although my uncle is usually a generous person, yesterday he gave *nothing* to a woman soliciting for a popular charity.

Were you able to guess what word fit the blank even before looking at the choices? If you could, that was a great way to answer the question. But that's something you can do on only the easiest sentence completion questions. So here's another strategy you can try.

SENTENCE COMPLETION STRATEGY 2.

Look for Flag Words

Certain words—called *flag words*—give important information about the "direction" of a sentence. For example, in the question above, the flag word is "although." "Although my uncle is usually a generous person, yesterday he gave nothing . . ." The first part of the sentence describes the uncle as generous, but in the second part he isn't generous at all. The word "although" *reversed* the direction of the sentence, signaling that the correct completion will be the opposite of generous.

Now suppose that instead of "although," the flag word was "since." Try completing this sentence: "Since my uncle is usually a generous person, yesterday he gave ________ to a woman soliciting for a popular charity." In this sentence the word "money" would fit.

The word "since" *continues* the direction of the sentence. The first part says that the uncle is generous, and the second part continues that thought. "Since my uncle is usually a generous person, yesterday he gave money to a woman soliciting for a popular charity."

So there are two kinds of flags:

Opposite flags.

These are words and phrases that reverse the direction of a sentence. Opposite flags include: although, despite, but, even though, instead of, nevertheless, contrary to, rather than, in spite of, however.

Same flags.

These are words that continue the direction of the sentence. Same flags include words like: since, thus, therefore, as, hence, because, for, for instance, and, moreover, so, due to, and—check this out—a semicolon (;), which also continues the thought of the sentence.

Let's look at this example:

Julia had spent the entire previous week studying; on her final examination, she encountered —— difficulties.

(A) myriad
(B) frequent
(C) formidable
(D) few
(E) remarkable

This sentence contains a semicolon, which is a same-flag. It indicates that the same feeling or thought continues throughout the entire sentence. In the first part of the sentence, you learned that Julia spent quite some time studying, and so the idea is that she's well prepared for the test. Now continue this thought. She was prepared, so what did she encounter on the test? Lots of difficulty? No. Continue the thought: Julia will find almost no difficulty on the test. The choice that gives that meaning is *few*.

SENTENCE COMPLETION STRATEGY 3.

Try the Second Blank First

Quite a few SAT sentence completion questions have two blanks instead of just one. Sometimes the second blank is easier to fill in than the first blank. Look at this example:

Even though he had not eaten all day and had —— money in his pocket, David —— the offer of a free meal.

(A) considerable..refused
(B) various..accepted
(C) extra..renegotiated
(D) little..declined
(E) enough..applauded

The flag words, "even though," tell you that the direction of the sentence will reverse. The first part of the sentence tells you that David hasn't eaten all day so he must be hungry. The flags "even though" tell you that in the second part of the sentence David will do the opposite of what his hunger would cause him to do. The two choices that work for the second blank are (A) refused, and (D) declined. So knock out choices (B), (C), and (E). Now try each of the remaining choices.

First (A). "Even though he had not eaten all day and had considerable money in his pocket, David refused the offer of a free meal." The second blank works well, but the first word, "considerable," doesn't make much sense. Remember that the flag "even though" tells you that the direction should change. If David had considerable money, he could refuse a free meal—nothing surprising about that. There's no change of direction.

So try choice (D). "Even though he had not eaten all day and had little money in his pocket, David declined the offer of a free meal." The second blank works as before, but now the first blank also works. Even though he had little money and was hungry, David said "no" to a free meal. With little money we would have expected him to jump at the chance for a free meal. But the flag words, "even though," tell you that the direction of the sentence will reverse and the opposite will happen. And so it did!

SENTENCE COMPLETION STRATEGY 4.

Try All the Choices

In the question above, you had to read in only two choices to find the winner. But for some questions you may have to read in all five choices. That happens when there are no flag words, or when the sentence is very long, or when it's just plain tough. Here's an example:

> The team members had few, if any, —— about postponing those long, arduous practice sessions that tended only to deflate their enthusiasm, —— their coach's frustration at their inconsistent execution.
>
> (A) desires..undermining
>
> (B) misgivings..increasing
>
> (C) hesitations..embracing
>
> (D) qualifications..ceasing
>
> (E) ideas..reducing

Hard to tell what's going on. On your test it may be better to come back to a question like this and do it at the end, since it's probably going to take a lot of time. But when you do come back to it, try reading in each choice to see which makes the most sense.

Let's try choice (A): "The team members had few, if any, *desires* about postponing those long, arduous practice sessions that tended only to deflate their enthusiasm, *undermining* their coach's frustration. . . ." Long practice sessions that deflate enthusiasm wouldn't undermine (or lessen) their coach's frustration, they would increase it. Forget this choice.

Choice (B): "The team members had few, if any, *misgivings* about postponing those long, arduous practice sessions that tended only to deflate their enthusiasm, *increasing* their coach's frustration at their inconsistent execution." This works. The team had no problem with postponing the dreaded practices, and these practices not only deflated the team's enthusiasm but also increased their coach's frustration at the team's lousy work. This is a winner, so mark it.

But try the others, just in case one of them is better than (B). Choice (C): "The team members had few if any *hesitations* about postponing those long, arduous practice sessions that tended only to deflate their enthusiasm, *embracing* their coach's frustration at their inconsistent execution." "Embracing their coach's frustration" doesn't make much sense in the context of this sentence, and besides, it's not nearly so good as (B). Strike it and keep going.

Choice (D): "The team members had few if any *qualifications* about postponing those long, arduous practice sessions that tended only to deflate their enthusiasm, *ceasing* their coach's frustration at their inconsistent execution." Here, too, the last phrase, "ceasing their coach's frustration" just doesn't make sense in this sentence. Strike this one and check the last one.

Choice (E): "The team members had few if any *ideas* about postponing those long, arduous practice sessions that tended only to deflate their enthusiasm, *reducing* their coach's frustration at their inconsistent execution." This also doesn't make much sense with the entire sentence. The team had no ideas about postponing a practice, and the tough practice reduced the coach's frustration at the team's lousy play? It just doesn't fit right. And certainly it doesn't make the kind of sense that choice (B) does.

Reading in each choice and checking for its meaning is time-consuming. But it's a last-ditch strategy that you'll probably need to use from time to time.

SENTENCE COMPLETION STRATEGY 5.

Read in Your Answer Choice

Even if you don't read all the answer choices into the original sentence, you should, at least, read in the one you picked as the correct answer. That will help you make sure it fits the meaning of the sentence.

Instant Replay: Sentence Completion Strategies

1. Use your own word.
2. Look for flag words.
3. Try the second blank first.
4. Try all the choices.
5. Read in your answer choice.

Day 6

Math Strategies: Problem Solving Section

Assignment for Today:

Learn problem-solving strategies for multiple-choice math questions.

MATH STRATEGY 1.

Scan Choices

The answer choices on the SAT tell us a lot about how to solve the problem. Many people are surprised when they find out that the answer choices give away a lot of information. Here's an example.

What is the sum of the lowest factors of 8 and 6?

(A) –48
(B) –14
(C) 2
(D) 10
(E) 24

Can you think of the answer? Before you find out whether you got the right answer or not, think about this important rule: Always scan the answers before you work on a problem.

Did you think about your answer again? You have probably guessed by now that the correct answer is not choice (C), 2. If you had scanned the answers before you solved this question, you would have seen that two of the answer choices were negative numbers. This should give you an important clue.

Yes, –6 is also a factor of 6 because $-6 \times -1 = 6$ and –8 is a factor of 8 because $-8 \times -1 = 8$. And so the correct answer is choice (B), –14.

Quite often, when you're asked to find the area or the circumference of a circle, you'll notice that the answer choices all have a π in them. This immediately tells you that you don't need to convert π to 3.14. You can leave π as π and work the problem.

So, remember this important strategy. Always scan the answers before you start a problem.

MATH STRATEGY 2.

See How It Ends

Here's a dandy shortcut to use when you multiply numbers. Suppose you were asked to multiply 356 and 39, and were given the following choices:

(A) 13,781
(B) 13,723
(C) 13,884
(D) 14,875
(E) 15,233

Before you even reach for your calculator, you should be able to tell that the right answer is choice

(C). How do you know? It's easy if you just "see how it ends." To show you how this works, let's take a problem that's more like the ones you'll find on the SAT.

Tickets to a concert cost \$36 each. What is the total cost of each ticket if there is a 6 percent sales tax?

(A) \$ 2.16
(B) \$36.00
(C) \$36.22
(D) \$38.16
(E) \$39.24

The first thing you should realize is that, because of the sales tax, the total cost will be more than \$36. At this point, you can knock out choices (A) and (B) because they are not more than \$36.

One way to solve this problem is to find 6% of \$36 and add that amount to \$36. Another way is to find 106% of \$36, and you would do that by multiplying 1.06 by 36.

$1.06 \times 36 =$

What happens when you multiply the two 6's together? Your answer will end in a 6 because $6 \times 6 = 36$. In other words, the correct answer should be greater than \$36 and it should end in a 6. Now look at the answer choices. Which answer choice is greater than \$36 and ends in a 6? Answer choice (D), \$38.16, has to be the correct answer. Notice that you could solve this problem without having to calculate the final answer!

Now back to the problem you saw at the beginning of this section:

$356 \times 39 =$

(A) 13,781
(B) 13,723
(C) 13,884
(D) 14,875
(E) 15,233

We know that 6 (from 356) × 9 (from 39) is 54, which means that the correct answer has to end in a 4. Only choice (C), 13,884, ends in a 4 and so it must be the right answer.

Don't forget. Scan the choices, and always check to see how they end.

Math Strategy 3.

Approximate

Sometimes you don't have to find the exact answer. You can approximate and get away with it. What's even better, if you approximate, you save time. And you can use that extra time on the more difficult problems.

Here's an example.

If the weight of 33 boxes is 65 pounds, what is the weight of 49 boxes?

(A) 88
(B) 97
(C) 98
(D) 103
(E) 137

Of course, you can use a calculator to do this problem. But, you could also do this problem by approximating. Notice that the weight of 33 boxes is just a little less than twice 33, which is 66. This tells you that the weight of 1 box is a little less than 2 pounds. So, 49 boxes must weigh just a little less than $49 \times 2 = 98$ pounds. So, choice (C), 98, is too high (because we want our answer to be *less* than 98), which means that only choice (B), 97, is close enough to be the answer.

So remember, you can save a lot of time if you get in the habit of approximating. Before you work a problem, see if you can approximate your answer. This is a good strategy to use if the five answer choices are not close in value. If the answer choices are spread apart, that tells you that the right answer can be approximated.

Math Strategy 4.

Work from the choices

In high school, you learned to set up equations whenever you saw a word problem. This may be a good strategy some of the time. But, most of the time, there's another strategy that is much faster. Suppose a problem goes like this:

In his wallet Bill has one-dollar, five-dollar, and ten-dollar bills. If he has a total of 12 bills, including 6 singles, that add up to $56, how many 10-dollar bills does he have?

(A) 1

(B) 2

(C) 3

(D) 4

(E) 5

One way to do this problem is to set up one equation for the total amount of money that Bill has:

$S + 5F + 10T = 56,$

where S is the number of singles, F is the number of 5-dollar bills and T is the number of 10-dollar bills.

Then, you'd need another equation for the number of dollar bills that he has:

$S + F + T = 12$

and then you have to solve the two equations.

This method works, but it's awfully slow. Here's a better way to do it. The secret is to work from the choices. To work from the choices, always start from choice (C) and then plug the answer back into the problem. So, let's plug in 3 as a possible answer.

Remember, we're looking for the number of 10-dollar bills. So, let's suppose Bill has three 10-dollar bills. Then, he has $30. Now, he has 6 singles, and so with 3 more bills he has 9 bills. That means he has to have three 5-dollar bills to get a total of 12 bills. But, how do these numbers add up?

6 singles	=	$6
3 tens	=	$30
3 fives	=	$15
Total	=	$51

But this total is not enough, because we need $56. Let's look at the choices again. We know that choice (C) is too low. Zap it. Well, if (C) is too low, we know that choices (B) and (A) are also too low. At this point, you should cross off choices (A), (B), and (C). Notice that if you wanted to guess, you now have a 50–50 shot. But, let's keep going.

We'll plug in (D). If it works, great. If it doesn't work, we know (E) has to be the answer. So, let's try (D) and plug in 4 as the number of tens that Bill has. If Bill has 4 tens, then he has 10 bills—6 singles and 4 tens. Since he has a total of 12 bills, he must have two fives.

6 singles	=	$ 6
4 tens	=	$40
2 fives	=	$10
Total	=	$56

This works, so we know that the right answer is choice (D), 4.

So remember: Whenever you see word problems, consider starting from the answers and working your way back to the problem instead of taking the time to set up and solve equations. When you plug in values, start from choice (C). However, you should be aware of a couple of exceptions to the "start with (C)" rule.

Exceptions.

If the problem says, "Find the *least* value," or "the smallest angle," or "the lowest integer," start from the lowest choice, usually choice (A). If the problem says, "Find the most, largest, or greatest, value," start from the highest choice, usually choice (E). Here's an example:

What is the lowest positive factor of 24?

(A) 0

(B) 1

(C) 2

(D) 12

(E) 24

Since we're looking for the lowest positive factor, we start from choice (A). Is 0 a factor of 24? No. Zap (A). Let's look at choice (B), 1. Is 1 a factor of 24? Yes, it is. Is 1 positive? Yes, it is. And so this is the winner. Notice, you don't need to go further. So, remember: Whenever you can, plug in values, and work from choices.

MATH STRATEGY 5.

Use Numbers for Unknowns

The people who write tests love things like P's and Q's and R's and X's. They talk about companies that manufacture T garments, about people who are X years older than their brothers, and about Q factors. The best way to make sense out of this weird test language is to say it in English.

To do that, whenever you see P's, or Q's or X's, change them to numbers. Let's look at an example.

If a company produces q items in d days, how many items can it produce in m days?

(A) $\frac{qd}{m}$

(B) $\frac{dm}{q}$

(C) $\frac{qm}{d}$

(D) $\frac{d}{qm}$

(E) $\frac{m}{qd}$

The easiest way to solve this problem is to change q to an easy number, say 10. Then, you can change d days to another easy number, like 1 day, and m to 2 days. Then, the question reads:

If a company produces 10 items in 1 day, how many items can it produce in 2 days?

Now, if 10 items are produced in 1 day, it's easy to see that in 2 days, 20 items can be produced. With the values of $q = 10$, $d = 1$, and $m = 2$, see which choice gives you 20.

Choice (A): $\frac{10\times1}{2} = 5$

We're looking for 20.

Choice (B): $\frac{1\times2}{10} = \frac{1}{5}$

Choice (C): $\frac{10\times2}{1} = 20$

Choice (C) works. But let's see what happens to the other choices.

Choice (D): $\frac{1}{10\times2} = \frac{1}{20}$

Choice (E): $\frac{2}{10\times1} = \frac{1}{5}$

As you can see, only choice (C) gives us 20, and so it is the right answer. So remember, if you find yourself staring at a, b, c, q, r, and so forth, just plug in your own numbers for these variables.

Instant Replay: Problem-Solving Strategies

1. Scan the choices.
2. See how it ends.
3. Approximate.
4. Work from the choices.
5. Use numbers for unknowns.

Day 7

Math Strategies:

Quantitative Comparison Section and Diagrams

Assignment for Today:

Learn strategies for Quantitative Comparisons and diagrams.

QUANTITATIVE COMPARISON SECTION

The quantitative comparison (QC) section of your math test looks something like this.

Common quantity

Quantity in Column A	Quantity in Column B

Your task is to evaluate the quantity in each column to determine which is greater. You have four options: Answer

- (A) if Column A is greater than Column B
- (B) if Column B is greater than Column A
- (C) if the two columns are equal
- (D) if you cannot determine a definite relationship from the information given

Never answer (E). There is no choice (E) for Quantitative Comparison questions.

Here's an easy example.

Column A		Column B
	$x = 2$ $y = 3$	
$x - y$		$y - x$

Notice that Column A is $2 - 3 = -1$, and Column B is $3 - 2 = 1$. This means that Column B is greater than Column A. So on your answer sheet you should fill in B as your answer.

Here are some strategies for the QC section.

QC STRATEGY 1.

Substitute Values for Variables

Whenever you see variables like x, y, z, a, b, c, and so forth in the QC section of your test, you should immediately start plugging in values for the variables to find out which column is greater.

Make sure that you plug in a wide range of values. First plug in 0 as a value of the variable, and see which column is greater. After that, plug in a positive number (1 is a good one) and then a negative number (–1, for example). If these three different values always give you the same answer, you've probably found the correct answer. However, as soon as you get two different results, you can stop because then the right answer is choice (D): it cannot be determined. Here's an example.

Column A	Column B

$-3 < t < 3$

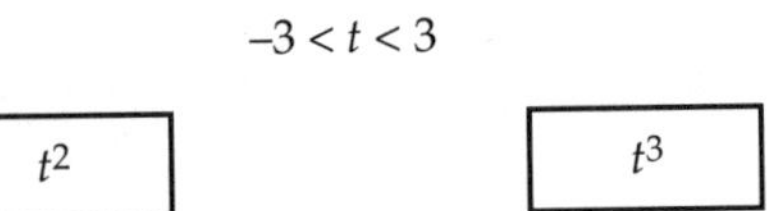

Start by plugging in values for t. We know that t can be 0 because we're told that t lies between –3 and 3. So plug in 0 for t. Then we get: Column A = 0 and Column B = 0.

This tells us that the right answer might be choice (C). But don't stop here. Plug in other values for t. For example, what happens if t is 3? Column A $= 3^2 = 9$ and Column B $= 3^3 = 27$.

Here Column B is greater than Column A. Bingo! We got two different results—first (C) and now (A). This immediately tells us that the correct answer is choice (D), it cannot be determined.

Notice that if you had stopped after plugging in 0 for t, your answer would have been incorrect. It's important to plug in a wide range of values, including negative numbers.

QC Strategy 2.

Cancel If You Can

The QC questions on your test are designed for speed. The more shortcuts you know, the faster you can do the problems. One important shortcut is canceling. Whenever you can, you should cancel common terms before you do any computations. Let's take an example. Suppose you are asked to compare the perimeters of the two figures shown.

Column A	Column B

All small triangles are equilateral with sides of length 1.

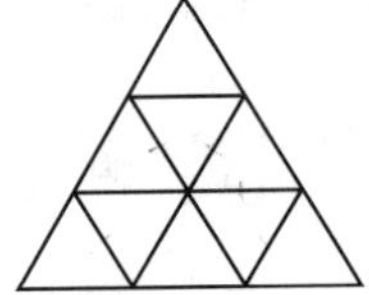

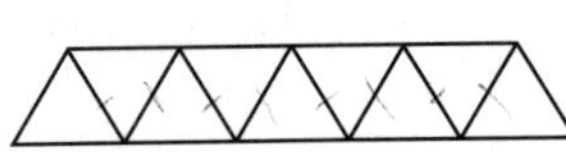

Perimeter of figure	Perimeter of figure

Perimeter simply means the distance around the outer edge of the figure. Before you actually calculate the distances, remember to cancel sides of triangles that are common to Column A and Column B. For every side that you consider in Column A, cancel a similar side in Column B. You will see that nine sides are common to both sides. Just cross them out.

Column A	Column B

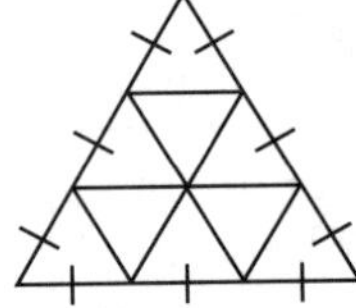

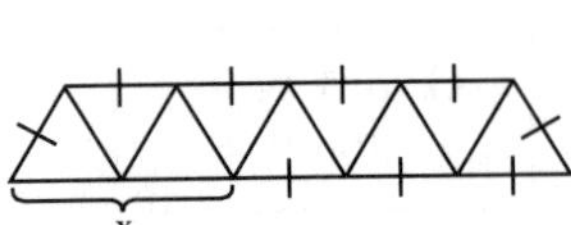

Now, you're left with just two sides (marked "x") that remain in Column B. Column B has two extra sides and so the right answer is (B). Notice that it wasn't really necessary to calculate the perimeter of each triangle. Canceling out the common terms made this an easy problem.

QC Strategy 3.

Factor Out Common Terms

Before you do any calculation, you should first see if common terms can be factored out. You can then cancel the common terms and simplify your work. Let's compare these two quantities.

Column A		Column B
	$x \neq -7$ $x \neq -4$	
$\dfrac{x^2-49}{x+7}$		$\dfrac{x^2-16}{x+4}$

Did you notice what is common? Let's factor the quantities on the top of both fractions. The top of Column A, $x^2 - 49$ can be written as:

$x^2 - 49 = (x + 7)(x - 7)$

So, Column A can be written as:

$$\frac{x^2-49}{x+7} = \frac{\cancel{(x+7)}(x-7)}{\cancel{x+7}} = (x-7)$$

We can cancel the $(x + 7)$ terms from the top and bottom to get $(x - 7)$ for Column A.

Similarly, in Column B, $(x^2 - 16)$ can be written as:

$(x^2 - 16) = (x + 4)(x - 4)$

So, Column B can be written as:

$$\frac{x^2-16}{x+4} = \frac{\cancel{(x+4)}(x-4)}{\cancel{x+4}} = (x-4)$$

We can cancel the $(x + 4)$ terms from the top and bottom to get $(x - 4)$ for Column B.

So we have $(x - 7)$ in Column A and $(x - 4)$ in Column B. No matter which value is taken by x, we can see that Column B will always be greater than Column A because Column B is only 4 less than x, whereas Column A is 7 less than x.

As you can see, factoring out the common terms will save you lots of time on the exam.

DIAGRAM STRATEGIES

Unfortunately, it's all too easy to make careless mistakes on your test, especially when a problem is long and wordy. One good strategy to help prevent careless mistakes is to make use of diagrams given in the problem. Feel free to mark on the diagram and write down the lengths of lines and values of angles. If no diagram is given to you, see if you can draw one yourself.

Before you work on these strategies, you should be aware of one special fact about your test: In the QC section of your test, do not assume that diagrams are drawn to scale. Angles that look perpendicular are not necessarily perpendicular; in fact, it's very likely that they're not perpendicular. Similarly, angles that look parallel may not be parallel.

Here are three very useful diagram strategies.

DIAGRAM STRATEGY 1.

Make a Sketch

It's very easy to drown in test language. To keep your head above water, you should get in the habit of drawing a diagram whenever you can. Use the margins of your test booklet for your sketches. Here's a good example of how a sketch can help:

> If the radius of a circle inscribed within a square is 5 feet, what is the perimeter of the square?

This question may look confusing, but it becomes simple if you draw a diagram. Let's see how we might do that.

We know that a circle of radius 5 is inscribed within a square. The diagram you draw may look something like this:

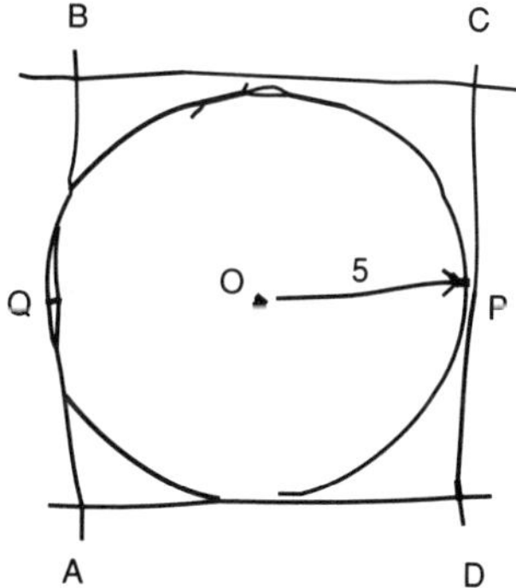

The problem asks us to find the perimeter of square *ABCD*. Because *ABCD* is a square, we know that all four sides have the same length. *OP* is the radius of the circle, and its length is 5. This means that *OQ*, which is another radius, is also 5. So, *QP* = 5 + 5 = 10. If *QP* is 10, then *AD* is also 10. Now we know that one side of the square is 10, which means that all sides of the square are 10. So the perimeter of the square is:

Perimeter $= AB + BC + CD + DA$

$= 10 + 10 + 10 + 10$

$= 40$

Notice that, even though the problem didn't come with a figure, you were able to draw one and simplify your work considerably.

Diagram Strategy 2.

Mark Up Given Diagrams

If a problem on your test comes with a diagram, you should get in the habit of marking on it. That way you minimize your chances of making careless mistakes. Marking on the given diagram also helps you keep focused and saves you time. Here's an example. Suppose a question on your test went something like this:

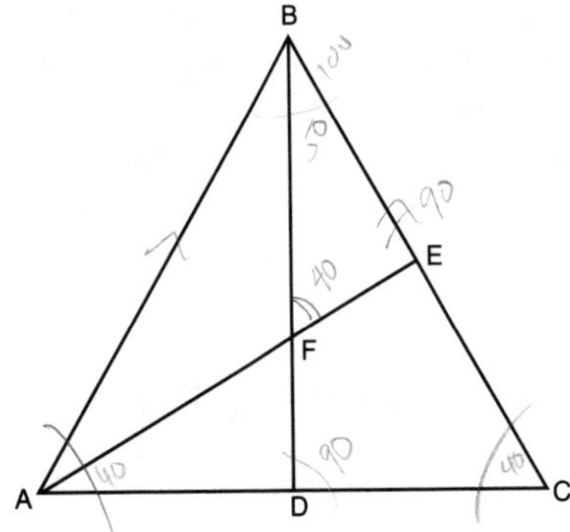

In the isosceles triangle ABC shown in the figure, angle BAC = angle BCA = 40 degrees. BD bisects angle ABC and AE is perpendicular to BC. What is angle BFE?

We're told that angle BAC is equal to angle BCA, and each one is 40 degrees. We also know that BD bisects angle ABC, which means that angle ABD is equal to angle DBC. Also, AE is perpendicular to side BC. Let's mark what we know.

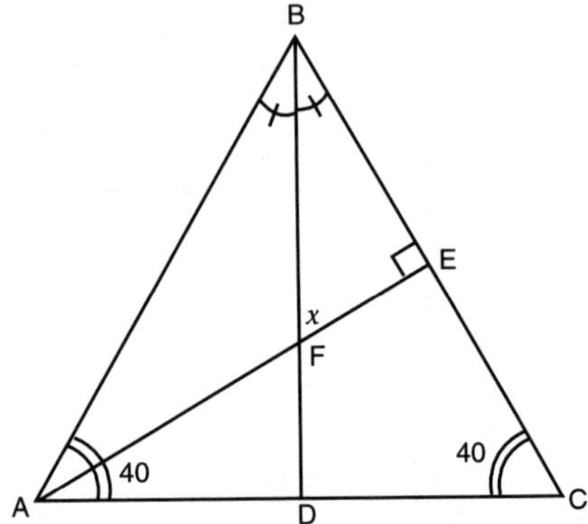

We want to find angle BFE, marked x in the figure. First, let's look at triangle ABC. If the two bottom angles are each 40 degrees, they add up to 80 degrees, which means angle ABC must be 100 degrees so that the three angles add up to 180 degrees. The two angles at the top are equal. So, each angle must be 50 degrees.

Now look at triangle BFE. We know that $\angle B = 50$ and $\angle E = 90$. Together, they add up to $90 + 50 = 140$ degrees. Because the three angles of any triangle must add up to 180 degrees, the measure of $\angle F$ must be $180 - 140 = 40$ degrees.

Notice how easy it becomes if you mark on the given diagram.

Diagram Strategy 3.

Distort Given Diagrams

On the SAT, looks can deceive. Angles that appear equal may not be equal and lines that look parallel may not be parallel. Every time you see two lines that look parallel, you should immediately assume they're not. In fact, you should distort those lines so that they look anything *but* parallel. In other words, don't hesitate to distort the given diagram. Here's an example.

Column A	**Column B**

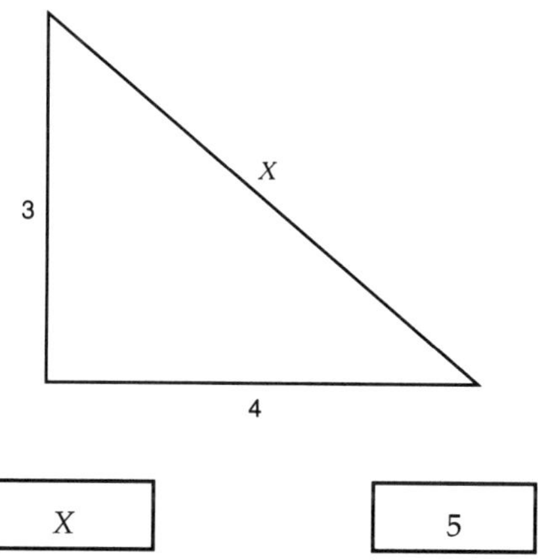

Suppose you're given a triangle as shown here. And you're asked to compare the length of the side marked X with 5. So, in Column A, you have X and in Column B, you have 5.

When you see two sides marked 3 and 4, you might be tempted to think that the third side, X, is 5. Right? X would be 5 if the given triangle were a right triangle. But nothing in the problem says that it is a right triangle. In fact, you should not assume that it is.

Let's see what happens if we distort the given diagram. Let's assume that the angle that looks like a 90-degree angle is, say, 30 degrees.

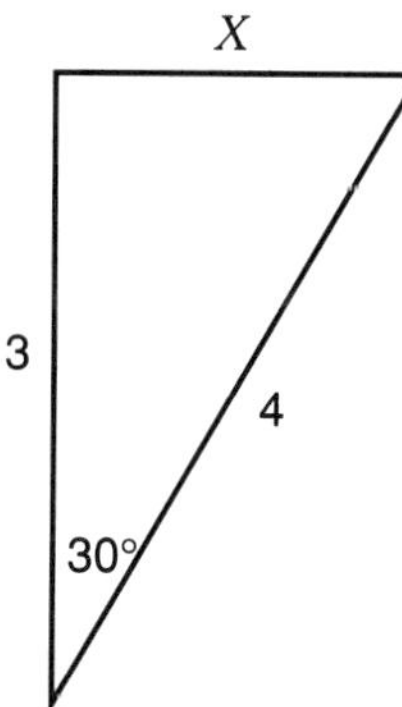

Notice that side X decreases from its original length if the bottom angle is 30 degrees. Similarly, watch what happens if the angle is, say, 120 degrees, instead.

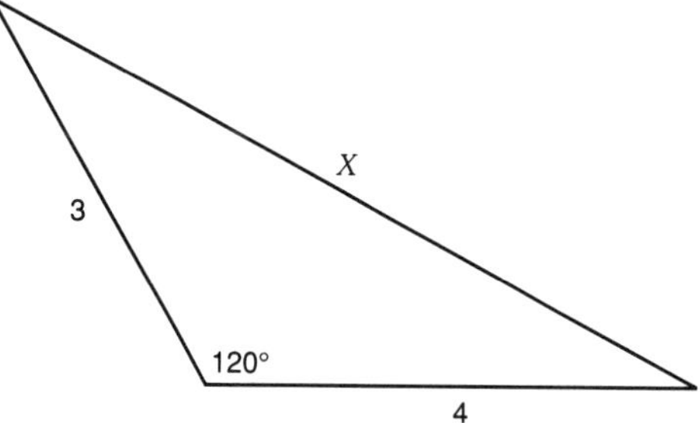

We can see that if the angle is 120 degrees, X becomes longer.

You've probably figured out by now that it's not possible to tell whether X is less than, equal to, or greater than 5, and so the right answer is choice (D), it cannot be determined. By distorting the given diagram, we were able to get the right answer.

Instant Replay: QC Strategies and Diagrams

QC Strategies

1. Substitute values for variables.
2. Cancel if you can.
3. Factor out common terms.

Diagram Strategies

1. Make a sketch.
2. Mark up given diagrams.
3. Distort given diagrams.

Day 8

Grid-in Section and Calculator Tips

Assignment for Today:

Learn how to use the answer grid and get some tips on calculators.

GRID-IN TIPS

The grid-in part of your test is a relatively new section on the SAT. It is the same as the other sections, except that no answer choices are provided for you. You have to solve the given problem and then provide your own answer by filling out a grid. Because this type of question requires you to come up with your own answer, you have to be extra careful in your calculations and in checking your answer.

The figure below shows an SAT math grid.

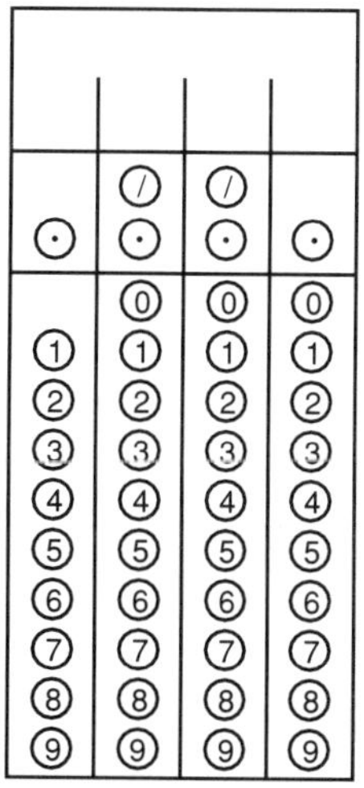

	/	/	
.	.	.	.
	0	0	0
1	1	1	1
2	2	2	2
3	3	3	3
4	4	4	4
5	5	5	5
6	6	6	6
7	7	7	7
8	8	8	8
9	9	9	9

GRID-IN TIP 1.

Write Your Answer First

Notice that the top row of each grid is blank. This is where you write your answer, one number per cell. But there's a catch you should be aware of: What you write in the top row of the grid will not be scored. The computer that evaluates your test scans only the darkened ovals in the grid. Then why do we recommend that you write your answers first? Because doing so will help you keep the numbers in their proper places.

The next row of the grid has a decimal point in the first cell, a slash "/" and a decimal point in the second and third cells, and a decimal point in the last cell. If your answer is in decimals, you must darken the appropriate decimal oval. If your answer is a fraction, darken the appropriate slash. For example, 3/7 can be used to show the fraction three-sevenths. This row of the answer grid is evaluated by the computer, so be careful to darken the correct space for the decimal or slash in your answer.

To record an answer, write the numbers in the top row, including decimals or slashes if necessary, and then fill in the corresponding spaces.

Grid-in Tip 2.

Start Whole Numbers in Any Column

Recording whole numbers is easy. Write the number at the top and then fill in the corresponding spaces. If your answer is shorter than four digits, you can start from the right or the left; it does not matter. For example, the number 25 can be recorded in any of the following ways:

2	5		

	2	5	

		2	5

Grid-in Tip 3.

Enter Your Answers as Fractions or Decimals

A proper fraction, such as $\frac{1}{2}$, can be recorded as 1–slash–2, or as 0–point–5, or as point–5, as shown in the figure. However, we recommend that, if your answer is in fractional terms, you should retain the fraction; do not convert your fractions to decimals (why do more work than necessary and risk making another mistake?).

1	/	2	

	0	.	5

.	5		

GRID-IN TIP 4.

Leave Improper Fractions as They Are

An improper fraction, or a top-heavy fraction such as $\frac{5}{3}$, should be recorded just as a proper fraction is recorded—5–slash–3. Do not convert improper fractions to mixed numbers.

GRID-IN TIP 5.

Change All Mixed Numbers to Improper Fractions

A mixed number, such as $1\frac{2}{3}$, should first be converted into an improper fraction, such as $\frac{5}{3}$, and the improper fraction should be entered in the grid. Do *not* record $1\frac{2}{3}$ as 1–2–slash–3 because the computer will read it as 12–thirds!

GRID-IN TIP 6.

Round Off Only at the Last Possible Digit

To avoid confusion and to guard against possible mistakes, do not convert fractions such as $\frac{1}{3}$ to their decimal equivalents. Simply grid in the answer as 1–slash–3. Similarly, grid in $\frac{2}{3}$ as 2–slash–3 without converting it to .667. However, if you get a recurring fraction such as .6667 as your answer, grid it in as .667, not as .7 because .7 will be taken as an error. In other words, you should fill in as many digits as is possible in the grid, rounding off the last digit.

A Word to the Wise

Notice that there is no space for a negative answer on your grid. This immediately tells you that you cannot have a negative answer. If you solve a problem and are left with a negative answer, check your work again. Notice also that you cannot get an answer longer than 4 digits.

CALCULATOR TIPS

As you probably know, calculators are allowed on the SAT. This is both good news and bad news. The bad news is that many questions on the SAT are designed so that you cannot solve the problem just by using your calculator. The good news: If you have a calculator, you don't have to waste time doing long and tedious arithmetic. So, bring a calculator with you. Here are a few tips on using the calculator to your advantage.

CALCULATOR TIP 1.

Buy New Batteries

Get fresh batteries for exam day. If you run out of batteries, you will not be able to borrow another calculator. And, you are not allowed to use the wall socket.

CALCULATOR TIP 2.

Bring a Familiar Calculator

Find a calculator you are comfortable with. Don't bring a calculator you haven't used before. And don't bring a fancy calculator that you don't know how to use.

What functions should your calculator have? Apart from standard addition, subtraction, multiplication, and division, your calculator should have the following functions:

Memory Function

Let's take an example to see why this is important. Suppose the question asks:

What is the value of $(x + 0.33) - (y + 0.58)$ if $x = 0.5$ and $y = 0.9$?

The fast way to do this problem is to first plug in the value of y in the second quantity, and put it in memory. So, take .9 plus 0.58, which equals 1.48. Then put 1.48 in memory. Now work the first set: x plus 0.33 is 0.5 plus 0.33, which equals 0.83. Now hit the minus sign and the memory release key (which is usually marked MR), hit equals . . . and there it is, negative 0.65.

Try another example on your own:

What is the value of $(x - 5) - 2(y - 3)$ if $x = .9$ and $y = .8$?

Go ahead and try it.

The fast way to do this is to take the value of y, 0.8 and subtract 3, to get negative 2.2, multiply it by 2, to get negative 4.4 and store this number in memory. Now, $x - 5$ is 0.9 minus 5, which is negative 4.1. Subtract from it the memory amount, and the answer is 0.3.

Inverse Function

Your calculator should also have an inverse function. This is usually shown as a $\frac{1}{x}$ key. This function is useful when you want to add fractions. Suppose you wanted to add $\frac{1}{5}$, $\frac{1}{7}$, and $\frac{1}{9}$. The fast way to do this is to use the inverse key.

Simply hit 5 and then inverse, plus, 7-inverse, plus, 9-inverse, and you get the answer!

Other Functions

Other useful functions that you might want include: percentage, exponents, and square root. The important thing is that you learn how to use these features before you enter the exam room. These features can also be used to check your work.

CALCULATOR TIP 3.

Write It Down

Even if you use your calculator, it's important that you write your rough work down. This way, if the answer you get does not appear as a choice, you can go back and check your work. If you don't make a note of your work, you'll have to start all over again.

Instant Replay: Grid-in and Calculator Tips

Grid-ins

1. Write your answer first.
2. Start whole numbers in any column.
3. Enter your answers as fractions or decimals.
4. Leave improper fractions as they are.
5. Change all mixed numbers to improper fractions.
6. Round off only at the last possible digit.

Calculators

1. Buy new batteries.
2. Bring a familiar calculator.
3. Write it down.

Test 1

Questions and Answers

Explanations and Strategies

Test 1, Section 1: Math

Questions and Answers

Assignment for Today

Take a sample SAT math test under actual test conditions. Allow yourself exactly 30 minutes to complete the 25 questions in this test.

Directions: *Solve each problem and select the appropriate answer choice from those given.*

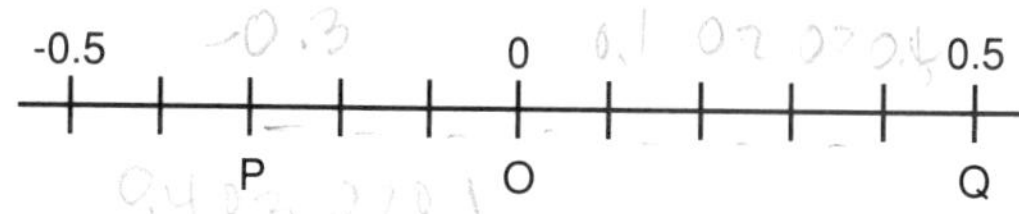

1. Tick marks in the figure above are equally spaced. If PQ is the diameter of a circle, what is the area of the circle?
   (A) 0.01π
   (B) 0.016π
   (C) 0.04π
   (D) 0.16π
   (E) 0.64π

2. Three boxes—A, B, and C—together weigh 26 pounds. Box A weighs one-third as much as box B and box C weighs three times as much as box B. How many pounds does box B weigh?
   (A) 2
   (B) $3\frac{5}{7}$
   (C) 6
   (D) $8\frac{2}{3}$
   (E) 13

3. If $\sqrt{y} = 9$, then $y^2 - \sqrt{y} =$
   (A) $\sqrt{3} - 9$
   (B) 0
   (C) $9 - \sqrt{3}$
   (D) 6552
   (E) 6561

4. What is the value of $(p + p^2 + p^4 + q^3)$ when $p = -1$?
   (A) 0
   (B) q^3
   (C) $p + q^3$
   (D) $(1 + q)^3$
   (E) $1 + q^3$

5. If $\frac{x+3}{6} = \frac{12}{x+4}$, what is the positive value of x ?
(A) 2
(B) 3
(C) 5
(D) $\sqrt{60}$
(E) 12

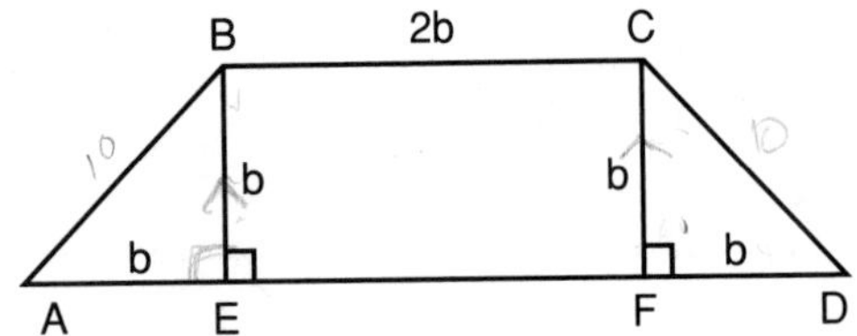

6. What is the perimeter of the trapezoid shown in the figure above if $AB = 10$?
(A) $30\sqrt{2}$
(B) $20 + 30\sqrt{2}$
(C) $20 + 40\sqrt{2}$
(D) 80
(E) 150

7. Cindy wants to paint her office. She can buy three cans of the same-priced paint and three identical brushes for \$21, or she can buy four cans of the same paint and one brush for \$22. How much does a can of paint cost?
(A) \$2
(B) \$3
(C) \$4
(D) \$5
(E) \$6

8. Which of the following must be true?
I. $(25 - 81) = (5 - 9)(5 + 9)$
II. $7(9 + 6) = 7(9) + 7(6)$
III. $6 \div (3 - 1) = (6 \div 3) - (6 \div 1)$
(A) I only
(B) II only
(C) III only
(D) I and II only
(E) I, II, and III

9. The sum of a and $9 - 2a$ is less than 8. Which of the following is (are) the value(s) of a?
I. $a < -1$
II. $a < 1$
III. $a > 1$
(A) I only
(B) II only
(C) III only
(D) I and II only
(E) I and III only

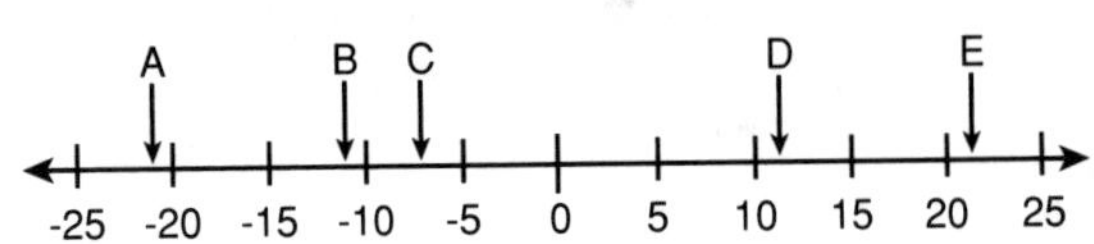

10. Which of the points shown in the figure above best represents $-\frac{A}{2}$?
(A) A
(B) B
(C) C
(D) D
(E) E

11. Susan is having a party. At 7:00 P.M., guests begin arriving at a uniform rate of 8 people every 15 minutes. If this pattern continues, how many guests will have arrived by 9:30 P.M.?
(A) 10
(B) 20
(C) 40
(D) 64
(E) 80

12. For positive integers p and q, if $p^2 + 2q^2 = 41$, and $2p^2 + q^2 = 34$, then $p^2 =$
(A) 2.5
(B) 7
(C) 3
(D) 9
(E) 16

13. If a:b is 7:6 and $3b$:$2c$ is 2:3, what is $\frac{c}{a}$?

(A) $\frac{14}{27}$

(B) $\frac{7}{9}$

(C) $\frac{6}{7}$

(D) $\frac{9}{7}$

(E) $\frac{27}{14}$

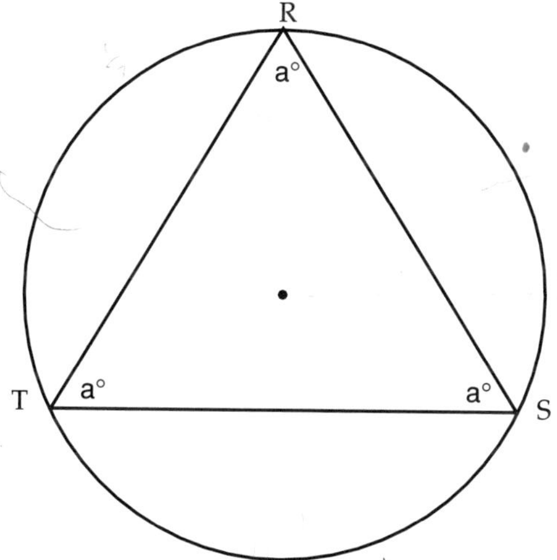

14. In the figure above, if the radius of the circle is 8, then the length of arc TRS is

(A) $\frac{16\pi}{3}$

(B) $\frac{32\pi}{3}$

(C) 16π

(D) $\frac{128\pi}{3}$

(E) 64π

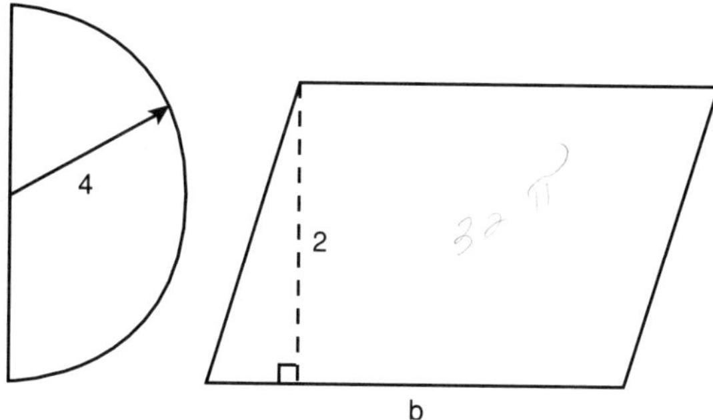

Note: Figure not drawn to scale

15. In the figure above, the area of the semicircle is equal to the area of the parallelogram. The semicircle has a radius of 4. What is b?

(A) 2

(B) 4

(C) 4π

(D) 8π

(E) 16π

16. For developing pictures, XYZ Photo Lab charges a service fee of \$3 for every order it receives in addition to a printing fee. If the order consists of 12 pictures or less, the printing fee per picture is \$0.36. If the order consists of more than 12 pictures, the printing fee per picture is \$0.24. What is the total cost per picture for an order consisting of 30 pictures?

(A) \$0.11

(B) \$0.24

(C) \$0.34

(D) \$0.46

(E) \$3.24

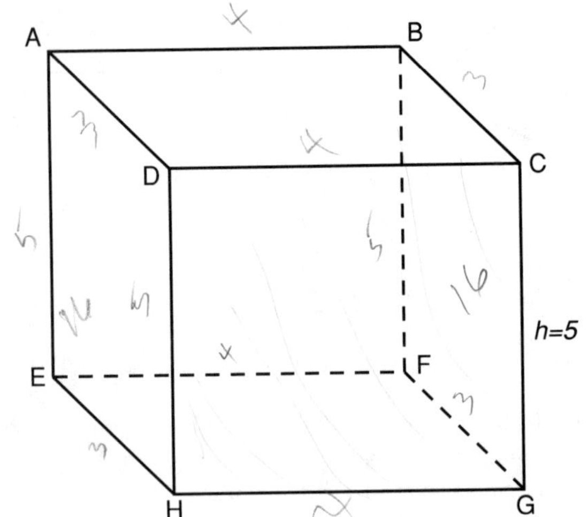

17. In the box shown above, $ABCD$ is a rectangle with perimeter 14, and $CGHD$ is a rectangle with perimeter 18. The height of rectangle $CGHD$ is 5. What is the total surface area of the box?

(A) 47
(B) 60
(C) 94
(D) 118
(E) 286

18. How many square concrete slabs of side $\frac{2}{3}$ feet can be cut out of another concrete slab 3 feet long and 3 feet wide?

(A) 13
(B) $13\frac{1}{2}$
(C) 16
(D) 20
(E) $20\frac{1}{4}$

19. Lisa found an easy way to add up a sequence of positive even integers with an even number of terms. She formed pairs of equal sums by adding the first integer to the last, the second integer to the next-to-last, and so on. She then computed the total by adding these equal sums. If the total Lisa obtained was 930, how many terms were there in the sequence of positive even integers if the sequence started with the number 2?

(A) 30
(B) 39
(C) 40
(D) 60
(E) 465

20. December is the busiest month at Lamont's Gift Shoppe, where sales in December are 40 percent higher than average. If sales in February are typically 20 percent lower than average, what is the ratio of February sales to December sales?

(A) 1:2
(B) 4:2
(C) 4:5
(D) 4:7
(E) 6:7

21. How many 4-digit numbers are there that consist of only *odd* digits?

(A) 20
(B) 625
(C) 1,024
(D) 4,500
(E) 5,000

22. For some integer m, let $\{m\}$ be defined by the equation $\{m\} = m(1 - m)$. If $n + 1 = \{n + 1\}$, then $n =$

(A) –2
(B) –1
(C) 0
(D) 1
(E) 2

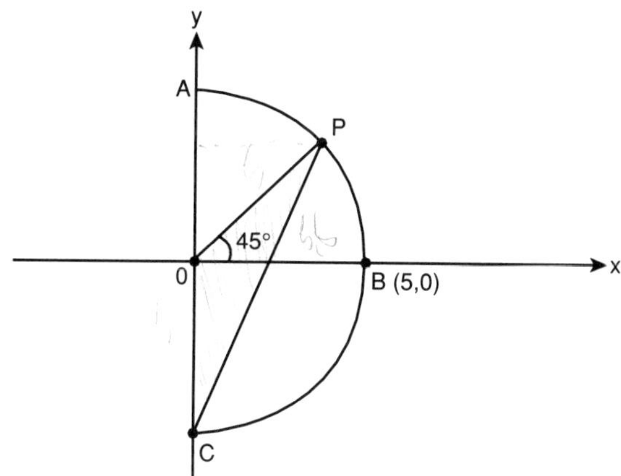

23. In the figure above, ABC is a semicircle with center at the origin. What is the area of triangle OPC?

(A) $\frac{25}{4}$

(B) $\frac{25}{4}\left(\sqrt{2}+1\right)$

(C) $\frac{25}{2\sqrt{2}}$

(D) $\frac{25}{2}$

(E) $\frac{25}{\sqrt{2}}$

24. Box A and box B have 6 cards each. Each card is marked with one integer, 1 through 6. Both boxes can have more than one card with the same integer, but the sum of all the integers in each box must be 18. Two of the cards in box A are 6's and two of the cards in box B are 5's. If one card is drawn from box A and one from box B, but neither a 6 nor a 5 is drawn, what is the *largest* possible sum of the integers on the cards drawn from the two boxes?

(A) 3

(B) 4

(C) 7

(D) 8

(E) 12

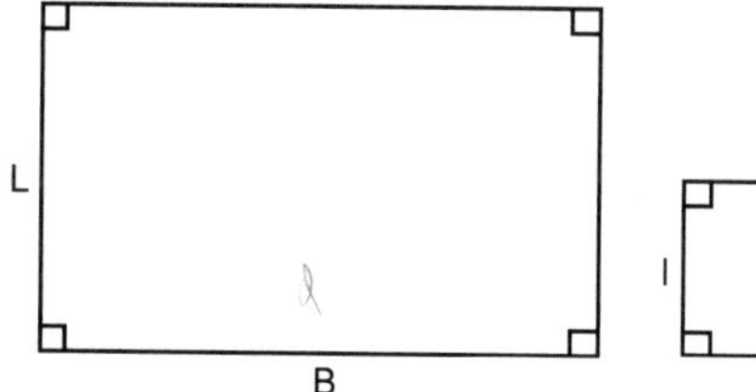

25. In the figure above, the ratio of the perimeter of the larger rectangle to the perimeter of the smaller rectangle is p.

If $\frac{L-B}{l-b} = d$, what is $\frac{L^2-B^2}{l^2-b^2}$ in terms of p and d?

(A) $p \times d$

(B) $\frac{p}{d}$

(C) $\frac{p^2-d^2}{p^2+d^2}$

(D) $\frac{p+d}{p-d}$

(E) $p-d^2$

Quick Answer Guide

Test 1, Section 1: Math

1. D
2. C
3. D
4. E
5. C
6. B
7. D
8. D
9. C
10. D
11. E
12. D
13. E
14. B
15. C
16. C
17. C
18. C
19. A
20. D
21. B
22. B
23. C
24. C
25. A

For explanations to these questions, see Day 10.

Day 10

Test 1, Section 1: Math

Explanations and Strategies

Assignment for Today

Review the explanations for the test you just took. See which answer is right and learn what makes each wrong answer wrong.

1. Correct choice (D) 0.16π

We're told that *PQ* is the diameter of the circle. We should first find the length of the diameter. From the figure we know that *PQ* is the sum of *PO* and *OQ*. *PO* is 0.3 (notice it's not –0.3 because distances cannot be negative) and *OQ* is 0.5. So, the diameter of the circle is $0.3 + 0.5 = 0.8$.

If the diameter is 0.8, the radius is half that, or 0.4.

If the radius is 0.4, the area $= \pi r^2 = \pi(0.4)^2 = 0.16\pi$.

(A) Missing key insight—Looks like you found the radius to be 0.1, possibly because you subtracted *OP* from *OQ* to find the diameter. Although point *P* has a negative value, when we find distances we take only the positive amount.

(B) Miscalc—You made a mistake in squaring 0.4. When you square 0.4, you should get 0.16, with only two places after the decimal point. You put down *three* places after the decimal point.

(C) Missing key insight—Looks like you found the radius to be 0.2. This is incorrect because you took the length of *OP* to be negative. Although *P* has a negative value, when we find distances we take only the positive amount. Also, you seem to have forgotten to divide the diameter by 2 to find the radius.

(E) Oversight—You did everything correctly, except you forgot to divide the diameter by 2 to find the radius. You used the formula for the area of a circle as πr^2, but you used the value of the diameter instead of the radius.

2. Correct choice (C) 6

Word problems like these are best solved by plugging in the answer choices. As usual, start from choice (C) 6. Because the question asked for the weight of box *B*, we plug in 6 pounds as its weight.

We're told that box *C* weighs 3 times as much as box *B*. So, if box *B* weighs 6 pounds, box *C* weighs $6 \times 3 = 18$ pounds. Now, box *A* weighs one-third as much as box *B*. So, if box *B* weighs 6 pounds, box *A* must weigh $\frac{1}{3} \times 6 = 2$ pounds.

Then, weight of box *A* = 2 pounds
weight of box *B* = 6 pounds
and weight of box *C* = 18 pounds
Then the total weight = 26 pounds

which works, so choice (C) is the right answer.

(A) Misread—If you chose 2 as your answer, you probably misread the question. This is the weight of box *A*, but the question asks for the weight of box *B*. Or, you may have taken the weight of box C to be three times the weight of box *A*. No, the weight of box C is three times the weight of box *B*.

(B) Misread—You may have misread the question and thought that the weight of box *A* was 3 times the weight of box *B*. No, the weight of box *A* should be one-third the weight of box *B*.

(D) Grabbing numbers—You may have been tempted to divide the total weight by 3. This, however, would be the weight of box *B* if all three boxes were of equal weight.

(E) Missing key insight—You may have incorrectly thought *B* accounted for half of the total weight and *A* and *C* combined accounted for the other half.

3. Correct choice (D) 6552

Let's start with what we know. We know that $\sqrt{y}$ = 9. Then, if we square both sides of this equation, $y = 81$.

Let's square this one more time to get: $y^2 = 81^2$.

Before we find the value of 81^2, note that the question asks for the value of $y^2 - \sqrt{y}$, which means we'll have to square 81 and then subtract 9. If we square 81, the last digit will end in a '1' (because when you multiply 81 by 81, the last digit will be $1 \times 1 = 1$). Then, when we subtract 9, the last digit will have to be $11 - 9 = 2$. Only one answer ends in a '2'—choice (D). Here's the calculation.

We know that $y^2 = 81^2 = 81 \times 81 = 6561$ (ends in a '1').

Now, we need to subtract 9 because we want the value of $y^2 - \sqrt{y} = 9$. So, $6561 - 9 = 6552$ (ends in a '2').

(A) Missing key insight—You probably found an incorrect value for y^2. If the given value is: $\sqrt{y} = 9$, then *y* is the *square* of 9, not its square root.

(B) Oversight—Looks like you found the value of y^2 as 9. If $\sqrt{y} = 9$, then *y* is 81, not the square root of 9.

(C) Missing key insight—You probably found the value of y^2 as 9 and the value of $\sqrt{y}$ as $\sqrt{3}$. This is incorrect because we're told that $\sqrt{y} = 9$, not 3.

(E) Misread—You found the value of y^2, but the question asked for the value of $y^2 - \sqrt{y}$. You need to go one step further.

4. Correct choice (E) $1 + q^3$

This problem required us to see that one of the terms is a *q*, not a *p* like the others. Then, because we are not given the value of *q*, our answer choice must have a *q*-term in it. We can zap (A) right away.

Let's plug in the value of (–1) for *p*. Then, we get:

$$\begin{aligned} p + p^2 + p^4 + q^3 &= (-1) + (-1)^2 + (-1)^4 + q^3 \\ &= -1 + 1 + 1 + q^3 \\ &= 1 + q^3, \text{ which is choice (E).} \end{aligned}$$

(A) Misread—Look at the problem carefully. You were asked to calculate the value of $p + p^2 + p^4 + q^3$, and not the value of $p + p^2 + p^4 + p^3$. That is, the last term is q^3, and not p^3, as you seem to have assumed.

(B) Careless—You seem to have started out well by canceling out the first two quantities (p and p^2) because they work out to –1 and +1 respectively when you plug in the value of *p*. But, you forgot to deal with the last quantity, p^4.

(C) Miscalc—You were close to the right answer, but not quite. You did a good job of isolating q^3, but you did not substitute –1 for all the *p*'s.

(D) Careless—In your hurry, you probably chose (D) when you meant to choose (E). Both look alike, but as you can see, they are not the same.

5. Correct choice (C) 5

You've probably been told to solve problems like this by cross-multiplying and solving for *x*. But here's a much faster method. Start from the choices and plug in values for *x*.

Remember, start with choice (C). So, let's plug in values for $x = 5$.

Then, we get $\frac{5+3}{6} = \frac{12}{5+4}$.

That is, $\frac{8}{6} = \frac{12}{9}$. Cross multiplying, we get

$$72 = 72$$

Hey, it works. So stop here. Of course, you can always cross multiply and solve as presented. But we think plugging in values is faster.

(A) Miscalc—Looks like you made a mistake in multiplying ratios. If you multiplied the top parts of two sides, you probably got $12(x + 3) = 6(x + 4)$

That is, $12x + 36 = 6x + 24$

Or, $6x = -12$

At this point, you probably found x to be –2, but decided to take its positive value because the question asked for the positive value of x.

But, remember, when you cross-multiply two ratios you multiply the top of the left side times the bottom of the right side and the top of the right side times the bottom of the left side.

(B) Grabbing numbers—Looks like you figured that if $x + 3$ is one of the terms, 3 must be one of the answers. Not so.

(D) Miscalc—You probably cross multiplied 12 and 6 to get 72 on one side and $(x + 3)(x + 4)$ to get $x^2 + 12$ on the other side of the equation. But, $(x + 3)$ times $(x + 4)$ does <u>not</u> equal $x^2 + 12$. Don't forget about the middle term $7x$ (because $4x + 3x = 7x$).

(E) Misread—Oh, no. Looks like you calculated the correct value, but you answered the wrong question. When you did the calculation, you probably got the equation:

$(x - 5)(x + 12) = 0$

And then you thought that the positive value of x is 12. No. For this equation, the value of x is –12. The *positive* value of x is 5. (It's also called the "positive root.")

6. Correct choice (B) $20 + 30\sqrt{2}$

Perimeter is the distance around the trapezoid. We first need to find the value of b. Let's look at right triangle AEB. AB (which, we're told, is 10) is the hypotenuse and $AE = BE = b$. Then, we can write:

$AB^2 = BE^2 + AE^2$

Or, $10^2 = b^2 + b^2 = 2b^2$

That is, $100 = 2b^2$

Or, $50 = b^2$

Taking the square root, $\sqrt{50} = b$

Or, $b = 5\sqrt{2}$

Now that we know the value of b, let's fill in all the distances in the figure, as shown in the second diagram.

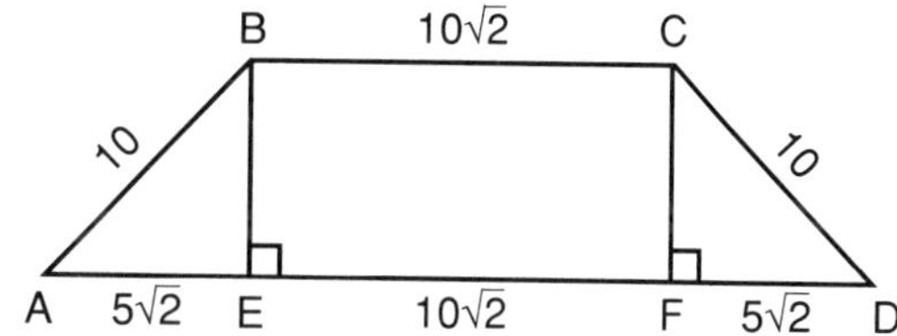

If AB equals 10, CD also equals 10.

$BC = 2b = 2 \times 5\sqrt{2} = 10\sqrt{2}$

Then, EF also $= 10\sqrt{2}$

$AE = FD = b$

So, $AE = FD = 5\sqrt{2}$

Then, the perimeter $= AB + BC + CD + DF + EF + EA$

$= 10 + 10\sqrt{2} + 10 + 5\sqrt{2} + 10\sqrt{2} + 5\sqrt{2}$

$= 20 + 30\sqrt{2}$

(A) Misread—This is the perimeter of the rectangular region $BCFE$. But, you were asked for the perimeter of the trapezoid $ABCDFE$.

(C) Oversight—You added BE and CF to the perimeter. To find the perimeter of the trapezoid (perimeter of anything, actually), you don't need to worry about what's *in* the figure. You're only concerned with the outer edge of the figure. So, no need to worry about BE and CF.

(D) Missing key insight—Did you get $b = 10$? No, b does not equal 10. Look at triangle AEB. If $AB = 10$, and angle AEB is 90 degrees, what is the value of b? (*Hint:* AEB is a 45-45-90 triangle.)

(E) Misread—You found the area of the trapezoid. But, you were supposed to find its perimeter. Remember, on the test, if you circle the ultimate question, you can guard against this mistake.

7. Correct choice (D) $5

To solve this problem, we can set up equations as follows, where p stands for the can of paint and b stands for a brush:

Call this the first equation: $3p + 3b = 21$

Call this the second equation: $4p + 1b = 22$

Then, we can get rid of the b-term in the second equation.

$$B = 22 - 4p$$

Let's plug this value of b into the first equation. We get:

$3p + 3(22 - 4p) = 21$

That is, $3p + 66 - 12p = 21$

Or, $-9p = 21 - 66 = -45$

So, $p = 5$, which is choice (D).

(A) Misread—Looks like you found the cost of a brush. But, you were asked for the price of a can of paint, not of the brush.

(B) Miscalc—Looks like you made a mistake when you subtracted the first equation, $3p + 3b = 21$, from 3 times the second. Did you subtract $3p$ from $12p$ to get $15p$? Check your work again.

(C) Missing key insight—Perhaps you made an educated guess after zapping the incorrect choices. However, the cost of a can of paint is not $4. Try setting up two sets of equations from the information given.

(E) Missing key insight—This answer is not possible because if each can of paint costs $6, 4 cans would cost $24. But we are told that 4 cans of paint *and* 1 brush together cost only $21. This was not a good guess, if in fact you did guess.

8. Correct choice (D) I and II only

The speed trick here is to look at each option and see what operation is being done. Of course, you can do the calculation on each side of the "=" sign, but that's slower.

Let's look at option I. Notice that 25 is really 5^2 and 81 is 9^2. Then, $25 - 81 = 5^2 - 9^2$. We know that the difference between two squares is: $(a^2 - b^2) = (a - b)(a + b)$. As you can see, option I is just that if you assume that $a = 5$ and $b = 9$. So, option I has to be true. Now knock out all choices that don't have numeral I in them. So we're left with choices (A), (D), and (E).

Option II is the distributive rule of multiplication. We know that $a(b + c) = ab + ac$. So, option II is also true and the right answer must have options I and II in it. We can knock out choice (A), and we're left with choices (D) and (E).

Let's look at option III. Let's work this one out:

$6 \div (3 - 1) = 6 \div 2 = 3$

But, $(6 \div 3) - (6 \div 1) = 2 - 6 \neq 3$

So, option III is not true. So, choice (E) should be crossed out and we're left with choice (D) as the right answer.

(A) Oversight—Option I is certainly true. But there's another option that is also true. Can you see which one?

(B) Oversight—Option II is certainly true. But there's another option that is also true.

(C) Misread—Maybe you thought you were to find the one that was *not* true. Can you see why option III is not true? Work out the equation and see if you get the left side to match the right side.

(E) Oversight—There is one option that is *not* true. If you don't see which one, solve both sides of each equation and see if you can get the left side to match the right side.

9. Correct choice (C) III only

We're told that the sum of a and $9 - 2a$ is less than 8. Then we can write:

$$a + 9 - 2a < 8$$

Or, $-a + 9 < 8$

Or, $-a < -1$

Now we need to multiply both sides by –1. Note that if we multiply by –1, we must reverse the inequality. That is, when we multiply by a negative number, "less than" becomes "more than." If you don't see why, take an example where, say, $x < -1$. Suppose $x = -2$. Then, when we multiply both sides by -1, we should get $-x > 1$. In other words, $2 > 1$.

Back to our problem. We have:

$$-a < -1$$

Then, $$a > 1$$

This tells us that only option III is true, which means the correct answer is choice (C).

(A) Miscalc—You made a calculation error in finding the value of $a - 2a$. Did you get $a - 2a$ as a, instead of minus a? Check your work again.

(B) Missing key insight—You forgot that when you multiply both sides of an inequality by -1, you have to reverse the inequality. For example, if $x < -1$, then when you multiply by -1, you get $-x > 1$, not $-x < 1$.

(D) Missing key insight—This is incorrect because you forgot that when you multiply both sides of an inequality by -1, you have to reverse the inequality. For example, if $x < -1$, then when you multiply by -1, you get $-x > 1$, not $-x < 1$.

(E) Oversight—One of the options in this answer choice is incorrect. To see which one, try plugging in your own values for a. For example, what happens if $a < -1$? Suppose $a = -2$. Does the sum of a and $9 - 2a$ become less than 8? Try it.

10. Correct choice (D)

Point A has an approximate value of -22. We are asked to find $-\frac{A}{2}$. Therefore, we have:

$$-\frac{A}{2} = -\frac{-22}{2} = 11$$

Notice that the answer isn't (B) because we need to find the *negative* of $\frac{A}{2}$.

(A) Missing key insight—This is the value of A itself. You were asked to find the value of $-\frac{A}{2}$. You should first estimate the value of A, and then multiply it by negative one-half.

(B) Misread—You found the value of $\frac{A}{2}$. But you were asked to find the value of $-\frac{A}{2}$. (Notice the negative sign.)

(C) Missing key insight—Hard to see why you chose this answer. Perhaps you were playing games with the computer. Did you notice that A has an approximate value of -22?

(E) Misread—Looks like you found the mirror image of point A. But the question asked for the value of $-\frac{A}{2}$. First estimate the value of A and then multiply it by negative one-half.

11. Correct choice (E) 80

We know that guests are arriving at the rate of 8 people per 15 minutes. So, in 30 minutes there are $8 \times 2 = 16$ people. And, in 1 hour (60 minutes) there are $16 \times 2 = 32$ people.

There are $2\frac{1}{2}$ hours between 7:00 P.M. and 9:30 P.M. If 32 people come in every hour, the number of people in $2\frac{1}{2}$ hours $= 32 \times 2\frac{1}{2} = 32 \times \frac{5}{2} =$ 80 people.

(A) Oversight—Looks like you multiplied 4 (the number of 15-minute segments in 1 hour) by $2\frac{1}{2}$, the number of hours. But you didn't take into account the number of people. You only found how many 15-minute segments there are in $2\frac{1}{2}$ hours.

(B) Miscalc—Looks like you multiplied $2\frac{1}{2}$ (the number of hours) by 8 (the number of people every 15 minutes). This is incorrect because $2\frac{1}{2}$ is in *hours* and 8 is in *minutes*.

(C) Misread—You forgot to multiply by 2 or you thought that 8 people came in every *half* an hour. You found the number of people per hour as 16, which isn't correct. If 8 people come in every 15 minutes, in just half an hour, there'll be 16 people.

(D) Careless—You took the time difference between 9:30 and 7:00 as only 2 hours, instead of $2\frac{1}{2}$ hours.

12. Correct choice (D) 9

We have two equations:

$$p^2 + 2q^2 = 41$$

and: $$2p^2 + q^2 = 34$$

We want to solve for p^2, so we should find a way to cancel the q^2 terms. Notice that if we multiply the second equation by 2, we will have identical

$2q^2$ terms in both the first and the second equations and then we'll be able to get rid of them.

So, let's copy the first equation: $p^2 + 2q^2 = 41$

and multiply the second one by 2: $4p^2 + 2q^2 = 68$

Now, let's subtract the first equation from the second: $3p^2 = 27$

Now let's divide by 3: $p^2 = 9$, choice (D).

(A) Miscalc—You probably meant to multiply the second equation by 2, but you forgot to multiply 34 by 2. Did you get the equation: $4p^2 + 2q^2 = 34$? It should be: $4p^2 + 2q^2 = 68$.

(B) Miscalc—Looks like you multiplied the first equation by 2, but forgot to multiply the "$2p^2$" term. Did you get the equation: $2p^2 + 2q^2 = 82$? It should be: $2p^2 + 4q^2 = 82$.

(C) Misread—You found the value of p. But the question asked for the value of p^2.

(E) Misread—This is the value of q^2. But the question asked for the value of p^2, not q^2.

13. Correct choice (E) $\frac{27}{14}$

First, let's write the given ratio as fractions:

$a:b = 7:6$ ====> $\frac{a}{b} = \frac{7}{6}$, and

$3b:2c = 2:3$ ====> $\frac{3b}{2c} = \frac{2}{3}$

We need to find the value of $\frac{c}{a}$. Notice that if we multiply the two fractions, $\frac{a}{b}$ and $\frac{3b}{2c}$, we can cancel the b-terms and we'll be left only with the a- and c-terms. So, let's do that:

$$\frac{a}{b} \times \frac{3b}{2c} = \frac{7}{6} \times \frac{2}{3}$$

Then, $$\frac{3a}{2c} = \frac{7}{9}$$

We're getting close. We need the value of $\frac{c}{a}$, which means we want c on top and a at the bottom. So, let's flip the equation:

$$\frac{2c}{3a} = \frac{9}{7}$$

If we multiply both sides by $\frac{3}{2}$, we will have only $\frac{c}{a}$ on the left.

So: $$\frac{c}{a} = \frac{9}{7} \times \frac{3}{2} = \frac{27}{14}$$

(A) Misread—You found the value of $\frac{a}{c}$, but the question asks for the value of $\frac{c}{a}$.

(B) Careless—Looks like you found the value of $\frac{b}{c}$ to be $\frac{2}{3}$ or $\frac{4}{6}$. This means you probably forgot about the "3" and the "2" on the left side of the given ratio: $3b:2c = 2:3$. Also you may have solved for the value of $\frac{a}{c}$, instead of $\frac{c}{a}$.

(C) Miscalc—Perhaps you found the ratio $b:c$ was 1:1. Actually, $b:c$ is 4:9. Check your math again.

(D) Miscalc—Looks like you found the value of $\frac{b}{c}$ to be $\frac{2}{3}$ or $\frac{4}{6}$. This means you probably forgot about the "3" and the "2" on the left side of the given ratio: $3b:2c = 2:3$.

14. Correct choice (B) $\frac{32\pi}{3}$

The triangle is equilateral because each corner angle ($a°$) is equal. This means that all sides of the triangle are also equal. Because each side of the triangle is equal, arc TR is equal to arc RS, which is also equal to arc ST.

Each arc then divides the total circumference of the circle into three equal thirds. We want the length of arc TRS, which is the sum of arc TR and arc RS, each of which is $\frac{1}{3}$ of the circumference. So, arc TRS is really $\frac{2}{3}$ of the circumference.

We know that the formula for the circumference of a circle is $2\pi r$. Then, $\frac{2}{3}$ of the circumference is $\frac{2}{3} \times 2\pi r$.

So, arc $TRS = \frac{2}{3} \times 2\pi r = \frac{4\pi r}{3}$

We're told that the radius of the circle is 8. Then,

$$\text{arc } TRS = \frac{4\pi 8}{3} = \frac{32\pi}{3}$$

(A) Oversight—You had the right idea, but forgot that the circumference of a circle is $2\pi r$, not πr.

(C) Oversight—You had the formula of circumference right, but you forgot that we want only $\frac{2}{3}$ of the circumference, not the whole thing.

(D) Careless—Looks like you used the formula for finding the area (πr^2) instead of the circumference ($2\pi r$).

(E) Missing key insight—You found the area of the circle. But, this isn't what the question asked for. See if you can first figure out what the total distance around the circle is.

15. Correct choice (C) 4π

Area of a circle = $\pi r^2 = \pi(4)^2 = 16\pi$. The area of a semicircle is half the area of a circle. So, the area of the semicircle = 8π. Area of a parallelogram is base × height. We know the height is 2. So, the area of the parallelogram = $bh = b(2) = 2b$.

We're told that the area of the semicircle is equal to the area of the parallelogram.

That is, $8\pi = 2b$

So, $b = 4\pi$

(A) Misread—Looks like you thought that the area of the semicircle was 4. But, 4 is the *radius* of the semicircle, not its area.

(B) Careless—You probably forgot the π in the formula for the area of the semicircle.

(D) Miscalc—You probably found the area of a full circle, rather than a semicircle. Or, perhaps you used the formula: $\frac{1}{2}$ base × height to find the area of the parallelogram. The area of the parallelogram is: base × height.

(E) Misread—You found the area of a circle. But the question asked for the base of the parallelogram, not the area of the circle.

16. Correct choice (C) \$0.34

We can solve this problem by setting up an equation, but the faster way is to scan our choices. (A) \$0.11 cannot be true because the cost per picture is more than \$0.24.

Similarly, because the printing fee *without* the service charge is \$0.24, *with* the service charge, the cost per picture has to be more than \$0.24. So, choice (B) \$0.24 is out.

The service charge of \$3.00 is to be spread across 30 pictures, which averages only 10 cents per picture. So, (E) \$3.24 is too high and can be zapped.

Now we are left with choices (C) \$0.34 and (D) \$0.46 as the only possible answers.

We just saw that the service charge of \$3.00 averages 10 cents per picture. Add to it the 24 cents per picture printing fee and we get 34 cents, choice (C).

(A) Missing key insight—If you add the \$3.00 service charge to \$0.24 and divide the sum (\$3.24) by 30, you get \$0.11. However, this is incorrect because the \$3.00 service charge applies to all 30 pictures and \$0.24 applies to only one copy and so you cannot add the two together.

(B) Missing key insight—If you do not include the service charge of \$3.00, you will be left with \$0.24 per picture. But the total cost per picture has to include the service charge, which, when spread across 30 pictures, averages 10 cents per picture.

(D) Misread—If you got \$0.46 as your answer, you probably took the wrong printing charge. If the order consisted of 30 pictures, the printing cost per page is only \$0.24, not \$0.36.

(E) Miscalc—An answer of \$3.24 probably means you made a calculation error. For example, you may not have divided by 30 to get the cost per picture, and instead added the service charge of \$3.00 (which applies to all 30 pictures) to the cost of printing, \$0.24 (which applies to each picture).

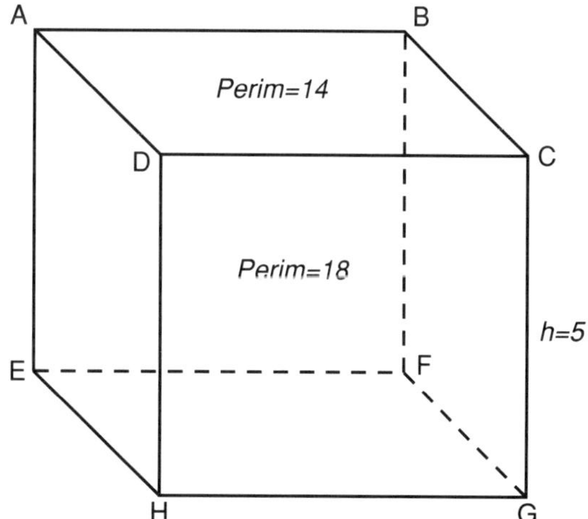

17. Correct choice (C) 94

Let's mark on the diagram. For the front surface *CGHD*, we know the perimeter and the height. We also know that the perimeter is the sum of all four sides.

Then, $CG + GH + HD + DC = 18$

But, we know that the height is 5.

That is, $CG = 5 = DH$

Then, $5 + GH + 5 + DC = 18$

We also know that GH and CD are equal.

So, $5 + DC + 5 + DC = 18$

Or, $2DC = 8$

So, $DC = 4$

Now the top of the box. DC is 4. Then AB is also 4.

Perimeter of $ABCD = 14$

Then, $AB + BC + CD + AD = 14$

Or, $4 + BC + 4 + AD = 14$

Also, $AD = BC$. So, $4 + BC + 4 + AD = 14$

Or, $2BC = 6$

So, $BC = 3$

Make sure you mark these on the diagram as shown.

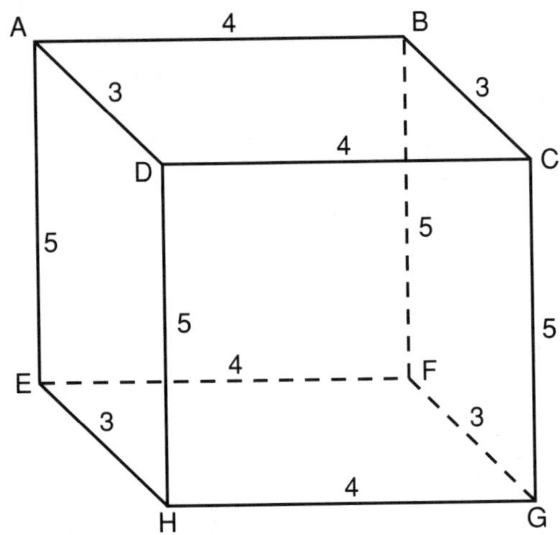

To find the total surface area, let's look at the top of the box. Its area = 3 × 4 = 12. So, the area of the bottom is also 12. The area of the front is 5 × 4 = 20. So, the area of the back is also 20. The area of the left side is 5 × 3 = 15. So the area of the right side is also 15.

Then, the total surface area = 12 + 12 + 20 + 20 + 15 + 15 = 94

(A) Oversight—You found all the dimensions of the box correctly, but you found the areas of only 3 of the 6 sides. To find the total surface area, you have to add the areas of all 6 sides.

(B) Missing key insight—This is the volume of the box. To find the total surface area, find the areas of each of the 6 surfaces and add them up.

(D) Careless—Looks like you got the perimeters mixed up. Perhaps you took the perimeter of the top to be 18 and the perimeter of the front to be 14. It should be the other way around.

(E) Missing key insight—Looks like you took half (7) of the perimeter of the top (14) and called it one of the 3 dimensions of the box. And you took half the perimeter of the front of the box and called it the other dimension. To solve this problem, start with the front of the box. Given that you know the perimeter and the height, you can find CD. Then, use this value of CD to find BC.

18. Correct choice (C) 16

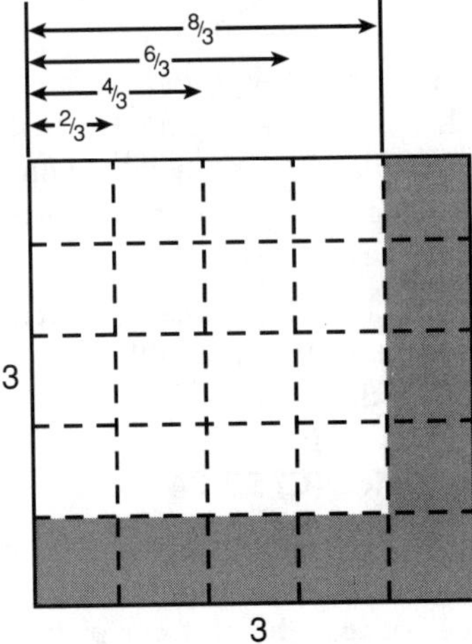

The key to solving this problem is to draw the figure. The larger concrete slab, 3 feet long and 3 feet wide, has been partitioned into smaller slabs, each of length $\frac{2}{3}$ and width $\frac{2}{3}$. As is shown in the figure, we can fit 4 smaller squares along the top row and thereby use up $(4 \times \frac{2}{3})$, or $\frac{8}{3}$ feet. This leaves $\frac{1}{3}$ feet along the edge that cannot be used. Similarly, we can fit four squares along the sides.

So, in total, we can fit four in one row. There are four rows and so the total number of squares is choice (C) 16.

Also, by scanning the choices, we could have eliminated choices (B) and (E), which have fractions. At this point, we could have guessed from among choices (A), (C), and (D).

Yes, this was a tricky problem. It is meant to be because it appears toward the end of the test.

(A) Miscalc—If you mistakenly assumed that the area of the smaller slab was $\frac{2}{3}$, and divided the larger area (9) by $\frac{2}{3}$, you probably got $13\frac{1}{2}$ as your answer, which you then rounded off to 13. Remember, the smaller square is of side $\frac{2}{3}$, which makes its area $\frac{4}{9}$. However, for problems of this nature, you should draw the figure and not simply divide the larger area by the smaller one; division does not take into account the strip of concrete at the edges that cannot be formed into squares.

(B) Miscalc—If you chose this answer, you probably took $\frac{2}{3}$ to be the area of the smaller slab. The area of the smaller slab is *not* $\frac{2}{3}$; it is $\frac{2}{3} \times \frac{2}{3}$, which is $\frac{4}{9}$. At any rate, you should not merely divide the larger area by the smaller area. Draw a figure.

(D) Missing key insight—If you got this answer, you probably divided the larger area, 9, by the smaller area $\frac{4}{9}$, and got $20\frac{1}{4}$, which you then rounded off to 20. This method does not take into account the fact that when you have cut out four small squares, you get a strip of concrete along the edge that cannot be used. The best way to solve this problem is to draw a figure.

(E) Missing key insight—If you got this answer, you probably divided the larger area, 9, by the smaller area, $\frac{4}{9}$ to get $20\frac{1}{4}$. This is incorrect because when you cut out four squares, you get a strip of concrete along the edge that cannot be used. The best way to solve this problem is to draw a figure.

19. Correct choice (A) 30

This is a difficult problem, one to come back to if there is enough time left on the test. But, let's say you have the time to solve it.

First of all, you can zap choice (B) 39 and choice (E) 465 because the problem says there should be an even number of terms in the sequence and 39 and 465 are both odd.

Suppose the sequence had only 4 terms. Then, the sequence would be: 2, 4, 6, and 8. Lisa's method would give us one sum of 10 by adding 2 and 8, and another sum of 10 by adding the two middle terms 4 and 6. Then, the total of the sequence would be 20. So, for 4 terms, the total is 20.

If there were 6 terms: 2, 4, 6, 8, 10 and 12, the paired sums would be:

$$\begin{aligned} 2 + 12 &= 14 \\ 4 + 10 &= 14 \\ 6 + 8 &= 14 \text{ and the overall} \\ \text{total} &= 14 + 14 + 14 = 42. \end{aligned}$$

Notice that when there are 4 terms,

$$\text{total} = 4 \times (4 + 1) = 4 \times 5 = 20$$

When there are 6 terms,

$$\text{total} = 6 \times (6 + 1) = 6 \times 7 = 42$$

So, to find the total, we need to multiply the number of terms by the number of terms plus 1, or $n(n+1)$, where n is the number of terms.

Now that we have this formula, let's start from the answers. As usual, we start from choice (C) 40. If there were 40 terms, then the total should be 40(41) = 1640. This is too high. So, if choice (C) is too high, choices (D) and (E) are also too high. We know that choice (B) cannot be the right answer because 39 is odd. Then choice (A) has to be the right answer. Let's check, anyway. We should get a total of 930 if we multiply 30 and 31. Well, 30 × 31 does equal 930, so this is correct.

(B) Repeated problem numbers—Looks like you picked this answer because of the digits 3 and 9 that appear in the problem. But remember, there has to be an *even* number of terms in the sequence. To solve this problem, see if you can form your own sequence of, say, 4 terms and another one of 6 terms. Then see what patterns emerge.

(C) Missing key insight—Looks like you took a wild guess. In a difficult problem like this, it's better to take a guess than to spend a lot of time working it and still get it wrong. To solve this problem, see if you can form your own sequence of, say, 4 terms and another one of 6 terms. Then see what patterns emerge.

(D) Oversight—Looks like you forgot to divide by 2 at the end. Check your answer. If there are 60 terms, the overall total will be 60 × 61, which is much higher than 930.

(E) Grabbing numbers—If you chose this answer, you probably divided 930 by 2. But, if you have 465 terms, the total will be 465 × 466, which is much higher than 930. Also, this cannot be the right answer because we're told that Lisa's sequence must have an even number of terms and 465 is odd. To solve this problem, see if you can form your own sequence of, say, 4 terms and another one of 6 terms. Then see what patterns emerge.

20. Correct choice (D) 4:7

It's important to remember what is meant by *x% higher* and *y% lower* in this context. An example is to say that "140 is 40% higher than 100," or "20% lower than 100 is 80."

So in this problem, we see that December sales are 40% higher than average, or to put it another way, December sales are 1.4 times the average monthly sales (100% + 40% = 140% = 1.4). Likewise, February sales are 0.8 (20% less than 1) times average sales.

So the ratio of February sales to December sales is $\frac{0.8}{1.4}$, which simplifies to $\frac{8}{14}$, or 4:7.

(A) Grabbing numbers—If you chose 1:2 as your answer, you probably just took 20% and 40%, two important numbers in the problem, and divided them. Be careful! Test writers often include answers that are simple manipulations of important numbers in the problem to distract you from the correct answer.

(B) Grabbing numbers—If you chose 4:2 as your answer, you probably just took 40% and 20%, two important numbers in the problem, and divided them. Be careful! Test writers often include answers that are simple manipulations of important numbers in the problem to distract you from the correct answer.

(C) Missing key insight—If you chose this answer, you may have thought that February sales were 20% lower than *December* sales, not 20% lower than average sales.

(E) Misread—If you chose this answer, you may have thought that February sales were 20% higher than average, rather than 20% lower.

21. Correct choice (B) 625

Recall that an *odd* digit is one that is not a multiple of 2. So the question is asking how many 4-digit numbers can we make using just the numbers 1, 3, 5, 7, and 9? To make a number, there are 4 digits that we have to fill, and there are 5 choices for what number to put in each position.

To calculate the total number of possible choices, we multiply the number of choices that we have for each position together—in this case $5 \times 5 \times 5 \times 5 = 5^4 = 625$ (if we could use even digits too, this number would be 10^4, or 10,000). Notice, you don't actually have to multiply this number. Once you figured out that it was 5 × 5 × 5 × 5, you can tell the answer has to be choice (B). Why? Because that's the only answer that ends in a 5.

(A) Too obvious—You probably figured out that there were 4 digits to fill and 5 choices for each digit. But you multiplied these two numbers together instead of taking 5 to the 4th power.

(C) Missing key insight—You probably figured out that there were 4 digits to fill and 5 choices for each digit. But you took 4 to the 5th power instead of taking 5 to the 4th power, which gave you a different answer.

(D) Misread—You probably just counted the odd 4-digit numbers, that is, the odd numbers between 1,000 and 9,999, but not the numbers that have only odd digits in them. So you counted numbers like 2,457, which is odd. But this number has even digits in it, which is not allowed.

(E) Misread—You probably just counted odd numbers with 4 digits or less, that is, the odd numbers between 1 and 9,999. This is not what the question asked for. Read the question again. It says the numbers *consist* of only odd digits, not that the numbers *end* in odd digits.

22. Correct choice (B) –1

To find an expression for $\{n + 1\}$, we apply the definition of the {} operator:

$$\{m\} = m(1 - m)$$

To find $\{n + 1\}$, rewrite this equation and put "$n + 1$" everywhere that an "m" appears:

$$\{n+1\} = (n+1)(1-[n+1])$$
$$= (n+1)(1-n-1)$$
$$= (n+1)(-n)$$
$$= -n^2 - n$$

So, to solve the problem $n + 1 = \{n + 1\}$, we will want to solve the equation

$$n + 1 = -n^2 - n$$

If we add $n^2 + n$ to both sides of this equation, we get

$$n^2 + 2n + 1 = 0$$

We recognize the left-hand side of this expression as $(n + 1)^2$, and conclude that this equation is true only if $n = -1$, choice (B).

(A) Miscalc—Did you miss a minus sign somewhere, and think that $\{n + 1\}$ was equal to $(n + 1)(n)$ instead of $(n + 1)(-n)$? Check your work again.

(C) Misread—You may have figured out that $\{0\} = 0$, and given the answer for $n = 0$ instead of $n + 1 = 0$, which is what the question asked.

(D) Oversight—Maybe you accidentally solved the problem $n + 1 = \{n\}$ instead of $n + 1 = \{n + 1\}$. Did you have an expression like $n + 1 = n(1 - n)$ somewhere in your solution? Check your work again.

(E) Miscalc—Perhaps you made a mistake in simplifying the quantity $(1 - n - 1)$ and found it to be equal to $-2 - n$, when it should've been equal to $-n$.

23. Correct choice (C) $\frac{25}{2\sqrt{2}}$

First, let's note that the radius of the semicircle is 5. We know this because the coordinates of B are (5,0), which means radius OB is 5. To find the area of the triangle, we need its base and its height. We can take OC as the base. We know that OC is also the radius of the semicircle, which is 5. So, the base of the triangle is 5. We now need its height.

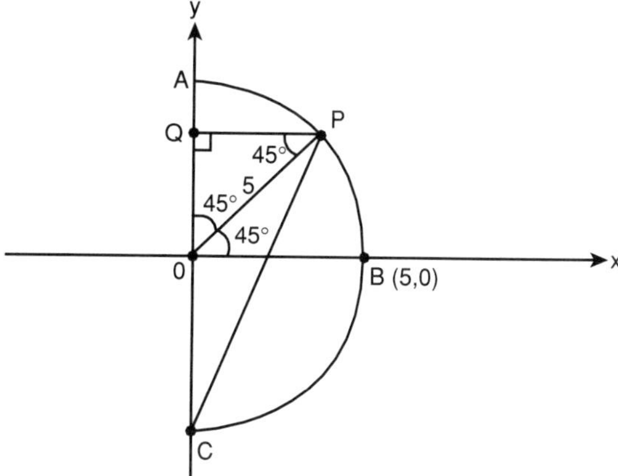

If we use OC as the base, we need a perpendicular from OC (or from an extension of OC) to the opposite corner. To find this perpendicular, let's draw PQ, 90 degrees on OA. Then, PQ is the height of the triangle. We need to find PQ.

Because $\angle POB$ is 45 degrees, $\angle POQ$ is also 45 degrees (because the 2 45-degree angles form the 90-degree angle between the x- and y-axes). If $\angle POQ$ is 45 and $\angle PQO$ is 45, then $\angle OPQ$ must also be 45 degrees so that the three angles sum to 180 degrees. So, triangle PQO is a 45–45–90 triangle. Notice also that OP is another radius, which means OP is 5.

We know that in a 45-45-90 triangle, the hypotenuse is $\sqrt{2}$ times each perpendicular side. In other words, the hypotenuse, 5, is $\sqrt{2}$ times the height PQ. So, $5 = \sqrt{2}(PQ)$.

And, $\frac{5}{\sqrt{2}} = PQ$

So now we have base = 5 and height = $\frac{5}{\sqrt{2}}$

Then, area of triangle OPC =

$$\frac{1}{2} \times 5 \times \frac{5}{\sqrt{2}} = \frac{25}{2\sqrt{2}}$$

(A) Missing key insight—Perhaps you thought that the height of the triangle was $\frac{5}{2}$. Maybe you assumed that point P is 2.5 units above the x-axis. To find the height of the triangle, drop a perpendicular from P to OA and work with the 45–45–90 triangle that you get.

(B) Oversight—You were almost there. You found the base of the triangle incorrectly. It looks like you dropped a perpendicular from *P* to *OA* (say, *PQ*) and then you added *OQ* to the base of the triangle. There's no need to add *OQ* because if you take *OC* as the base, and *PQ* as the height, you can find the area of triangle *OPC*.

(D) Missing key insight—Looks like you assumed that the base and the height of the triangle were equal. The base is 5, but the height isn't 5. You have to find the height by dropping a perpendicular from P to *OA*.

(E) Careless—You almost had it. You forgot the "$\frac{1}{2}$" term in the formula for the area of a triangle.

24. Correct choice (C) 7

We know that the total sum of all the cards in each box must be equal to 18. Box *A* has two cards that are already determined for us. Two of the cards are 6's. Therefore, the sum of the 2 cards in box *A* is 12. Thus the other 4 cards must sum to 6. Each card is numbered 1 through 6. We want 3 of the 4 cards to be as small as possible. Therefore, the 3 cards should be 1's. This leaves us with the fourth card as 3.

Sum of cards in box *A*: 6 + 6 + 1 + 1 + 1 + 3 = 18

For box *B*, two of the cards are 5's. This leaves us with four cards. Again, we want 3 of the 4 cards to be as small as possible. Let the 3 cards be 1's. This leaves the fourth card as 5. But recall that neither card was a 5 or a 6. Thus, the fourth card must be smaller than 5. We see that if the fourth card is 4 and one of the other cards is 2, we have:

Sum of cards in box *B*: 5 + 5 + 1 + 1 + 2 + 4 = 18

So, the largest possible sum of the two cards is 3 + 4 = 7.

(A) Misread—You probably found the largest numbered card in box *A*. But you were asked to find the largest possible *sum* of the two cards.

(B) Misread—You probably found the largest numbered card in box *B*. But you were asked to find the largest possible *sum* of the two cards.

(D) Miscalc—You probably forgot that neither of the two cards was a 5.

(E) Oversight—You probably forgot that neither of the two cards was a 6.

25. Correct choice (A) p × d

There are a number of ways of working this problem. But first, let's use the given information to write an equation. We are told that the ratio of the perimeter of the larger to the smaller rectangle is p. That is,

$$\frac{\text{perimeter of larger rectangle}}{\text{perimeter of smaller rectangle}} = p$$

In terms of length and width, we know that the perimeter is $2(L + B)$ for the larger rectangle, and $2(l + b)$ for the smaller rectangle. Then the ratio of the two perimeters is

$$\frac{2(L+B)}{2(l+b)} = p, \text{ which can be reduced to}$$

$$\frac{(L+B)}{(l+b)} = p. \text{ Call this Equation (1).}$$

We are also told that $\frac{(L-B)}{(l-b)} = d$. Call this Equation (2). Now multiply Equation (1) and Equation (2) so that we get

$$\frac{(L+B)}{(l+b)} \times \frac{(L-B)}{(l-b)} = p \times d$$

Ah, both the numerator and the denominator are of the form

$(a + b) \times (a - b)$ which is equal to $(a^2 - b^2)$.

Using the same formula, we multiply the numerators together and the denominators together to get

$$\frac{(L^2 - B^2)}{(l^2 - b^2)} = p \times d, \text{ which is choice (A).}$$

Don't be surprised that this was a difficult problem. It appears at the end of the section; it is meant to be difficult.

But, let's see if there is an easier way to do the problem. If you don't like to deal with variables like p and d, give values to L, B, l, and b. To make calculations easy, let $L = 4$, $B = 2$, $l = 2$, and $b = 1$. Then, the ratio of the two perimeters is given by:

$$\frac{(L+L+B+B)}{(l+l+b+b)} = \frac{(4+4+2+2)}{(2+2+1+1)} = \frac{12}{6} = p = 2$$

$$\text{Similarly, } \frac{(L-B)}{(l-b)} = \frac{(4-2)}{(2-1)} = \frac{2}{1} = d = 2$$

We are asked to find $\frac{(L^2-B^2)}{(l^2-b^2)}$. Substituting our own values,

we get $\frac{(4^2-2^2)}{(2^2-1^2)}=\frac{16-4}{3}=\frac{12}{3}=4$

Now look at the answer choices. Choice (A) is $p \times d$, which is equal to $2 \times 2 = 4$. As you can see, choice (A) gives us the required value, and so it is the right answer. At this point, we don't need to try the other choices.

(B) Too obvious—Quantity $\frac{p}{d}$ is simply the ratio of the two given quantities. It's too obvious. It's also wrong.

(C) Missing key insight—This choice looks plausible simply because it is expressed in a fancy mathematical form. Again, you have to remember that this problem is a difficult one and such answers, though they may look attractive, are usually incorrect.

(D) Repeated problem numbers—This answer choice looks very much like the two ratios p and d. It is meant to be an attractive choice for those making a random guess. Watch out for numbers and patterns in answer choices that copy those found in the problem.

(E) Missing key insight—This is misleading because it presents the p quantity without squares and the d quantity as a squared amount, which corresponds to the values of p and d given in the problem.

Day 11

Test 1, Section 2: Verbal

Questions and Answers

Assignment for Today:

Take a sample SAT Verbal Reasoning Test under actual test conditions. Allow yourself exactly 30 minutes to complete the 35 questions in this test.

Directions: *For questions 1–10, one or more words have been left out of each sentence. Circle the answer, A–E, which contains the word or words which best fit the meaning of the entire sentence.*

1. While at the party, the actress lived up to her reputation for being —— when she jumped onto the piano and began to dance.
   (A) stodgy
   (B) insincere
   (C) exuberant
   (D) terse
   (E) urbane

2. To the food server, her work was just a job; she did it for the sake of —— and nothing else.
   (A) approbation
   (B) remuneration
   (C) emulation
   (D) exoneration
   (E) procrastination

3. Because the bulk of tax revenue comes from various sales taxes, the burden of payment falls —— on the shoulders of poor and middle-income Americans who spend roughly 16 percent of their incomes on taxable goods, while the richest Americans spend only about 3.1 percent.
   (A) disproportionately
   (B) diminutively
   (C) lightly
   (D) inadequately
   (E) equitably

4. According to the minority political party, the major problem with national health insurance reform, as a —— alternative to more government spending, is that it's a tax ——.
   (A) purported..increase
   (B) cheery..standard
   (C) feasible..revolt
   (D) sarcastic..statement
   (E) toxic..shelter

5. When he declined the knighthood offered him by a corrupt government, even the libertarian press ceased to label him a —— rabble-rouser and lauded him as a man of courage and ——.
   (A) troublesome..bravery
   (B) cowardly..duplicity
   (C) social-climbing..integrity
   (D) motivated..disrepute
   (E) royalist..hauteur

6. After the wind blew away the musician's music, she —— so cleverly that the people watching were not —— of the mishap.
   (A) extemporized..cognizant
   (B) digressed..unappreciative
   (C) improvised..warned
   (D) wafted..aware
   (E) denigrated..mindful

7. The dermatologist was —— in his belief that the new surgical procedure he had worked ten years to perfect would —— all signs of a tattoo.
   (A) unwavering..expunge
   (B) incredulous..erase
   (C) sentient..obliterate
   (D) timorous..eradicate
   (E) euphoric..exacerbate

8. When the mayor announced her candidacy for the next term, she —— the virtues of her past term while the reporters took copious notes and wished she weren't so ——.
   (A) explained..taciturn
   (B) expatiated on..garrulous
   (C) expounded on..insidious
   (D) gibbered about..erudite
   (E) noted..talkative

9. After work, Miriam would go home and enjoy —— with her husband and children, but at work she talked in lofty tones that were reminiscent of a ——.
   (A) bantering..colloquy
   (B) housework..discourse
   (C) discussion..eulogy
   (D) hoopla..secretary
   (E) quibbling..scholar

10. What had started out as good-natured ——, developed into a brawl, with the larger man getting his front tooth broken.
   (A) intuition
   (B) raillery
   (C) bickering
   (D) veracity
   (E) virulence

Directions: *For questions 11–23, determine the relationship between the two words given in capital letters. Then, from the choices listed A–E, select the one pair that has a relationship most similar to that of the capitalized pair. Circle the letter of that pair.*

---

11. HIGHWAY:VEHICLE::
   (A) window:frame
   (B) nest:bird
   (C) garage:automobile
   (D) path:hiker
   (E) engine:magnet

12. FLATTER:COMPLIMENT::
   (A) request:solicit
   (B) deceive:delude
   (C) forswear:swindle
   (D) withhold:release
   (E) splurge:spend

13. CEMETERY:MOURN::
   (A) park:feed
   (B) zoo:stroll
   (C) church:worship
   (D) bank:save
   (E) airport:travel

14. CAVE:SHELTER::
    (A) valley:sun
    (B) tree:sapling
    (C) river:delta
    (D) wind:mill
    (E) peak:lookout

15. STATESMAN:GOVERNMENT::
    (A) teacher:faculty
    (B) potter:art
    (C) raconteur:anecdote
    (D) dowager:marriage
    (E) shepherd:farm

16. SURREPTITIOUS:CANDOR::
    (A) stealthy:mystery
    (B) confident:honesty
    (C) fearless:pride
    (D) fatuous:sense
    (E) subtle:cunning

17. STAGGER:INEBRIATED::
    (A) devour:famished
    (B) enhance:ecstatic
    (C) enact:apathetic
    (D) muscle:lethargic
    (E) drift:posh

18. COBBLER:OXFORDS::
    (A) mason:mortar
    (B) lapidary:stones
    (C) haberdasher:linen
    (D) chandler:candles
    (E) agronomist:fertilizer

19. PAGE:TOME::
    (A) ink:paper
    (B) tree:forest
    (C) rose:petal
    (D) sky:sun
    (E) thespian:stage

20. GALAXY:EPHEMERAL::
    (A) fanatic:vehement
    (B) dolt:sagacious
    (C) dinosaur:antediluvian
    (D) connoisseur:epicureal
    (E) ocean:voluminous

21. FORUM:DISCUSSION::
    (A) papacy:absolution
    (B) space:exploration
    (C) parliament:legislation
    (D) rostrum:peroration
    (E) speakeasy:gossip

22. EXCORIATE:ABRADE::
    (A) consent:decree
    (B) demur:agree
    (C) mar:burnish
    (D) eschew:avoid
    (E) proscribe:support

23. MNEMONIC:REMEMBER::
    (A) amnesiac:forget
    (B) euphoria:relax
    (C) nostril:smell
    (D) audio:hear
    (E) glasses:see

Directions: *Answer each question based only on what is stated or implied in the passage and any introductory material given.*

Questions 24–35 are based on the following passage.

In the following selection, a journalist muses on the nature of the readers' queries that he has received.

Before I became law editor for a farm paper, I used to doubt the genuineness of some of the absurd queries one occasionally sees propounded in the "Answers to Correspondents" columns of newspapers. Now I am almost prepared to believe that a Utah man actually wrote Bill Nye for information concerning the nature and habits of Limburg cheese, as a basis for experiments in the use of that substance as motive power.

Of the hundreds of queries that come to my office in the course of a year, most of them are commonplace enough, including such questions as what constitutes a lawful fence in Connecticut. But one correspondent in fifty unconsciously sends in a gem that gives the editor a smile with which to rest his tired countenance, albeit there is often concomitant pathos in the letters.

Many a pathetic domestic snarl is disclosed in amusing language. For instance, one woman wrote, "My husband's health is very poor and he is stubborn about making a will." She sought advice concerning her property rights, contingent upon her spouse's "stubbornness" remaining with him to the end.

Sometimes the wife holds the upper hand, as illustrated by a Wisconsin farmer who complained: "Came to Wis., bought 160 A, put it in my Wife's name, and as soon as she found out that the law of Wis. gave the husband absolutely nothing, she will not give me *one cent*, or go a single place, or will not buy me any clothe, only working clothe. Now, can I compell her to pay me a salary, without leaving her. And I shopped three horses, one cow, one calf, one brood sow, wagon and harness, buggy and harness, and can *I* dispose of them?" This Mr. Bumble was told that he was at liberty to "go places" as he saw fit, could control the stock enumerated, and dictate the terms on which he would work in his wife's vineyard, but that the Wisconsin law makes her secure in the sole ownership of the farm which he unadvisedly caused to be conveyed to her.

Another rebellious husband wrote that he conveyed his property to his wife to defeat his judgment creditors. "Now I want my wife to Deed some of it back to me but she refuses to do that on account the feeling is not at best between us." He wanted to know if it wouldn't be a good plan to confess to the creditors, and get the property deeded "back to me as it was before as the hole Deal was a Fraud." The main objection to this plan being that it would enable the creditors to get the property, it was suggested that Friend Wife be permitted to retain control, especially since he could not compel her to revest title in him.

Another case was stated as follows: "The contents of case are—A newly married couple, the young lady having come to the decision that life is unbearable to live with her husband because she hates him and cannot bear his ways of manners. She wishes them to part, and he will not agree to it. And she thinks of going to her parents to live, and take her belongings that she had before being married with him, and the husband says no—what has she a right to do? Or does the belongings belong to him also?" Without encouragement to a domestic rupture, the correspondent was told that a woman's ownership of personal property is not affected by her marriage.

A jilted girl sought advice on how to "fix" her unfaithful sweetheart. He promised marriage three times, but as the wedding day approached he "always had some excuse. If it weren't the crops, it was the widow-women. If it weren't the widow-women, it was something else. He never had written his love for me in a letter. But when I was with him he was all love and kisses and so on. He said in one of his letters, 'Make all you can this fall in no matter what kind of work as it may not last forever.' But he has backed out now for good."

But problems of the heart are by no means the only cause for correspondence. Rights between employer and employee are frequently called into question. One indignant woman employed on a farm objected that the "landlord brought out a large worthless dog and we have been feeding him, have been paying thirty dollars a sack for flour and twenty-two dollars per week for corn meal to feed him. We have asked several times to take him away as we cannot afford to feed him. This mutt is no earthly account for any thing and he seldom gets up. He just lies there, wagging his tail, eager for his meals. We don't need or want him here and have told him so."

I disclaim any intention to unduly discredit the intelligence or high-mindedness of any of my correspondents for, as already intimated, the freak letters are few as compared with the general run of submissions. My observations in reading thousands confirm my belief that most people, regardless of their wealth or walk in life, stand upon an equal plane intellectually and morally, when fair allowance is made of individual opportunities and environment. I may smile for a moment or two over the occasional rude spelling or unschooled language of one writer out of fifty, but I sober up when I reflect that he or she may have earned a larger percentage of dividend on the opportunities presented than I have on mine.

24. The main purpose of this passage most likely is to
    (A) examine the different types of commonly occurring domestic disputes
    (B) describe the failed schemes of people who try to outwit the law
    (C) analyze the legal recourse available to people in oppressive situations
    (D) determine the role of a newspaper in helping its readers through advice columns
    (E) validate the authenticity of strange but heartfelt submissions that newspapers publish

25. The word "countenance" in line 17 most likely means
    (A) head
    (B) tolerate
    (C) composure
    (D) encourage
    (E) visage

26. The author probably wades through submissions to the paper with
    (A) incessant laughter
    (B) weary disillusionment
    (C) restrained contempt
    (D) profound disbelief
    (E) infrequent smiles

27. The author relates the story of Mr. Bumble the farmer in order to
    (A) warn farmers that Wisconsin law can be dangerous
    (B) emphasize that some wives are suffering in silence while waiting for a chance to gain the upper hand
    (C) highlight a turning point in the forces that brought about the liberation of women
    (D) illustrate the pitfalls of not taking legal advice before trusting someone even as close as a wife
    (E) entertain the reader with a pathetic but amusingly worded domestic dispute

28. The word "conveyed" in line 43 most likely means
    (A) trusted
    (B) transported
    (C) transferred
    (D) bequeathed
    (E) bypassed

29. The common thread that ties together every anecdote in the passage is
    (A) advocacy solicited
    (B) freak letters
    (C) property rights
    (D) punitive measures
    (E) editorial responses

30. The essential difference between the Limburg cheese letter and the letter in paragraph three is that the Limburg cheese letter was
    (A) a freak letter whereas the other letter was commonplace
    (B) merely absurd whereas the other letter was amusing
    (C) written by an Utah man and the other letter by a Connecticut woman
    (D) an information query while the other letter was for legal advocacy
    (E) concerned with powerful odors and the other letter with stubbornness

31. What makes the author disinclined to sneer or mock at letters he receives is that
    (A) although strange or funny, the letters depict a heartfelt pathos
    (B) most people dwell within an equal moral sphere, and to mock one would be to mock himself
    (C) he may be suspected of trying to portray correspondents as fools
    (D) the strange correspondent has probably made more of his or her circumstances than the author
    (E) submissions in general, except for the occasional freak letter, are more wearying than amusing

32. In this passage, the author probably uses excerpts from submissions
    (A) so readers may judge for themselves the extent to which farming communities are petty and illiterate
    (B) because they possess an amusing flavor that is lost if converted to polished prose
    (C) to lend authenticity to what might otherwise be unconvincing narrative
    (D) to show, if only linguistically, that pathetic snarls can have an amusing facet
    (E) so the reader may not misinterpret the information or suspect the author of fabrication

33. From the various examples used in the passage the reader can conclude that
    (A) the farm paper is based in Utah or Wisconsin
    (B) Wisconsin law stipulates that on a farm the wife secures sole ownership
    (C) hating your husband's unbearable manners is sufficient grounds for divorce
    (D) large dogs are capable of consuming 62 dollars' worth of meal in a week
    (E) some farm people were not hesitant to solicit advice from newspapers.

34. Which of the following can be inferred from the advocacy given in one or more of the cases mentioned?
    (A) The farm and livestock do belong to his wife, but Mr. Bumble may decide how he wants to work on it.
    (B) If a deal was based on fraud, it can be rendered null and void.
    (C) A wife retains control over her personal property even if her husband raises a dispute.
    (D) A general statement in a letter is not legally considered as a sign of intent to marry.
    (E) A landlord has the right to add livestock or animals to a farm without the tenant's consent.

35. The word "rude" as used in line 110 most likely means
    (A) violent
    (B) harsh
    (C) impolite
    (D) rough
    (E) nasty

Quick Answer Guide

Test 1, Section 2: Verbal

1. C
2. B
3. A
4. A
5. C
6. A
7. A
8. B
9. A
10. B
11. D
12. E
13. C
14. E
15. C
16. D
17. A
18. D
19. B
20. B
21. C
22. D
23. E
24. E
25. E
26. E
27. E
28. C
29. B
30. D
31. D
32. C
33. E
34. C
35. D

For explanations to these questions see Day 12.

Day 12

Test 1, Section 2: Verbal

Explanations and Strategies

Assignment for Today:

Review the explanations for the test you just took. See which answer is right, and learn what makes each wrong answer wrong.

1. Correct choice (C) exuberant

How would you describe someone who jumps onto a piano and begins to dance? Lively and full of fun, right? So look for a word that describes this behavior. The best choice is *exuberant*, which means joyously unrestrained.

While at the party, the actress lived up to her reputation for being *exuberant* when she jumped onto the piano and began to dance.

(A) *Stodgy* means "dull and stuffy." This doesn't work with someone who's the life of the party.

(B) *Sincerity* has little to do with dancing on a piano at a party.

(D) *Terse* means "concise or abrupt." Terse people aren't necessarily prone to dancing on pianos.

(E) *Urbane* means "cultured," which might be exactly the wrong choice for someone so unrestrained.

2. Correct choice (B) remuneration

The sentence makes it clear that the server is working just for the money. So to find the right answer, select the word that has something to do with earning money. Choice (B) fits; *remuneration* means compensation or money.

To the food server her work was just a job; she did it for the *remuneration* and nothing else.

(A) *Approbation* means "approval." It's unlikely that a food server would be working only for approval.

(C) *Emulation* means "imitation." To say that the server is working for the sake of imitation makes no sense.

(D) *Exoneration* means "freedom from blame." Is the server working simply so she can be free from blame? No, she's working for money.

(E) Do you think the server is working because she is *procrastinating*, which means "putting something off"? In that case, she's either not working or working at some activity other than what needs to be done now. Such an interpretation is possible but not likely.

3. Correct choice (A) disproportionately

Note the flag word, "because," at the beginning of the sentence. This tells you that the last part of the sentence is caused by the first part.

The sentence tells us that the tax burden is nearly five times greater for poor and middle-income Americans than for rich Americans. In other words, the tax load is lopsided. An adverb that means "uneven or inequitable" would fit the context nicely. So choice (A), *disproportionately*—which means "unevenly distributed"—is the correct answer.

Because the bulk of tax revenue comes from various sales taxes, the burden of payment falls *disproportionately* on the shoulders of poor and middle-income Americans who spend roughly 16 percent of their incomes on taxable goods, while the richest Americans spend only about 3.1 percent.

(B) *Diminutively* means "small or minute," but the sentence tells us that the tax burden is larger for poor and middle-class Americans than for rich Americans. This choice doesn't work.

(C) The sentence is describing an unevenly distributed tax burden, not a light burden. The choice *lightly* doesn't work.

(D) *Inadequately* means "insufficiently." The sentence claims that poor and middle-class Americans are unfairly taxed, not insufficiently taxed.

(E) *Equitably* means "fairly or evenly." The sentence claims that poor and middle-class Americans are unfairly, not fairly, taxed.

4. Correct choice (A) purported..increase

You can find the right answer to this question by using a different strategy for each blank. First, think of what word you might use for the second blank. The sentence should tell you that having national health care is going to raise taxes. Choice (A) fits beautifully here. Now try the elimination strategy for the first blank. Again, nothing works very well here except *purported* in choice (A).

According to the minority political party, the major problem with national health insurance reform, as a *purported* alternative to more government spending, is that it's a tax *increase*.

(B) *Cheery* might fit, but national health insurance has nothing to do with a tax *standard*.

(C) *Feasible* works well, but a tax *revolt* makes no sense at all.

(D) *Sarcastic* alternative doesn't work well, and tax *statement* is not right in this sentence.

(E) Although tax *shelter* may seem right, the idea of having a *toxic* alternative should tell you this choice is not right.

5. Correct choice (C) social-climbing..integrity

Plug in and check each answer choice. No flags here, but there are other clues.

". . . *ceased to label* him a —— rabble-rouser and *lauded* him as a man of courage and ——." A *rabble-rouser* is negative, so the first blank must be negative. The second blank must be positive just as *courage* is positive. That means it's either choice (A) or choice (C).

"The . . . press ceased to label him" something "when he declined the knighthood." This indicates that turning down the knighthood showed that he wasn't ——. It must be choice (C), because social climbers don't refuse knighthood. Social climbers are status seekers, blue-blood wannabes.

When he declined the knighthood offered him by a corrupt government, even the libertarian press ceased to label him a *social-climbing* rabble-rouser and lauded him as a man of courage and *integrity*.

(A) This choice fits the sentence in that the first blank is negative, and the second blank positive. But would refusing a knighthood make the press think of him as less *troublesome?* Not really.

(B) *Duplicity* is deceitfulness, or double-dealing. "When he declined the knighthood offered him by a corrupt government, even the libertarian press lauded him as a man of courage and *deceitfulness*." Doesn't make sense. *Courage* is positive, *duplicity* is negative.

(D) *Disregard* means "neglect; lack of due respect or regard." It is negative. It doesn't mean "he was not concerned with honors." It means he was a disrespectful sort. The press wouldn't *laud* him as *both* a man of courage and lacking proper respect. They would praise his *courage* but chide his *disregard*.

(E) A *royalist* is a strong supporter of the monarchy. Royalists don't refuse knighthood. They also don't rouse rabble in revolt. That's like management starting a labor strike. Besides, *hauteur* means arrogance, snobbery, or disdainful pride, something the press wouldn't *laud* him for.

6. Correct choice (A) extemporized..cognizant

The sentence itself gives you some major clues. First off, if a musician loses her music, she will either have to stop playing or make stuff up as she goes along. The sentence indicates that the musician is clever, so you can be fairly sure she made stuff up. The people watching did not notice what she did. So look for words that fit these ideas. Choice (A) works best.

After the wind blew away the musician's music, she *extemporized* so cleverly that the people watching were not *cognizant* of the mishap.

(B) To *digress* means to wander off track. While a musician without music may likely not play the notes that were scored, *digress* doesn't accurately describe this musician's troubles. Close, but just not right.

(C) *Improvise* fits perfectly in the first blank; however, to say that the "people watching were not warned of the mishap" doesn't make logical sense.

(D) *Waft* means to move gently by wind or breeze and usually refers to smells. It doesn't work here. But *aware* works well. This answer is half right, which isn't good enough.

(E) To *denigrate* is to belittle, so this doesn't fit the meaning of the rest of the sentence. However, *mindful* works well.

7. Correct choice (A) unwavering..expunge

The easy part about this question is deciding what kinds of words will adequately fill the blanks—something like "hopeful" and "erase." The hard part is knowing which words have these meanings. Choice (A) offers *unwavering*, which means solidly confident, and *expunge*, which means to remove all evidence of existence. This is the best choice.

The dermatologist was *unwavering* in his belief that the new surgical procedure he had worked ten years to invent would be able to *expunge* all signs of having a tattoo.

(B) *Incredulous* means "doubtful," only stronger. It's unlikely the doctor would doubt his own work. *Erase* does work well, however, so well that many people will select this choice on the strength of the second word, which is exactly what the test maker would like you to do.

(C) *Sentient* means "conscious or aware." This really doesn't work well in the first blank because *sentient* is usually used to describe something as being alive, such as a *sentient* being. *Obliterate* means "to wipe out" and works fine.

(D) *Timorous* means "fearful." It's unlikely that the doctor would be fearful about his new procedure. *Eradicate* means "to destroy" and works well in the second blank.

(E) *Euphoric* means "feeling extremely happy" and works well enough, but *exacerbate*, meaning "to make worse," does not. A surgical procedure that makes the situation worse would not be good.

8. Correct choice (B) expatiated on..garrulous

The best bet for finding the correct choice is to simply read in the choices, eliminating those that don't work well. Then you will have to make some fine distinctions about which choice fits the context the best. All in all, (B) works best. To *expatiate* is to elaborate. This works well for a politician. *Garrulous* means talkative—another good word for a politician.

When the mayor announced her candidacy for the next term, she *expatiated on* the virtues of her past term while the reporters took copious notes and wished she weren't so *garrulous*.

(A) *Explained* is okay but lacks the energy a politician would give to an announcement to seek a second term. *Taciturn*, however, means reluctant to talk, which makes no sense if the reporters were taking copious (lots of) notes.

(C) *Expound* means "to explain in detail" and fits fine. *Insidious* means "seductive but harmful," which doesn't really fit the context: a seductive but harmful re-election speech?

(D) To *gibber about* is to talk foolishly, which might be okay except that the reporters thought she was *erudite*, which means scholarly. These two phrases don't go together.

(E) *Noted* is much too neutral. To note is to make a brief remark. The reporters thought the mayor was too *talkative*. This pair of words doesn't go together very well.

9. Correct choice (A) bantering..colloquy

The sentence clues and the flag word "but" indicate that the first blank is best filled by a word that means "light talk," while the second word should mean "serious talk." (A) is the best choice here. *Bantering* means playful kidding. A *colloquy*, in contrast, is a serious conference.

After work, Miriam would go home and enjoy *bantering* with her husband and children, but at work she talked in lofty tones that were reminiscent of a *colloquy*.

(B) So you think she's going to enjoy *housework?* Probably not. But *discourse* is okay.

(C) *Discussion* fits, but is too formal for the context. The sentence seems to want something a little more relaxed. *Eulogy*, a formal statement of praise, works well, however.

(D) *Hoopla*, excited commotion, fits the first blank. It gets the idea of fun across. But *secretary* is odd because you don't usually think of *secretaries* talking in lofty tones.

(E) *Quibbling* isn't right because it means "fighting with words," which most people don't enjoy. *Scholar* fits the second blank. But an answer that's only partly right is the wrong answer.

10. Correct choice (B) raillery

If you can't figure out which word should go in the blank, eliminate the words you know won't work and then choose from the ones that remain. Doing this (and with some luck), you just may choose the right answer: (B) *raillery*, which means playful teasing.

What had started out as good-natured *raillery* developed into a brawl, with the larger man getting his front tooth broken.

(A) *Intuition* is knowing something without solid evidence. Good-natured intuition doesn't lead to violent fights.

(C) *Bickering*, arguing about trivial things, works to a small degree, but *bickering* usually isn't good-natured. Question-mark this choice, but look for a better answer.

(D) *Veracity* is truthfulness. This makes little sense. Why would good-natured truthfulness develop into a fight?

(E) *Virulence* means bitterness or hostility. As you can see, virulence does not have a good-natured aspect to it. Find something better.

11. Correct choice (D) path:hiker

highway—a place where vehicles travel

vehicle—a machine that transports people and things

A *highway* is a place where *vehicles* travel.

(A) Is a *window* a place where *frames* travel? No. A *window* rests in a *frame*.

(B) Is a *nest* a place where *birds* travel? No, a *nest* is a home for a bird.

(C) Is a *garage* a place where *automobiles* travel? No, *automobiles* are stored in a *garage*.

(D) Is a *path* a place where *hikers* travel? Yes, *vehicles* travel on *highways* in the same way as *hikers* travel on *paths*. **Correct choice.**

(E) Is an *engine* a place where *magnets* travel? No, *magnetic* fields cause electrical *engines* to work, but there's no traveling involved.

12. Correct choice (E) splurge:spend

flatter—to compliment extravagantly

compliment—to express admiration

To *flatter* is to *compliment* extravagantly.

(A) Is *request* to *solicit* extravagantly? No. The two words mean roughly the same thing: to ask.

(B) Is *deceive* to *delude* extravagantly? No. The two words mean about the same thing: to trick.

(C) Is *forswear* to *swindle* extravagantly? No. To *forswear* is to reject under oath. To *swindle* is to cheat someone out of his or her property.

(D) Is *withhold* to *release* extravagantly? No, these two are opposites—to *release* is to let go, whereas to *withhold* is to keep.

(E) Is *splurge* to *spend* extravagantly? Yes. Therefore, *flatter* is to *compliment* in the same way that *splurge* is to *spend*. **Correct choice.**

13. Correct choice (C) church:worship

cemetery—a place where dead people are buried

mourn—to feel sad or to grieve

A *cemetery* is a common place where people *mourn*.

(A) Is a *park* a common place where people go to *feed?* Not really. But they may go there to eat or to feed the animals.

(B) Is a *zoo* a common place where people go to *stroll?* Sort of. But people usually go to the zoo to see the animals, not to stroll. Question-mark this choice, but look for a better one.

(C) Is a *church* a common place where people go to *worship?* Yes! So *cemetery* is to *mourn* as *church* is to *worship*. **Correct choice**.

(D) Is a *bank* a common place where people go to *save?* Sort of. But the difference here is that in a cemetery people mourn while they are still there; in a bank, people don't stand around saving. A better answer would have been *bank:deposit*. This was a tricky one.

(E) Is an *airport* a common place where people go to *travel?* Sort of. However, people usually don't remain at a airport when they travel; they just start their traveling there.

14. Correct choice (E) peak:lookout

cave—an enclosure in a hill or mountain

shelter—a structure that protects

A *cave* can be used as a *shelter*.

(A) Can a *valley* be used as a *sun?* No. This doesn't work.

(B) Can a *tree* be used as a *sapling?* No. Saplings are small trees.

(C) Can a *river* be used as a *delta?* No. A delta can be part of a river (its end).

(D) Can a *wind* be used as a *mill?* No, but wind can be used to power a mill.

(E) Can a *peak* be used as a *lookout?* Yes. So *cave* is to *shelter* as *peak* is to *lookout*. **Correct choice**.

15. Correct choice (C) raconteur:anecdote

statesman—a person skilled in the art of government

government—the control of the actions of a community or nation

A *statesman* is a person skilled in the art of *government*.

(A) Is a *teacher* skilled in the art of *faculty?* No. A *faculty* is the teaching body, a group of teachers.

(B) Is a *potter* skilled in the art of *art?* No. Not all art. Probably just in making pots and stoneware.

(C) Is a *raconteur* skilled in the art of *anecdote?* Yes. A *raconteur* is a person skilled in relating *anecdotes* interestingly (an expert teller). **Correct choice**.

(D) Is a *dowager* skilled in the art of *marriage?* Not necessarily. A *dowager* is a wealthy, dignified woman or a royal widow.

(E) Is a *shepherd* skilled in the art of *flock?* No. If you figured a *shepherd* takes care of the flock, that comes close. But a *statesman* doesn't have to take care of *government*.

16. Correct choice (D) fatuous:sense

surreptitious—to be secretive

candor—honesty and sincerity

To be *surreptitious* means to lack *candor*.

(A) Does being *stealthy* mean to lack *mystery?* No. *Stealthy* has to do with being secretive, which is part of *mystery*.

(B) Does being *confident* mean to lack *honesty?* No.

(C) Does being *fearless* mean to lack *pride?* No.

(D) Does being *fatuous* mean to lack *sense?* Yes. To be *fatuous* is to be silly and inane. **Correct choice**.

(E) Does being *subtle* mean to lack *cunning?* No.

17. Correct choice (A) devour:famished

stagger—to walk unsteadily

inebriated—intoxicated

Stagger is an action resulting from being *inebriated*.

(A) Is *devour* an action resulting from being *famished?* Yes! *Devour* means to eat ravenously, and *famished* means to be suffering severely from hunger. **Correct choice**.

(B) Is *enhance* an action resulting from being *ecstatic?* No, to *enhance* means to improve something. *Ecstatic* means utter happiness. One does not necessarily improve something merely because one is happy.

(C) Is *enact* an action resulting from being *apathetic*? No, since to *enact* means to perform an action, and *apathetic* means to be inactive due to lack of concern.

(D) Is *muscle* an action resulting from being *lethargic?* No, to *muscle* means to physically exert oneself. *Lethargic* means tired and without energy.

(E) Is *drift* an action resulting from being *posh?* No, *drift* means to wander off course, and *posh* means luxurious. These are not necessarily related.

18. Correct choice (D) chandler:candles

cobbler—a person who makes shoes

oxfords—shoes, something worn on the foot

A *cobbler* makes *oxfords.*

(A) Does a *mason* make *mortar?* Maybe, but a *mason* is really someone who works with stones or bricks, so this isn't 100 percent. Question-mark it but look for a better answer.

(B) Does a *lapidary* make *stones?* No. A *lapidary* is someone who works with *stones.*

(C) Does a *haberdasher* make *linen?* No. A *haberdasher* sells men's socks and shirts.

(D) Does a *chandler* make *candles?* Yes! A *chandler* is a candlemaker. Therefore, *cobbler* is to *oxfords* as *chandler* is to *candles.* **Correct choice.**

(E) Does an *agronomist* make *fertilizer?* No. An *agronomist* is one who specializes in crops and may *use fertilizer* but doesn't make it. Horses and other barnyard animals are the ones that "make" fertilizer!

19. Correct choice (B) tree:forest

page—a single sheet of paper in a book

tome—a large or scholarly book

A *tome* consists of many *pages.*

(A) Does *paper* consist of many *inks?* No. Many inks may be used to print a page. This is a same-category attractor, but it's an incorrect choice. Remember: You are looking for the same *relationship*, not the same category.

(B) Does a *forest* consist of many *trees?* Yes. Therefore, a *tome* consists of many *pages* in the same way that a *forest* consists of many *trees.* **Correct choice.**

(C) Does a *petal* consist of many *roses?* No, but had it been *petal:rose*, this would have been correct, since a *rose* consists of many *petals.*

(D) Does the *sun* consist of many *skies?* No, although during the day the *sun* can be seen in the *sky.*

(E) Does a *stage* consist of many *thespians?* No. A *thespian* is an actor. A *stage* (the place where a play or musical is performed) may be *occupied* by many actors, but does not *consist* of actors.

20. Correct choice (B) dolt:sagacious

galaxy—aggregate of stars, space, and dust

ephemeral—lasting a very short time

A *galaxy* is not *ephemeral.*

(A) Is a *fanatic* not *vehement?* No. *Vehement* means emphatic or intense. Many fans of professional sports or music are this way about their "stars."

(B) Is a *dolt* not *sagacious?* Right! *Sagacious* means wise. A *dolt* is a stupid person. Therefore, *galaxy* is to *ephemeral* as *dolt* is to *sagacious.* **Correct choice.**

(C) Is a *dinosaur* not *antediluvian?* No. *Antediluvian* means ancient, so *dinosaurs* are indeed *antediluvian.*

(D) Is a *connoisseur* not *epicureal?* No. A *connoisseur* is indeed *epicureal*, which means having refined tastes.

(E) Is an *ocean* not *voluminous?* No. An *ocean* is *voluminous*, which means having a huge quantity—which in this case is water.

21. Correct choice (C) parliament:legislation

forum—an assembly for the discussion of public affairs

discussion—debate, exchange of views, examination by argument

A *forum* is a body of people assembled for *discussion.*

(A) Is a *papacy* a body assembled for *absolution?* No. The *papacy* is the office of the pope, the successive line of popes, or the ecclesiastic government headed by the pope. You could consider it an assembly. But it's an assembly for organized *religion,* not specifically to relieve people of sin by *absolution.*

(B) Is *space* a body assembled for *exploration?* No.

(C) Is a *parliament* a body assembled for *legislation?* Yes. *Parliament* is the legislative body of representatives that makes or enacts laws. **Correct choice.**

(D) Is a *rostrum* a body assembled for *speech?* No. A *rostrum* is a platform, pulpit, or lectern for public speaking. *Peroration* is the concluding part of a speech.

(E) Is a *speakeasy* a body assembled for *gossip.* No. A *speakeasy* is a place where alcoholic beverages are sold illegally. *Gossip* is idle talk or rumors, not alcohol.

22. Correct choice (D) eschew:avoid

excoriate—to wear off the skin

abrade—to rub away by friction

To *excoriate* is the same as to *abrade.*

(A) Is to *consent* the same as to *decree?* No. To *consent* is to agree, which rhymes with *decree* (a lawful order), but doesn't have the same meaning.

(B) Is to *demur* the same as to *agree?* To *demur* is to reject or disagree, the opposite of agree.

(C) Is to *mar* the same as to *burnish?* No, they're opposites. To *mar* is to blemish. To *burnish* is to polish.

(D) Is to *eschew* the same as to *avoid?* Yes. **Correct choice.**

(E) Is to *proscribe* the same as to *support?* No. To *proscribe* is to prohibit, the opposite of *support.*

23. Correct choice (E) glasses:see

mnemonic—a device used to aid memory

remember—to recall

A *mnemonic* is a device used to help one *remember.*

(A) Is an *amnesiac* a device used to help one *forget?* No. An *amnesiac* is an individual who has partially or completely lost the ability to remember.

(B) Is *euphoria* a device used to help one *relax?* No. *Euphoria* is not a device. It's the state of extreme happiness or elation.

(C) Is a *nostril* a device used to help one *smell?* Hmmm. A *nostril* is an opening of the nose, which is the organ of smell. Is it a "device"? Not really. Better question-mark this choice, but look for a better one.

(D) Is *audio* a device used to help one *hear?* No. An *audio* is something having to do with the production, transmission, or reception of sound.

(E) Are *glasses* a device used to help one *see? Glasses* are a device used to correct poor vision, thus enabling a person to *see* more clearly. **Correct choice.**

24. Correct choice (E)

This passage seems to contain a series of anecdotes or different incidents. In this case, the first paragraph contains clues that tie them together.

In the first sentence, the author admits he used to question the genuineness of submissions in newspaper columns. The author then describes a number of strange queries he has received, all of which served to convince him that unusual submissions were authentic.

(A) Too specific—The cases mentioned are wide-ranging: domestic disputes, love affairs, employee rights.

(B) Too specific—Only one case (fifth paragraph) describes how a husband tried to circumvent the law.

(C) Not addressed—Some advice given to correspondents is disclosed in this passage. But the author does not analyze legal situations or solutions or alternatives. The passage is descriptive, not analytical.

(D) Not addressed—The role of a newspaper is not mentioned in this passage.

25. Correct choice (E)

Many words have several meanings. If you know the meanings, you can find the correct one by looking at the context (how it's used in the sentence): "One letter in fifty gives the editor a *smile* with which to rest his tired countenance . . . ." The only meaning that fits in is face or *visage*, which is (E).

(A) "Countenance" doesn't mean "head." Even if it did, would a smile help rest your tired head?

(B) " . . . tired *tolerate*?" Doesn't even sound right.

(C) Can you have a "tired *composure*"? Composure is tranquillity, usually mental. But there's a better choice.

(D) " . . . tired *encourage*?" This makes no sense.

26. Correct choice (E)

Lines 15–17 tell us that "one correspondent in fifty unconsciously sends in a gem that gives the editor a smile with which to rest his tired countenance." This implies that 49 out of 50 submissions don't make the editor smile. "*Infrequent* (or occasional) smiles" describes this nicely. The other choices don't come close.

(A) Contradiction. "Incessant laughter" means laughing continuously. But lines 15–17 tell us that the editor usually has a "tired countenance."

(B) A "tired countenance" is quite different from "weary disillusionment." The editor has no illusions or expectations that are being shattered.

(C) The last paragraph tells us that the editor thinks that his correspondents may have made better use of their opportunities than he did of his. Not exactly contemptuous, or showing spite toward these people.

(D) Lines 11–13 tell us that "of the hundreds of queries . . . most . . . are commonplace enough . . ." If most submissions are so ordinary, the editor probably doesn't read them with "profound disbelief."

27. Correct choice (E)

The author is trying to tell the reader that advice columns describe real problems or situations, even if they seem funny or strange. Given this purpose, only choice (E) makes sense. The other choices assume that the author is trying to give advice.

(A) True, but—This doesn't answer the question: What is the purpose of telling the Bumble story?

The author tells this strange and funny story to entertain readers and convince them that advice columns are not made up. If he wanted to give advice, he'd say, "Farmers, watch out for your wives and the law."

(B) Not addressed—Although Mrs. Bumble did gain the upper hand, the story does not imply that other wives are waiting for a chance or are suffering in silence.

(C) Not addressed—Women's liberation is not mentioned in the passage.

(D) True, but—This doesn't answer the question. The question is, "What is the purpose of telling the Bumble story?" not "What does the story tell us?"

28. Correct choice (C)

Convey can mean "transport, transmit, communicate" or, in a legal context, "transfer" (titles, deeds, property, and so forth). The context here is legal. Besides, none of the other choices make sense when you talk about property, such as a farm.

(A) *Trusted* doesn't make complete sense. The husband can't get the property back because he transferred it legally. If you just trust someone to keep something for you, it doesn't become their property.

(B) *Transported* usually implies carrying something from one place to another. "He carried the farm to his wife"? Weird, huh?

(D) *Bequeathed* usually implies passing on property through a will, usually after dying.

(E) A *bypass* is a detour. It can also mean "to neglect or ignore your superior."

29. Correct choice (B)

In this passage the author describes some of the freak—or unusual—letters he gets to prove that advice columns are not made up. Therefore, the common thread is "freak letters."

(A) Too general—This choice is close, but there's a better one. Although all the letters seek advice, what really ties them together is that they are freakish letters, used to show that advice columns are strange but genuine.

(C) Too specific—The "jilted girl" story and the "worthless dog" story are not about *property rights*.

(D) Too specific—*Punitive measures* means "ways of punishing." Except perhaps for the "jilted girl" story, none of the stories mention punishments.

(E) Too specific—All of these stories have been submitted by correspondents. Some, but *not all*, include *editorial responses*.

30. Correct choice (D) information query

This choice sounds too superficial or easy. But all the other choices have something wrong with them. We know the former was written for "information concerning the nature and habits of Limburg cheese" (line 8). We know the latter was for "advice concerning her property rights" (line 23). That's enough evidence to support this choice.

(A) Contradiction—The letter in paragraph three is not described as commonplace. It follows a statement about some letters being gems (line 16).

(B) Not addressed—The author considers both these letters to be freak letters. We know he considers the latter as amusing, but he says nothing about the Limburg letter being merely absurd. Steer away from unnecessary inferences, especially if there's a better choice (and there is!).

(C) Not addressed—We don't know that the letter was written by a *Connecticut* woman. The passage does not tell us. Don't get misled. Recheck for specific information.

(E) Contradiction—The "Limburg cheese" letter did not deal with *powerful odors*. It dealt with using Limburg cheese as a "power source" in experiments—quite different. Don't let the wording trip you up.

31. Correct choice (D)

Questions like this usually spring from a particular piece of information in the passage. Make life easy. Find it.

Lines 108–114 tell us, "I may smile for a moment . . . but I sober up when I reflect that he or she may have earned a larger percentage of dividend on the opportunities presented than I have on mine."

That's exactly choice (D), or pretty darned close.

(A) True, but—You, or the author, probably wouldn't "sneer at or mock" "strange or funny" letters. You would laugh.

(B) Too specific—Although this sounds like a reasonable inference, the author doesn't say this specifically. In lines 103–108, the author gives you a reason. Check it out.

(C) True, but—In lines 99–101, the author disclaims any intention to portray correspondents as fools. He identifies these as freak letters, not as general submissions. But this doesn't answer the question.

(E) True, but—This doesn't answer the question. "Wearying submissions" do not make the author unwilling to mock or sneer at the letters. They might make him tired or glum, however.

32. Correct choice (C)

What sounds like a personal judgment really has to do with the author's main purpose in the passage. The author is out to entertain readers and convince them that advice columns are not made up. Keeping this in mind, it becomes obvious that choice (C) is the best answer.

(A) Contradiction.

In lines 99–101, the author disclaims any intention to discredit the high-mindedness or intelligence of correspondents. So (A) can't be right.

(B) True, but—The amusing flavor may be lost if the submissions are converted to polished prose. The question isn't, "Why does the author retain the original language?" but "Why does the author use parts of actual letters?"

(D) True, but—This moves away from the purpose of the passage. While pathetic snarls can have amusing facets, that is not why the author uses actual excerpts.

(E) True, but—This choice may be a hidden purpose. But how does using excerpts stop misinterpretation?

33. Correct choice (E)

This choice may seem too simple, but the other choices can be ruled out because of obvious inaccuracies. The passage speaks of farm people who asked for advice. Logical inference: some farm people were not hesitant to solicit advice from newspapers.

(A) Too general—While Utah, Connecticut, and Wisconsin are mentioned, you can't tell where the editorial offices of the newspaper are located.

(B) Contradiction—The wife secures sole ownership only if the farm is put in her name.

(C) Contradiction—The lady wanted to separate from her husband, but keep her personal property, because she hated her husband's manners. The advice given was that personal property remains personal property when you part. It did not mention anything about grounds for divorce.

(D) Contradiction—If you believed the passage, you would add "thirty dollars a sack for flour and twenty-two dollars per week for corn meal." That's fifty-two dollars, not sixty-two. And is flour the same as meal? Maybe. But the passage seems to make a distinction between them.

34. Correct choice (C)

The question is very specific. Which of the following can be inferred from the advocacy given? not from the descriptions or disputes. Examine each choice carefully against the passage.

In lines 70–72, " . . . the correspondent was told that a woman's ownership of personal property is not affected by her marriage." So a wife's dispute with her husband cannot affect personal property.

(A) Contradiction—Only the farm was put in Mrs. Bumble's name. In line 39 "Mr. Bumble was told that he could control the stock . . .."

(B) Contradiction—In line 55, the farmer is advised that "Friend Wife be permitted to retain control, especially since he could not compel her to revest title in him." This implies that the deal between the husband and the wife is not affected by the fraud of the husband upon the creditors.

(D) True, but—This choice may be true, but we don't know what advice was given in that particular case.

(E) True, but—The passage doesn't tell us what advocacy was given in that case.

35. Correct choice (D)

Always try to fit the choice into the sentence to see if it makes sense. Only choice (D) works here. "I may smile . . . over the occasional *rough* spelling or unschooled language . . ." Many of the words in the submissions have an approximate, or "rough," spelling.

(A) *Rude* can mean "violent." But "violent spelling" doesn't make sense.

(B) *Rude* can mean "harsh." But "harsh spelling" doesn't make sense.

(C) *Rude* can mean "impolite." But "impolite spelling" doesn't make sense.

(E) *Rude* can mean "nasty." But "nasty spelling" makes no sense.

Day 13

Test 1, Section 3: Math

Questions and Answers

Assignment for Today:

Take a sample SAT Math Test under actual test conditions. Allow yourself exactly 30 minutes to complete the 25 questions in this test.

Directions: *For questions 1–15, each question contains two quantities—one on the left (Column A) and one on the right (Column B). Compare the quantities and answer*

(A) if Column A is greater than Column B
(B) if Column B is greater than Column A
(C) if the two columns are equal
(D) if you cannot determine a definite relationship from the information given

Never answer (E).

In some questions, information appears centered between the two columns. Centered information concerns each of the columns for that question only. For each question, any symbol used in one column represents the same value if it appears in the other column.

	Column A	Column B
1.	$(\sqrt{20})(\sqrt{5})-(\sqrt{2})(\sqrt{8})$	$(\sqrt{50})(\sqrt{2})-(\sqrt{6})(\sqrt{6})$
2.	Interest owed on a loan of $6,000 at an annual rate of 10%.	Interest owed on a loan of $12,000 at an annual rate of 5%.

Stefan misread a math problem and took the square root of x when he should have taken the square of x. He made no other mistake and his answer was a positive integer. Maria did the same problem correctly.

	Column A	Column B
3.	$(\text{Maria's answer})^{\frac{1}{2}}$	$(\text{Stefan's answer})^2$

Column A	Column B

AOB is a line segment

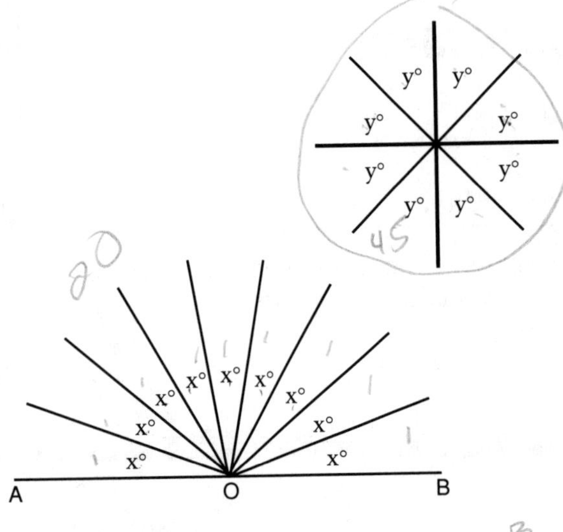

4. | $2x$ | y |
|---|---|

Each boxer in the Lightweight category weighs 150 pounds or less. The average weight of 4 Lightweight boxers is 140 pounds and the combined weight of 2 of them is 290 pounds.

5. | Weight, in pounds, of the lightest of the 4 Lightweight boxers | 120 pounds |
|---|---|

Column A	Column B

Assume the tick marks are equally spaced.

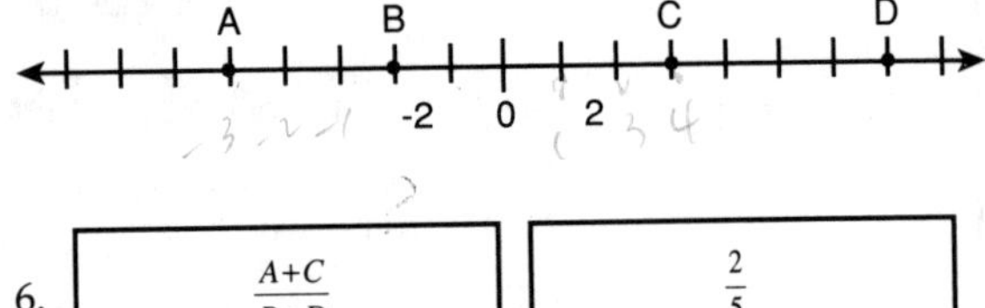

6. | $\frac{A+C}{B+D}$ | $\frac{2}{5}$ |
|---|---|

3 balanced coins are tossed at the same time.

7. | Probability of getting 2 heads and a tail | Probability of getting only 1 head |
|---|---|

Perimeter of the rectangle *ABCD* is 24 and *AD* is twice *CD*.

8. | CD^2 | AD |
|---|---|

Column A	Column B

Perimeter of parallelogram $BCDE = 30$

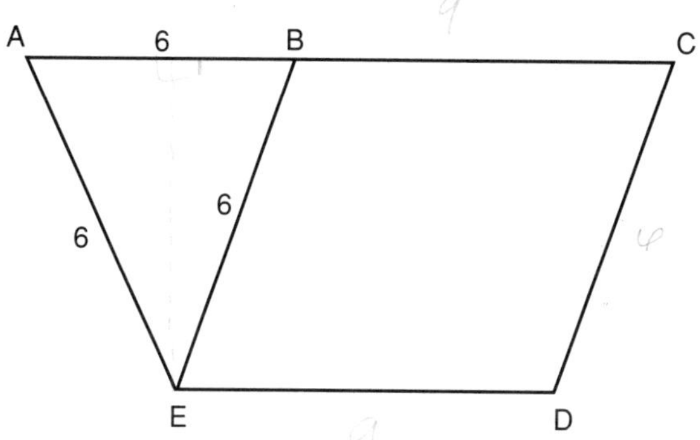

	Column A	Column B
9.	Area of $BCDE$	$27\sqrt{3}$

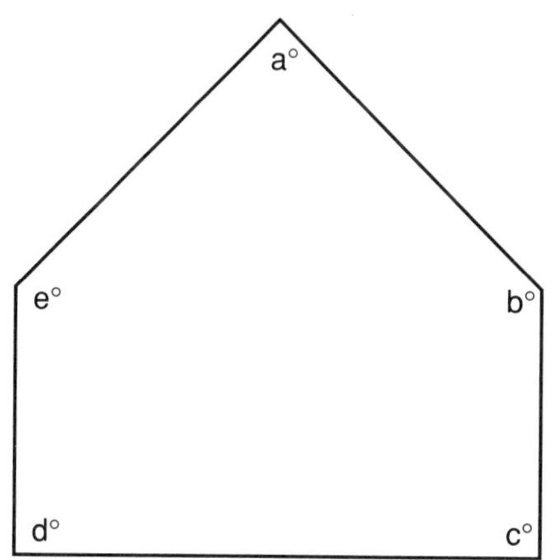

$$a^\circ = b^\circ = c^\circ$$

$$d^\circ = \frac{a^\circ + b^\circ + c^\circ}{2}$$

$$e^\circ = 2d^\circ$$

	Column A	Column B
10.	c°	72

Column A	Column B

$x < y - 1$

	Column A	Column B
11.	$x^2 - y^3$	$x^3 - y^2$

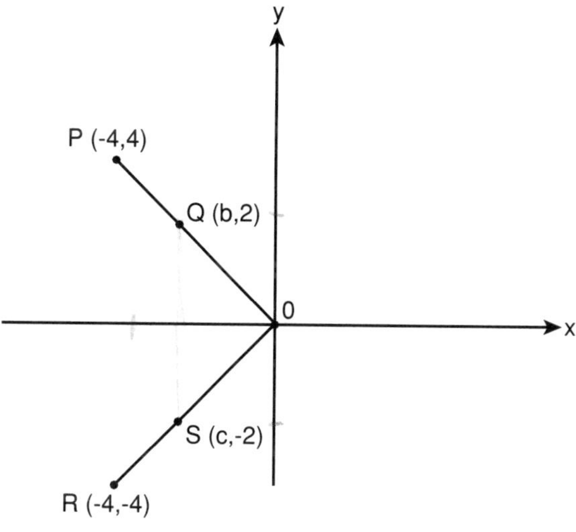

	Column A	Column B
12.	$b + c$	-4

Column A	Column B

AC and *BD* are perpendicular bisectors

Radius of circle = 5

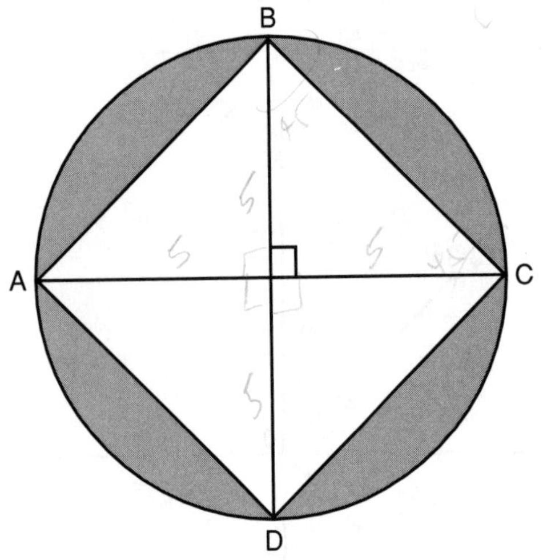

	Column A	Column B
13.	Area of shaded portion	25

Column A	Column B

$a = g$
$b = c = d = e = f$
$a = 3d$

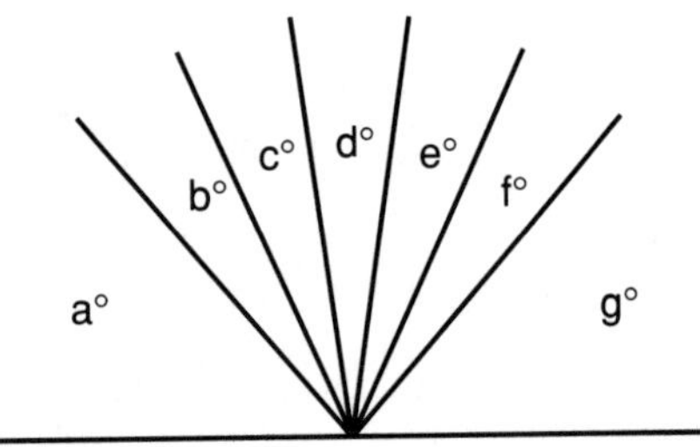

	Column A	Column B
14.	$a + b$	65

A credit card PIN number consists of 4 digits from 0 through 9. The first digit cannot be 0.

	Column A	Column B
15.	The total number of different possible PIN numbers	9^4

Directions: *For questions 16–25, solve each problem, and enter your answer in the grid provided.*

---

16. If $\frac{6p-(2p-1)}{2} = 5.5$, then $p =$

17. To get to the city zoo, Ralph has to drive 30 miles on the highway and 15 miles on the state turnpike. If Ralph drives 60 miles per hour on the highway and 30 miles per hour on the state turnpike, how many minutes will it take him to drive to the zoo?

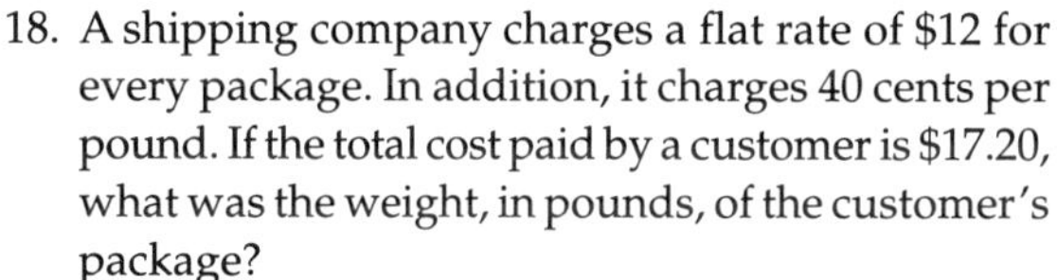

18. A shipping company charges a flat rate of \$12 for every package. In addition, it charges 40 cents per pound. If the total cost paid by a customer is \$17.20, what was the weight, in pounds, of the customer's package?

19. Mary is exactly 30 years younger than Judy. In 5 years, Judy will be exactly twice as old as Mary. What is Mary's current age, in years?

16.

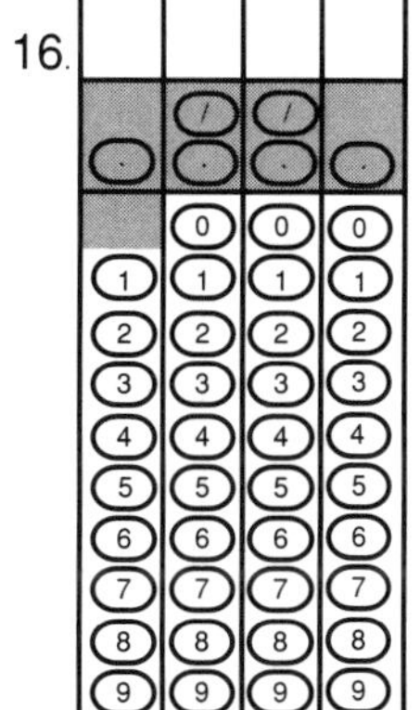

17.

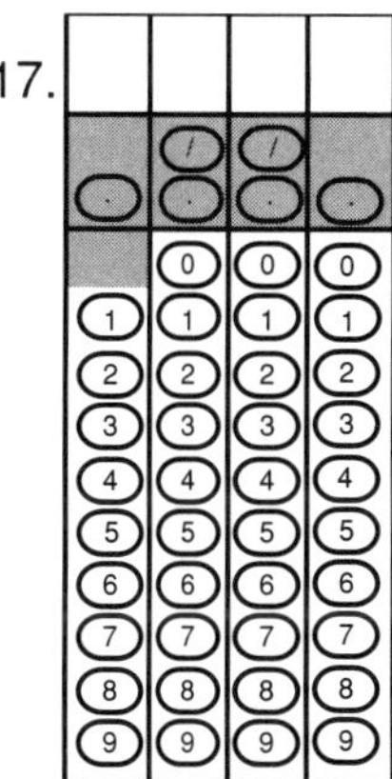

18.

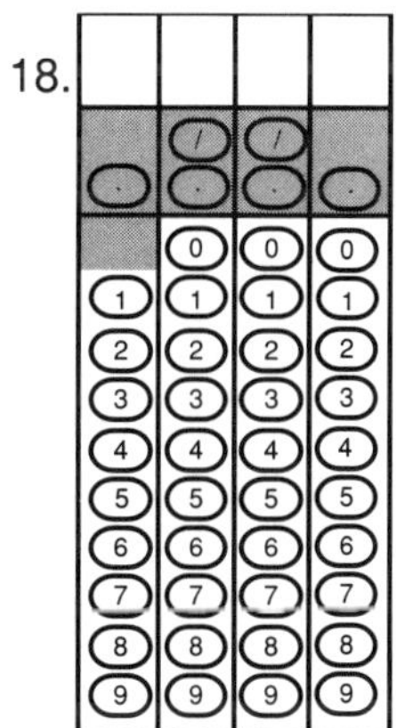

19.

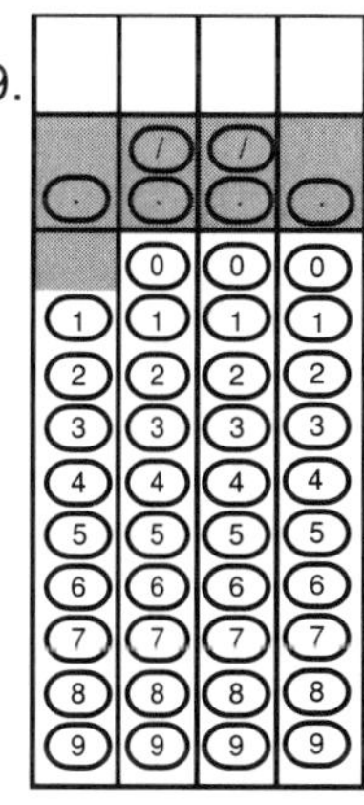

20. Towns A, B, and C are shown in the diagram below. The distance between Town A and Town B is 30 miles and the distance between Town A and Town C is 50 miles. Tom drives from Town A to Town C via Town B, and Jerry drives directly from Town A to Town C. Tom drives how many miles more than Jerry?

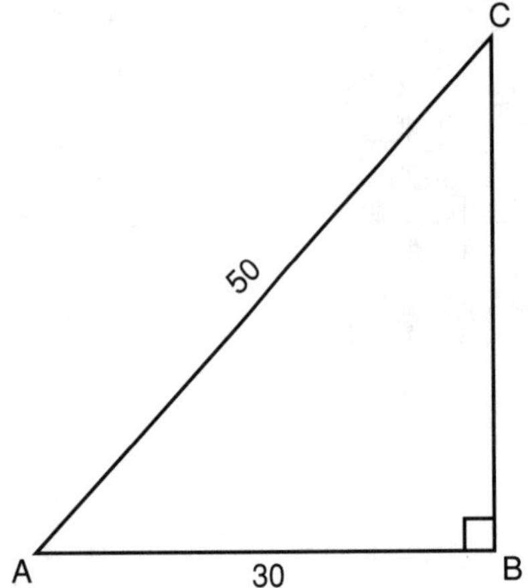

21. George and Heidi each bought a box of 24 computer disks at the same price. Four of George's disks were defective. The cost per usable disk for George was 32 cents. If 8 of Heidi's disks were defective, what was the cost per usable disk, in cents, for Heidi? (Disregard the symbol for cents when gridding your answer.)

22. How many different multiples of 4 are there from 4,044 to 4,104, inclusive?

23. Photographs in a studio are printed in various sizes, but the length-to-width ratio is always maintained at 1.5. If the area of a rectangular photograph is 216, what is its length?

20.
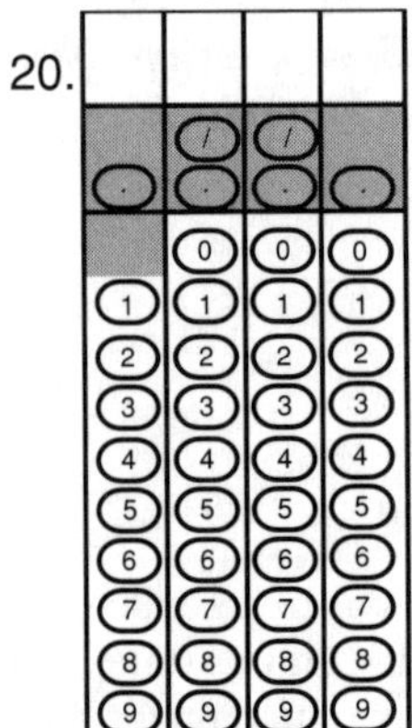

21.
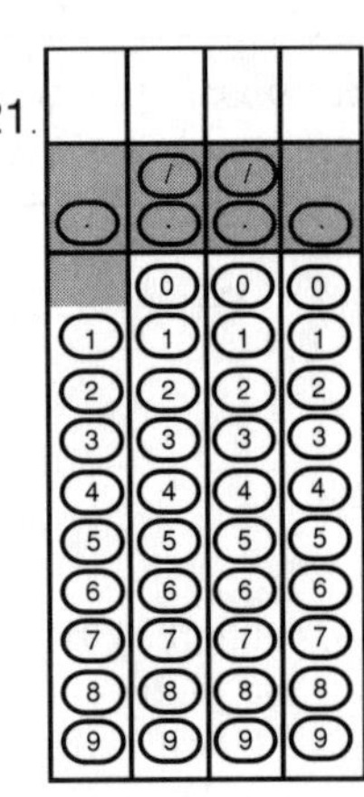

22.
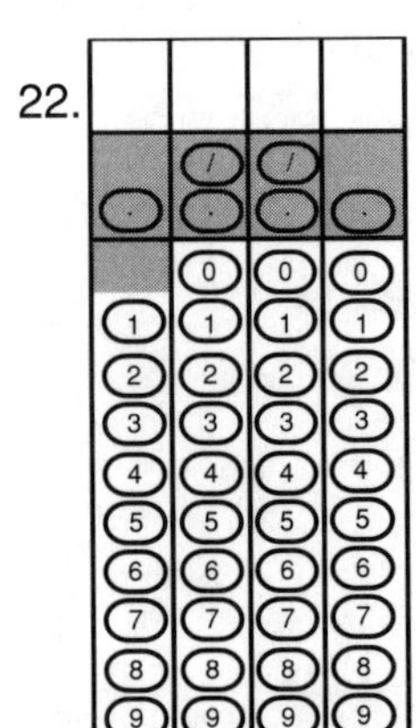

23.
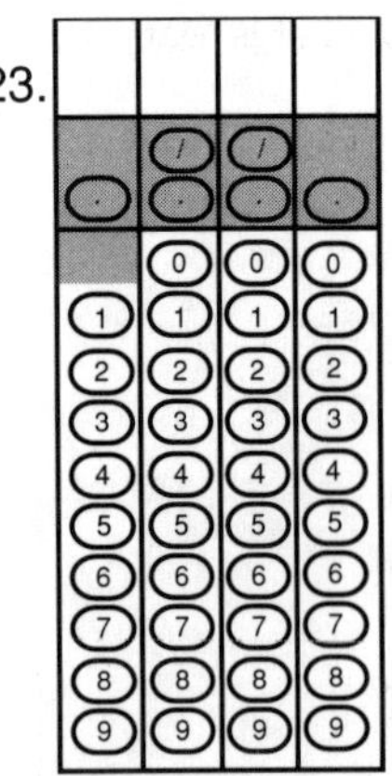

24. If $2p - 4q + 3r - 4s = 10$, and $p - 2q = 4$, then what is the value of $6r - 8s$?

25. In the figure below, the perimeter of rhombus *PQRS* is 60 and its area is 180. What is the area of triangle *RTS*?

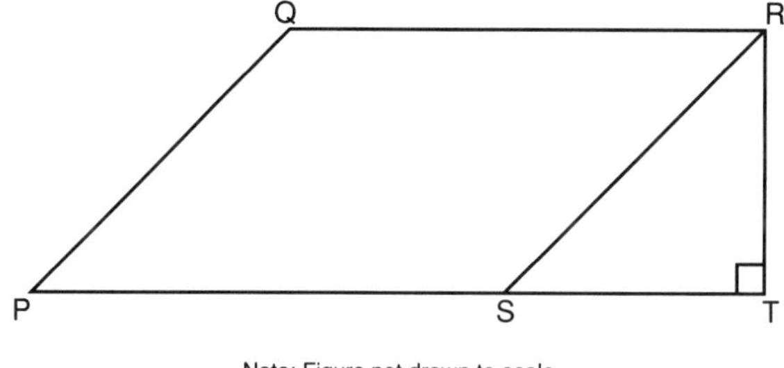

Note: Figure not drawn to scale.

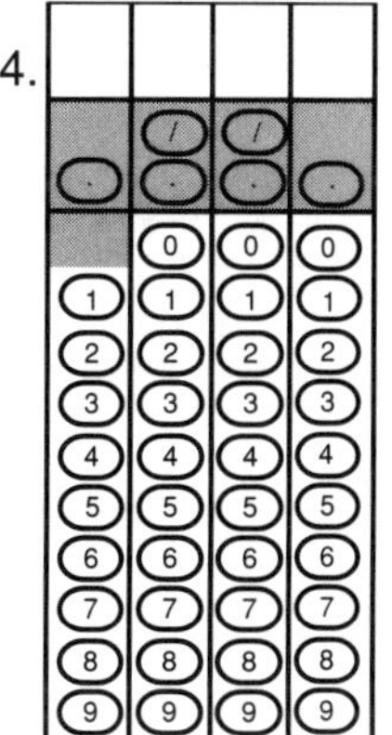

25.

Quick Answer Guide

Test 1, Section 3: Math

1. A
2. D
3. C
4. B
5. C
6. B
7. C
8. A
9. C
10. C
11. D
12. C
13. A
14. A
15. A
16. 2.5
17. 60
18. 13
19. 25
20. 20
21. 40
22. 16
23. 18
24. 4
25. 54

For explanations to these questions see Day 14.

Day 14

Test 1, Section 3: Math

Explanations and Strategies

Assignment for Today:

Review the explanations for the test you just took. See which answer is right, and learn what makes each wrong answer wrong.

1. Correct choice (A)

As with most quantitative comparison problems, there are at least two ways to work to an answer: in this case, a fast way and a faster way! One fast way is to multiply the square roots in parentheses. So, in column (A), you get $\sqrt{100} - \sqrt{16}$ which equals 10 – 4, or 6. In column (B), you get $\sqrt{100} - \sqrt{36}$, which equals 10 – 6, or 4. So column (A) is greater.

A faster way is to realize that the first set of parentheses are the same for each column (they both equal $\sqrt{100}$). So all you have to do is compare the second sets of parentheses: In column (A), you have $-\sqrt{16}$, which equals –4. In column (B), you have $-\sqrt{36}$, which equals –6. Since –4 is greater than –6, column (A) is greater. (Don't forget about those minus signs!)

(B) Careless—Did you eliminate the equal $\sqrt{100}$ in both columns, but forget about the minus signs in front of the radicals that were left? Check your work again.

(C) Miscalc—In column (A), under the radical signs, you have 8 times 2, whereas in column (B), also under the radical signs, you have 6 times 6. So, the two columns cannot be equal.

(D) Missing key insight—Since you have only numerical values in both columns, choice (D) cannot be the correct answer.

2. Correct choice (D)

The formula for finding interest is:

interest = loan amount × rate × time

Notice that we are given the loan amount ($6,000 for Column A and $12,000 for Column B), and the annual rate (10 percent in Column A and 5 percent in Column B), but we don't know anything about the time period. That means we cannot determine either quantity, so the answer is choice (D).

(A) Oversight—Perhaps you noticed that the interest rate was double in Column A, compared to Column B. But then, the loan amount was half in Column A, compared to Column B. An important piece of information is not given in this problem.

(B) Oversight—Perhaps you noticed that the loan amount in Column B was twice the amount in Column A. But then, the interest rate in Column B was only half, compared to Column A. An important piece of information is not given in this problem.

(C) Missing key insight—Ah, this was somewhat of a trick problem. You may have chosen this answer because you noticed that one quantity was double its counterpart in the other column and the other quantity was one-half. But, an important piece of information is not given in the problem.

3. Correct choice (C)

To solve this problem, plug in values for the unknowns. Let's assume that x is 25. Then, Stefan took the square root of 25, which means his answer was 5. Then Column B is:

(Stefan's answer)$^2 = 5^2 = 25$

The correct answer required Maria to square x. So, with x as 25, Maria's answer was 25×25.

Then, Column A is:

$$(25 \times 25)^{\frac{1}{2}} = \sqrt{25 \times 25} = 25$$

So, both columns are equal.

(A) Misread—Looks like you compared Maria's answer with Stefan's answer. But the problem asked you to compare the square root of Maria's answer with the square of Stefan's answer.

(B) Miscalc—Looks like you did not plug in values to solve this problem. The best way to solve this problem is to think of a number for x and figure out Stefan's answer and Maria's answer.

(D) Oversight—Perhaps you plugged in negative numbers or decimal values for x. But, we are told that after taking the square root of x, Stefan was left with a positive integer. This tells us that x has to be a positive integer, too.

4. Correct choice (B)

Let's look at Column A first. We know that AOB is a straight line, which means that the total angle enclosed by AOB is 180 degrees. There are 9 angles, each x degrees. So each x is $180 \div 9 = 20$ degrees. So, if $x = 20$, $2x = 40$. Then, Column A = 40.

The 8 equal angles in Column B form a circle.

We know that a circle has 360 degrees.

So, if $8y = 360$, $y = 360 \div 8 = 45$

Then, Column B = 45.

So, Column B is greater than Column A.

(A) Misread—Perhaps you counted only 8 xs. Actually, there are 9 of them. You know that AOB is 180 degrees. You can find x.

(C) Oversight—Perhaps you thought that AOB (which is 180 degrees) is half of the circle in Column B and so each x in Column A is equal to half of y in Column B. But this is true only if there are as many xs in Column A as there are ys in Column B. There are 9 xs in Column A and only 8 ys in Column B.

(D) Missing key insight—Perhaps you chose this answer because you didn't see any numbers in the problem. But you can use your knowledge of geometry to solve this problem. You know that a circle has 360 degrees and a line has 180 degrees. Knowing this, you can find the value of each x and y.

5. Correct choice (C)

Work with total weights, not with average weights, because averages have to be added with caution. We know that the average weight of the 4 boxers is 140 pounds. This means the total weight of the 4 boxers is $140 \times 4 = 560$. (*Remember:* total weight is the average weight times the number of boxers.)

We know that 2 of the boxers have a combined weight of 290 pounds. The heaviest possible weight that any boxer can have is 150 pounds. This means the lighter of the two can weigh a minimum of $290 - 150 = 140$ pounds. Now let's find the lighter of the other two boxers.

We know that 4 of them weigh 560 pounds and two of them weigh 290 pounds. Then, the other two must weigh $560 - 290 = 270$ pounds. Again, the lighter of these two boxers can weigh a minimum of $270 - 150 = 120$ pounds.

In both groups of two, to find the lighter boxer, we assume that the heavier boxer weighs the maximum possible amount, which is 150 pounds. This is the only way to make sure that the lighter boxer has the least possible weight.

So, Column A is 120 pounds, which is equal to Column B.

(A) Miscalc—Perhaps you made a mistake in finding the total weight of the 4 boxers. Or maybe you figured that if the average is 140 pounds, each boxer must weigh more than 120 pounds. To solve this problem, find the combined weight of the other two boxers.

(B) Oversight—Perhaps you figured that the lightest of the boxers could weigh any amount less than 120. But you forgot that the heaviest boxer can't weigh more than 150 pounds. This also restricts the weight of the lightest boxer. To solve this problem, you should find the combined weight of the other two boxers.

(D) Missing key insight—Perhaps you thought you couldn't answer this question because the individual weights of the boxers aren't given to you. You don't need to know the weight of each boxer. To solve this problem, you should work with "total" weights and not with "average" weights. Try to find the combined weight of the other two boxers.

6. Correct choice (B)

We can determine the coordinates of the points we are interested in by just using the number line. Note that each tick mark is 2 units long.

$$\left.\begin{aligned} A &= -10 \\ B &= -4 \\ C &= 6 \\ D &= 14 \end{aligned}\right\} \Rightarrow \frac{A+C}{B+D} = \frac{-10+6}{-4+14} = \frac{-4}{10} = -\frac{2}{5}$$

So, Column A is a negative value and Column B is a positive value, which means Column B is greater than Column A.

(A) Missing key insight—Perhaps you didn't get negative numbers as the coordinates of *A* and *B*. Also note that each tick mark is 2 units long, not 1.

(C) Miscalc—You probably miscalculated $\frac{A+C}{B+D}$. Be careful of the sign of $\frac{A+C}{B+D}$. Two of these quantities have negative values.

(D) Missing key insight—It's possible to find the exact values, based on the number line, of points *A*, *B*, *C*, and *D*, which means it *is* possible to compare the two columns. See if you can first find the values of all four points *A*, *B*, *C*, and *D*.

7. Correct choice (C)

If we toss 3 coins, we notice that there are a total of 8 possible different outcomes: HHH, HHT, HTH, HTT, THH, THT, TTH, and TTT.

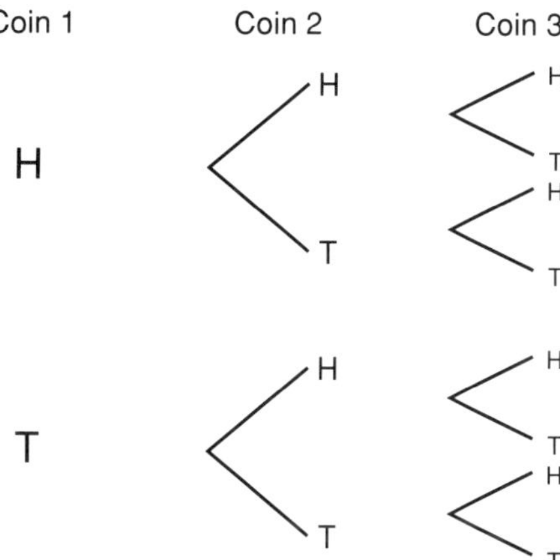

There are 3 outcomes with 2 heads and a tail (HHT, HTH, and THH) and so the probability is $\frac{3}{8}$, which is Column A.

There are 3 outcomes with only 1 head (HTT, THT, and TTH) and so the probability is $\frac{3}{8}$, which is Column B.

The two probabilities are equal, so the answer is choice (C).

(A) Missing key insight—You may have picked this answer because it looked as if there would be more favorable outcomes in Column A than in Column B. The best way to answer this question is to draw a chart that shows all possible outcomes.

(B) Missing key insight—You may have picked this answer because it looked as if there would be more favorable outcomes in Column B than in Column A. The best way to answer this question is to draw a chart that shows all possible outcomes.

(D) Missing key insight—It *is* possible to find the probability in each column. Remember, probability is the ratio of the number of favorable outcomes to the number of total outcomes.

8. Correct choice (A)

If the perimeter is 24, then the sum of the length and width is 12 (because the perimeter is twice the sum of the length and width). That is,

$AD + CD = 12$

But, AD is twice CD. That is, $AD = 2(CD)$. So, let's plug in this value of AD in the equation.

$2(CD) + CD = 12$

or, $3\ CD = 12$

that is, $CD = 4$ If CD is 4, AD has to be 8. Then,

Column A = $4^2 = 16$ and Column B = 8

So, Column A is greater.

(B) Misread—Perhaps, when working the equation, you assumed that $CD = 2(AD)$. It should be the other way around. That is, $AD = 2(CD)$.

(C) Oversight—Did you assume that $AD = CD^2$? Remember, the proper relationship is: AD = 2(CD).

(D) Missing key insight—Here, the main thing you need to know is that $AD + CD + BC + AB = 24$. Since $AD = BC$, and $AB = CD$, we can write: $AD + CD + AD + CD = 24$

Or, $2\ AD + 2\ CD = 24$

Or, $AD + CD = 12$

Try it again with this insight, and remember that $AD = 2(CD)$.

9. Correct choice (C)

To find the area of the parallelogram $BCDE$, we need its base, ED, and its height. Side BE is 6. Then, side CD is also 6 (in a parallelogram, opposite sides are equal). Together, these two sides sum to 12. We know the perimeter of $BCDE$ is 30. If two of the sides add up to 12, the other two sides must add up to $30 - 12 = 18$. So, side BC must be 9 and the base, ED must also be 9. Got base, need height.

On to triangle ABE. It has the same height as the parallelogram. Each side of the triangle is equal in length and it's an equilateral triangle.

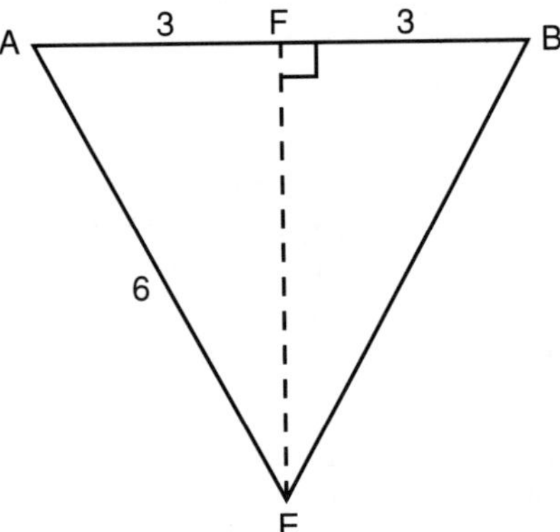

We can draw a perpendicular from E to AB. Then, $AF = BF = 3$. Then, from the right triangle AFE, we can find FE by using the Pythagorean theorem.

$AE^2 = AF^2 + FE^2$

Or, $6^2 = 3^2 + FE^2$

Or, $27 = FE^2$

So, $FE = \sqrt{27} = \sqrt{9 \times 3} = 3\sqrt{3}$

So, the height of the parallelogram is $3\sqrt{3}$. We know its base is 9. Then, its area = base × height $= 9 \times 3\sqrt{3} = 27\sqrt{3}$.

So, Column A is equal to Column B.

(A) Missing key insight—Perhaps you thought that the area of the parallelogram was 6×9. The base of the parallelogram is 9, but the height is not 6. Triangle ABE should help you find the height.

(B) Missing key insight—Perhaps you used $\frac{1}{2}$ base × height as the formula for the area of the parallelogram. Or, maybe you thought that the base of the parallelogram was 6. The perimeter of the parallelogram should help you find the base.

(D) Oversight—Maybe you weren't able to find the height of the parallelogram. Triangle ABE is an equilateral triangle. That should tell you how to find the height of the triangle. And, the height of the triangle is the same as the height of the parallelogram.

10. Correct choice (C)

First, find the sum of all interior angles of the given figure. The sum of the interior angles of a polygon is $180 \times (n - 2)$, where n is the number of sides.

So, the sum of the interior angles of the figure shown (with 5 sides) is: $180 \times (5 - 2) = 180 \times 3 = 540$.

We're asked to compare the value of angle c with 72 degrees. Let's suppose that c *is* 72 degrees. Let's see what happens if we plug this value back into the problem.

If c is 72, then $a = 72$ and $b = 72$ (because we're told: $a^\circ = b^\circ = c^\circ$).

We also know that $d^\circ = \frac{a^\circ + b^\circ + c^\circ}{2}$. If a, b, c, are all 72 each, then, $d = \frac{(72+72+72)}{2} = \frac{216}{2} = 108$

And, we know that $e = 2d$. So, if $d = 108$, then $e = 2 \times 108 = 216$.

Now, let's add up these values and see if they give us a total of 540 degrees.

$a + b + c = 216$

$d = 108$

$e = 216$

Then, total = 540

So, the value of c *is* 72 degrees and the two columns are equal.

(A) Missing key insight—If you chose (A), you may have solved for d° or e°, or you may have thought the sum of all internal angles was greater than 540°. The formula for finding the sum of all interior angles is $180(n - 2)$, where n is the number of sides in the polygon.

(B) Missing key insight—You may have assumed the sum of internal angles was less than 540°. Or, maybe you tried to eyeball the value of c. Remember, the diagram is not drawn to scale.

(D) Missing key insight—You may have been unable to get started on the problem. ***Hint:*** the sum of all interior angles of any figure is $180(n - 2)$, where n is the number of sides in the polygon.

11. Correct choice (D)

The best way to solve this problem is to plug in values for x and y. Let's try the greatest possible value for y, which is 1, and 0 for x (which must be less than y).

Then, Column A = $0 - 1 = -1$, and Column B = $0 - 1 = -1$.

This implies that the two columns are equal. Now, let's try $x = -1$ and $y = 0$.

Then, Column A = $1 - 0 = 1$, and Column B = $-1 - 0 = -1$. Here, Column A is greater.

Because we get two different values, the correct choice is (D).

(A) Too limited—Maybe you did not try a wide range of values for x and y. For example, if you tried -1 for x, and 0 for y, Column A = 1 and Column B = -1, in which case Column A is greater. But what about when $x = 0$ and $y = 1$?

(B) Missing key insight—Looks like you did not plug in values for x and y. Maybe you thought that Column B is greater because there the cubed term comes first. Remember, the best way to solve problems like this is to plug in values. Try different values for x and y such that x is less than y and y is either 1 or less than 1.

(C) Too limited—Maybe you plugged in 0 for x and 1 for y and stopped there. If x is 0 and y is 1, you are right—both sides are equal. But see what happens when x is, say, -1 and y is 0.

12. Correct choice (C)

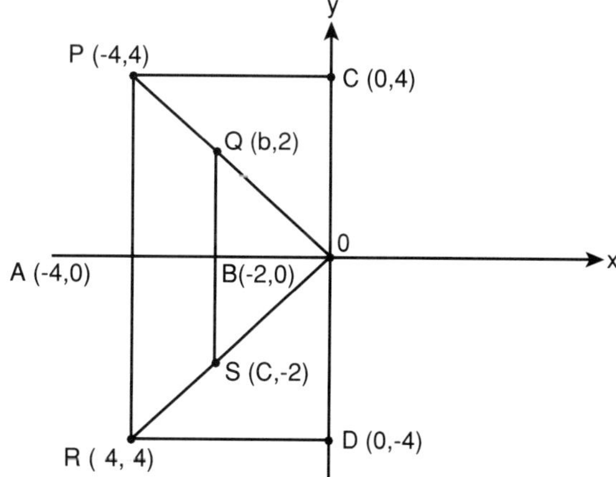

Let's first find the slopes of OP and OR. A slope is simply the ratio of the y-distance to the x-distance.

From point O to point P, there is a y-distance of 4 (shown as OC), and there is a x-distance of –4 (shown as OA).

Then, slope of $OP = \frac{y - \text{distance}}{x - \text{distance}} = \frac{4}{-4} = -1$

This means, along the entire line OP, if we move 1 to the left, we have to move 1 upwards. Notice that to get to point Q, we need to move 2 upwards from the origin. This means we have to move $-1 \times 2 = -2$ on the x-axis. So, $b = -2$.

The slope of line OR is: $\frac{y - \text{distance}}{x - \text{distance}} = \frac{-4}{-4} = 1$

This means, along line OR, if we move 1 to the left, we have to move 1 downwards. To get to point S, we move 2 downwards from the origin. So, we also need to move 2 to the left, which means the value of c is –2.

So, $b = -2$ and $c = -2$. Then, $b + c = -2 + -2 = -4$, and the two columns are equal.

(A) Miscalc—Perhaps you found the values of b and c as 2. Actually, each one is –2 because both points lie on the left side of the y-axis.

(B) Missing key insight—Perhaps you got values of b and c as –3 each. Did you find slope of line OP as –1 and slope of line OR as 1? Now use these values to find b and c.

(D) Missing key insight—Perhaps you thought that it wasn't possible to pin down the exact location of points Q and S. Actually, if you find the slopes of OP and OR, you can find the exact values of b and c.

13. Correct choice (A)

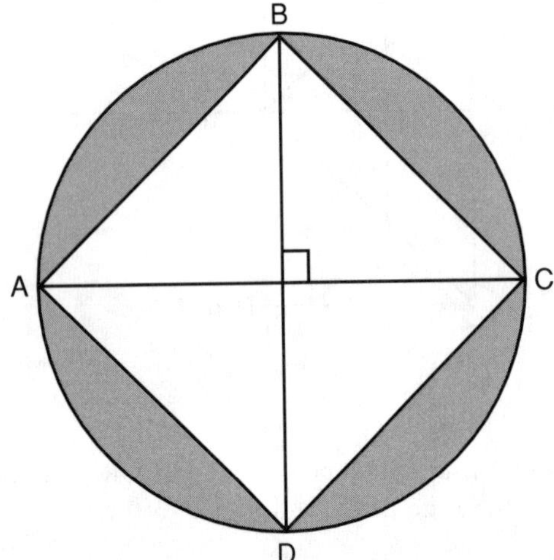

To find the area of the shaded portion, first let's find the area of the circle. Once we find the area of the circle, we can subtract from it the area of rectangle $ABCD$ (because everything is symmetrical, angle A = angle B = angle C = angle D and so $ABCD$ is a rectangle) and we'll be left with the area of the shaded portion.

Area of circle $= \pi r^2 = \pi(5^2) = 25\pi$.

Notice that rectangle $ABCD$ can be divided into 4 right triangles, each with height = base = radius = 5.

Then, area of each triangle $= \left(\frac{1}{2}\right)$ base $\times$ height

$= \left(\frac{1}{2}\right)$ radius $\times$ radius

$= \left(\frac{1}{2}\right) 5 \times 5 = \frac{25}{2}$

There are 4 such triangles in rectangle $ABCD$.

So, area of rectangle $ABCD = 4 \times$ area of each triangle

$= 4 \times \frac{25}{2} = 50$.

So, area of shaded portion =
area of circle – area of $ABCD = 25\pi - 50$

We have to compare this quantity in Column A with 25 in Column B. Notice that 25π is more than 75 because the value of π is a little more than 3 (it's roughly 3.14). We can approximate 25π to 78 or so. So, the area of the shaded portion is about 78 – 50, which is about 28. No matter what its exact value, the area of the shaded portion is going to be more than 25, and so Column A is greater.

(B) Oversight—Perhaps you figured that because the radius is 5, the area of the circle is 25π (which is true), and so the area of the shaded portion has to be less than 25. This would be true if the value of π was close to 1. But, it's not. See if you can approximate the value of π to find the area of the shaded portion.

(C) Missing key insight—Perhaps you got this answer by guessing. One way to find the area of the shaded portion is to find the area of the circle and subtract from it the area of rectangle $ABCD$.

(D) Missing key insight—Perhaps you picked this answer because you didn't know how to find the area of the shaded portion. Find the area of the circle and then subtract it from the area of rectangle $ABCD$.

14. Correct choice (A)

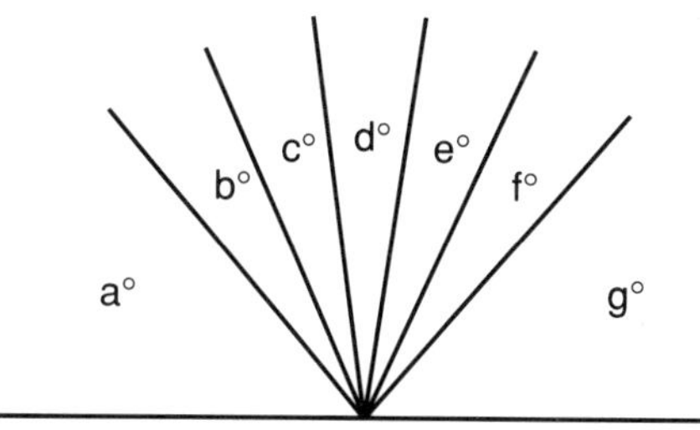

To solve this problem, we need to find the value of a and b. We see that all angles add up to 180° because they form a straight line.

So, $a + b + c + d + e + f + g = 180$

Let's rewrite this equation using only a and b because we need to compare $a + b$ in Column A with 65 in column B.

Then, we can write $c = b$, $d = b$, $e = b$, and $f = b$, and $g = a$.

So, $a + b + c + d + e + f + g = 180$ can be written as:

$$a + b + b + b + b + b + a = 180$$

Or, $2a + 5b = 180$

We also know that $a = 3d$ and $d = b$. So, $a = 3b$.

Then, $2(3b) + 5b = 180$

Or, $6b + 5b = 180$

Or, $11b = 180$

Or, $b = \frac{180}{11}$

Because $a = 3b$, $a = \frac{180}{11} \times 3$

To get the value of $a + b$, we note that a is $3\left(\frac{180}{11}\right)$ and b is $1\left(\frac{180}{11}\right)$. So, together, $a + b = 4\left(\frac{180}{11}\right) = \frac{720}{11}$

If you divide this expression, you will find that it is 65 plus some (we don't need the exact amount, we only need to know that it's a bit more than 65). So Column A is 65 plus some and Column B is 65. The answer then is choice (A).

(B) Oversight—Perhaps you solved for b and forgot to add a. Or, you solved for a and forgot to add b.

(C) Careless—Perhaps you rounded off some numbers and approximated. There's a danger here if you round off some decimals.

(D) Missing key insight—Looks like you chose this answer because there were no numbers in the problem. But, did you remember that a straight line is 180°?

15. Correct choice (A)

Column A first. A PIN number has 4 positions and has a number in each position. In all positions except the first one, there are 10 possible numbers (0 through 9) that can fill that position. In the first position, since 0 is not allowed, there are 9 possible choices. To get the total number of possible PIN numbers, we multiply these numbers together:

9 possibilities in the first position
$\times$ 10 possibilities in the 2nd position
$\times$ 10 possibilities in the 3rd position
$\times$ 10 possibilities in the 4th position
= 9,000 total possibilities

There are a couple of ways we can see that 9,000 is greater than 9^4, the quantity in Column B. We could compute 9^4 directly (Yuck!), and see that it is less than 9,000 ($9^4 = 6{,}561$), or we could express Column A as 9×10^3 and column B as 9×9^3, and choose Column A because $10^3 > 9^3$.

(B) Missing key insight—You probably didn't understand how to find the total number of different possible PIN numbers. To find the number of possible combinations of a sequence of digits such as this, remember to count how many digits are acceptable in each position, and then multiply these numbers together.

(C) Missing key insight—You probably didn't understand how to find the total number of different possible PIN numbers. Count how many digits are acceptable in each position, and then multiply these numbers together.

(D) Missing key insight—You probably didn't understand how to find the total number of possible PIN numbers. In any case, remember to use the "Cannot be determined" response sparingly. This is usually not the correct answer, especially for the more difficult problems of the test.

16. Correct answer 2.5

We're given: $\frac{6p-(2p-1)}{2} = 5.5$

Cross-multiplying: $6p - 2p + 1 = 11$

Or, $4p + 1 = 11$

Or, $4p = 10$

Then, $p = 2.5$

17. Correct answer 60

On the highway, Ralph has to drive 30 miles. If he travels at 60 miles per hour, the 30-mile ride will take him half an hour. (Because, in 1 hour, he can travel 60 miles, so in half an hour, he can travel 30 miles.)

On the state turnpike, he can drive at 30 miles per hour. That means, to travel 15 miles, he needs half an hour.

So, Ralph needs to spend half an hour on the highway and half an hour on the state turnpike. This means his total driving time is 30 minutes + 30 minutes = 60 minutes.

18. Correct answer 13

The total charge was $17.20. Of this amount, $12 was the "flat rate." That means if we subtract $12 from the total charge, the remaining amount will be the charge for the weight of the package.

So, the charge for the weight of the package = $17.20 – 12 = $5.20.

We know that the cost per pound is 40 cents. So, if we divide $5.20, or 520 cents, by 40, we'll get the weight of the package.

So, weight of the package = $\frac{520}{40} = \frac{52}{4} = 13$ pounds

We can check our work. If the weight of the package is 13 pounds, the charge for the weight is 13 × 40 = 520 cents = $5.20. Add the "flat rate" to find the total cost. 5.20 + 12 = 17.20, which is the amount we started with. So, 13 pounds is the correct answer.

19. Correct answer 25

Set up equations from the information given.

We know that Judy is 30 years older than Mary. So we can write:

$$J = M + 30$$

In 5 years, Judy will be (J + 5) years old and Mary will be (M + 5) years old. At that time, Judy will be twice as old as Mary.

So, $J + 5 = 2(M + 5)$

But we know that $J = M + 30$. Let's substitute this value for J.

Then, $(M + 30) + 5 = 2(M + 5)$

Or, $M + 35 = 2M + 10$

Or, $M - 2M = 10 - 35.$

Or, $-M = -25$

Or, $M = 25.$

So, Mary's current age is 25.

20. Correct answer 20

Using the Pythagorean theorem, we can find the distance from Town B to Town C.

In a right triangle, we can write the formula: $(\text{hypotenuse})^2 = (\text{base})^2 + (\text{height})^2$. Let's say that *BC* is x.

Then we can write:

$$50^2 = 30^2 + x^2$$

Or, $2{,}500 = 900 + x^2$

Or, $1{,}600 = x^2$

So, $40 = x^2$

Notice that we could have found this distance using the 3–4–5 right triangle rule. If the hypotenuse is 10(5) and one of the perpendicular sides is 10(3), the other perpendicular side has to be 10(4). For your test, you should be familiar with the common 3–4–5, 6–8–10, 30–40–50 triangles.

So, if the distance from Town B to Town C is 40 miles, Tom has to drive 30 + 40 = 70 miles. Jerry, on the other hand, has to drive only 50 miles. So, Tom has to drive 70 – 50 = 20 miles more than Jerry.

21. Correct answer 40

Let's first look at the price George paid. He bought 2 dozen, or 24, disks, out of which 4 were defective. This means 20 disks were usable. We're told that the price George paid was 32 cents per usable disk. This means the price for the box of disks must have been 32 × 20 = 640 cents. (Notice that it's not 32 × 24, because the price per *usable* disk means we have to multiply by 20.)

Now we know that the price for the box of 24 disks was 640 cents. This must also be the price Heidi paid for her disks. We know that 8 of Heidi's disks were defective. In other words, $24 - 8 = 16$ disks were usable, for which she paid 640 cents. So, the cost per usable disk for Heidi was:

$$\frac{\text{Total cost for disks}}{\text{Usable disks}} = \frac{640}{16} = 40 \text{ cents.}$$

Notice that one way to check your answer is to see that, because more of Heidi's disks were unusable (compared to George's), she ends up paying more per usable disk.

22. Correct answer 16

First, let's find the difference between these two numbers: $4{,}104 - 4{,}044 = 60$

The common mistake is to say that the number of multiples is $60 \div 4 = 15$. To see why the answer isn't 15, think what would happen if the two numbers were 16 and 4. The difference is 12, but the number of multiples of 4 isn't $12 \div 4 = 3$, it's 1 more than 3. The multiples are 4, 8, 12, and 16. In other words, we have to add 1 to 3.

Similarly, if the difference between 4,104 and 4,044 is 60, then the number of multiples of 4 is $(60 \div 4) + 1 = 16$.

23. Correct answer 18

The area of a rectangle is length × width. We're told that the length to width ratio is always 1.5. In other words,

$$\frac{\text{length}}{\text{width}} = 1.5$$

So, length = 1.5(width)

So, the area of the photograph can be written as:

area = length × width

= 1.5(width) × width.

= $1.5(\text{width})^2$

We know that this value is 216

So, $216 = 1.5(\text{width})^2$

Or, $\frac{216}{1.5} = (\text{width})^2$

Or, $(\text{width})^2 = \frac{2160}{15} = 144$

Then, width = 12

If the width is 12, the length must be 1.5 times the width. So, the length = $12 \times 1.5 = 18$.

24. Correct answer 4

This isn't an easy problem, is it? We have 4 unknowns, p, q, r, and s, and only 2 equations. Remember, on grid-in questions, there are no "none of the above" or "it cannot be determined" choices. This means the problem *can* be solved. Let's see what we can do.

Notice that the second equation, $p - 2q = 4$, gives us the relationship between p and q. So, let's work with the p and q terms in that long and ugly equation, $2p - 4q + 3r - 4s = 10$.

The p and q terms have a factor of 2 that's common to them. So, we can write the equation as:

$$2(p - 2q) + 3r - 4s = 10$$

But, from the second equation given to us, $p - 2q = 4$, we know that the p and q terms inside the parentheses are equal to 4.

So, $2(4) + 3r - 4s = 10$

Or, $8 + 3r - 4s = 10$

Or, $3r - 4s = 2$

We know the value of $3r - 4s$, but we need the value of $6r - 8s$. But notice what happens if we multiply both sides of the equation by 2:

$$2(3r - 4s) = 2(2)$$

Or, $6r - 8s = 4$

And so our answer is 4.

25. Correct answer 54

A rhombus has 4 equal sides. In other words, you can think of a rhombus as a square whose two opposite corners are pulled away from each other. If the perimeter of the rhombus is 60, it means that the sum of the 4 equal sides is 60. So, the length of each side of the rhombus is $60 \div 4 = 15$.

We're also told that the area of the rhombus is 180. The area of a rhombus is equal to the base × the height. We can take side PS to be the base (which is 15). Then the height of the rhombus can be taken to be side RT (remember, the height is simply a perpendicular drawn to the opposite corner). So we can write the equation:

$$PS \times RT = \text{area}$$

Or, $15 \times RT = 180$

Or, $RT = \frac{180}{15} = 12$

Now let's look at triangle *RTS*. It's a right triangle, with hypotenuse, $RS = 15$ and height, $RT = 12$. Then, using the Pythagorean theorem, we can find the length of base, *ST*. After we find the length of the base, we can find the area of the triangle.

Then, $RT^2 + ST^2 = RS^2$

Or, $12^2 + ST^2 = 15^2$

Or, $ST^2 = 225 - 144 = 81$

Then, $ST = 9$

Now, to find the area of triangle RTS, we have its height and the base. So,

Area of triangle $= \frac{1}{2}$ base $\times$ height

$= \frac{1}{2} \times 9 \times 12 = 54$

Test 1, Section 4: Verbal

Questions and Answers

Assignment for Today:

Take a sample SAT Verbal Reasoning Test under actual test conditions. Allow yourself exactly 30 minutes to complete the 33 questions in this test.

Directions: *For questions 1–9, one or more words have been left out of each sentence. Circle the answer, A–E, which contains the word or words which best fit the meaning of the entire sentence.*

1. The biggest merger ever in the communications industry has —— a monster that will make —— intrusions into our privacy.
   (A) informed..unsupervised
   (B) terrorized..indigent
   (C) engineered..genetic
   (D) unleashed..trivial
   (E) spawned..frightening

2. The fins of a plane generate a(n) —— or whirling airflow like a small tornado on each side of the aircraft and control spinning during sharp ——.
   (A) swirling..descents
   (B) updraft..inclinations
   (C) whirligig..ascents
   (D) vortex..maneuvers
   (E) orthogonal..turns

3. After the movie star had been —— by the press, she yearned to make herself more ——, so she moved out to the desert where no one could find her.
   (A) pursued..accessible
   (B) ignored..infamous
   (C) lambasted..insular
   (D) slandered..vulnerable
   (E) followed..discreet

4. The famed conductor can —— the titles of Verdi's operas as deftly as a(n) —— can enumerate the works of the great scholars.
   (A) destroy..child
   (B) write..librarian
   (C) articulate..pagan
   (D) list..academician
   (E) outlive..mortician

5. The —— architects of twentieth-century Manhattan sought to relieve creative people of the drudgery of cooking by designing apartment buildings without kitchens, instead connecting each apartment to a restaurant below through a(n) —— invention called the dumbwaiter.
   (A) unimaginative..artificial
   (B) lethargic..space-saving
   (C) futuristic..revolutionary
   (D) irresponsible..enervating
   (E) innovative..hackneyed

6. Strong, independent women have long —— that men have been paying mere lip service to feminist ideas or, for that matter, have rarely manifested common ——.
   (A) anticipated..courtesy
   (B) suspected..decency
   (C) concealed..ground
   (D) denied..sense
   (E) asserted..roots

7. The —— of traditional cultures through the twentieth century has —— early expectations that the colonial and post-colonial expansions of the West could lead only to an inevitable Westernization of the world.
   (A) disappearance..frustrated
   (B) spread..confirmed
   (C) preservation..fulfilled
   (D) disintegration..confounded
   (E) resilience..belied

8. The —— woman criticized her family about so many petty things that they eventually —— all overtures she made toward them.
   (A) captious..repudiated
   (B) sagacious..considered
   (C) acrimonious..endorsed
   (D) implacable..embraced
   (E) conciliatory..rejected

9. Ms. Gerber, who will succeed the ailing paleontologist, is widely recognized as the leading authority in the modest field of —— animal development.
   (A) geological
   (B) abiotic
   (C) prehistoric
   (D) coniferous
   (E) Pleistocene

Directions: *For questions 10–15, determine the relationship between the two words given in capital letters. Then, from the choices listed A–E, select the one pair that has a relationship most similar to that of the capitalized pair. Circle the letter of that pair.*

---

10. TELLER:BANK::
    (A) sheriff:badge
    (B) nurse:needles
    (C) ophthalmologist:cataract
    (D) epidemiologist:hatchery
    (E) scholar:academy

11. AMUSING:HILARIOUS::
    (A) sad:clever
    (B) unfair:unclear
    (C) small:microscopic
    (D) painful:frustrating
    (E) cold:furious

12. NOVELIST:NOVEL::
    (A) troubadour:doggerel
    (B) bard:epic
    (C) litterateur:literature
    (D) pedagogue:essay
    (E) minstrel:psalm

13. SURFEIT:EXCESS::
    (A) dearth:glut
    (B) morass:quagmire
    (C) zenith:nadir
    (D) synonym:homonym
    (E) forfeit:savings

14. CONTUSION:INJURY::
    (A) amputation:tourniquet
    (B) italic:typeface
    (C) zipper:snap
    (D) suture:surgeon
    (E) leaf:photosythesis

15. SYMPATHETIC:ANTIPATHETIC::
    (A) sympatric:antiquarian
    (B) consecrated:sanctified
    (C) philanthropic:misanthropic
    (D) choleric:anthropic
    (E) truculent:antiseptic

Directions: *For questions 16–33, answer the questions that follow each passage. Base your answers only on what is stated or implied in the passage and any introductory material given.*

Questions 16–21 are based on the following passage.

The following passage, written at the turn of the twentieth century, extols the virtues of the often overlooked dictionary.

One does not ordinarily pick out dictionaries for light reading. They are supposed to be heavy, didactic works, manifestly devoid of plot or what certain reviewers like to call "heart interest." Bulky in form, they traditionally are cumbersome in spirit, rather like the domestic furnace, which, for all its utility, can never be converted into a parlor ornament.

The dictionary, however, is grossly maligned. Rightly considered, even the most prosaic variety, the boiled-down Webster or Worcester or Standard for household use, has within it the possibilities of unlimited delight. To go no further than the pictures, what other work published in this day and generation would ever presume to edify its readers through the agency of such preposterous woodcuts, which are still orthodox in the dictionary? My own Webster, of the crop of 1884, is a gallery of priceless art treasures. Consider the Moose, manifestly drawn from a melancholy donkey, to the head of which the artist, in a flight of poetic imagination, has affixed a pair of angel's wings. Behold the Gila Monster, note the gaping jaws of *Crocodilis vulgaris*, and then try to maintain that the dictionary is not a work of fancy.

Even the small dictionary has pictures; the large one has, in addition, innumerable examples of how one would use all the words if one only knew what they meant. Poetry and philosophy, prose and verse, have been ransacked for these illustrations; they range from Milton to Billingsgate—not as long a jump as it looks. Most people resolutely ignore these quotations, which are to a dictionary what color is to a landscape. For example, the word "shoe" does not suggest vast illumination, yet I read: "sometimes used in derisive phrases; e.g., in the Towneley 'Noah's Flood' (about 1400), Noah's wife replies to her husband's exhortation to enter the ark: 'Yei, Noah, go cloute thy shoon, the better will they last.'" And there is the whole character of Mrs. Noah in a nutshell.

As for the etymologies—at which people look still less than at the literary examples—they tell half the history of civilization. Why, for instance, should the French language, which inherited almost its whole vocabulary from the Latin, have gone, some eight centuries ago, to the Germans for its word for "war"? Our own "warrior," acquired in the first place from the French "*guerrier*," goes back to an old German form. So the dictionary proves the thoughts which best fitted the German speech in the days of the Crusades.

The fact is, of course, that words live, and a true dictionary is a vast collection of biographies. It will tell you how Caesar's legionaries found the Celtic natives using a clumsy, two-wheeled vehicle which, in the Celtic dialect, was called a "*karr*." The soldiers commandeered the wagon, and with it the word; it became a part of the camp slang that traveled the length and breadth of the empire. In many regions it died, as slang so often does; in some, and notably in France, it lived and traveled to Britain as "char" so that today it carries us and out belongings up and down the land. You can look up either "car" or "cart" in any dictionary that gives thorough etymologies, and read the word's biography in full.

16. The main point of the passage is that
    (A) people don't use dictionaries enough
    (B) dictionaries are useful as sources of artwork
    (C) dictionaries are more stimulating than most people think
    (D) word origins are good indicators of history
    (E) dictionaries are difficult to enjoy

17. In line 3 the word "didactic" is used to mean
    (A) ponderous
    (B) massive
    (C) profound
    (D) depressive
    (E) crushing

18. The author cites "the Moose" (line 20) and "the Gila Monster" (line 23) to support the point that
    (A) dictionaries can teach a lot about nature
    (B) dictionary artwork can be considered highly imaginative
    (C) the drawings in the dictionaries belong in art galleries
    (D) woodcuts are a poor excuse for artwork
    (E) many drawings in dictionaries are unfortunately inaccurate

19. When the author writes in paragraph three that "they range from Milton to Billingsgate," the author is refering to
    (A) illustrations in the dictionary
    (B) authors of dictionary definitions
    (C) editors for his favorite dictionary
    (D) quotations cited in dictionaries
    (E) publishers of dictionaries

20. The word "etymologies" (line 44) means
    (A) literary examples
    (B) synonym list
    (C) word histories
    (D) pronunciation guide
    (E) diacritical markings

21. The author of the passage would most likely *disagree* with which of the following statements?
    (A) Dictionaries are a necessary but cumbersome part of a person's education.
    (B) The history of a word tells a lot about the history of a civilization.
    (C) Language is constantly evolving.
    (D) Our word for "war" ultimately comes from Germanic origins.
    (E) Dictionaries are fun.

Questions 22–33 are based on the following passage:

This passage discusses what happens when an element is burned and its flame examined under a "spectroscope," the Zeeman effect, and other important discoveries in science.

If you take a lump of dry salt between your thumb and fingers, you may readily reduce it to an impalpable powder. If you were to dust some of the almost invisible grains of this powder upon a glass slide and examine them through a microscope, you would find that the smallest of the dust-like particles now seems rather like a rough and jagged piece of rock than like the infinitesimal thing that it appeared to the naked eye. It is easy to believe that this fragment of matter is built up of smaller particles and is nowhere near the limits of divisibility.

If now you put a few drops of water on the slide, you will see the rock-like particle of salt fade away and dissolve into nothingness. It has become absolutely invisible. If the microscope you are using is a powerful one, this means that there remains no particle of the salt of the size of one-hundred-thousandth of an inch.

In point of fact, the portion of salt has now been separated into molecules so small that many millions of them must be massed together to form the smallest visible particle of matter. These molecules are moving about freely in the solution among the molecules of water. Individually they are so small that they do not obstruct the light waves; hence, the transparency of the solution of which they now form a part.

But if you were to thrust a platinum wire into the solution and then hold the wire in the flame of a Bunsen gas burner, the flame will instantly take on a peculiar green color which proves to the discerning eye that the particles of salt have been rendered luminous. If this green flame is examined through a spectroscope, the rays of light coming from it will be observed to be split up into a characteristic series of lines.

This particular series of spectral lines would not appear in light emanating from anything but sodium. No other substance in the world can duplicate that record. The same series of lines might appear in the light coming from the sun or from a star, but they would prove the presence of sodium at the source of light. These lines *spell* sodium in the language which any chemist in the world can read, and the signature of the spectrum cannot be forged or duplicated.

What is true of sodium is true of every other element. Each has a signature which it writes as a series of lines in the spectrum. The chemical test thus afforded is exquisitely delicate. There may be but the smallest trace of a given substance present, as in the case of our infinitesimal droplet of salt solution, but the telltale lines of the spectrum will record the trace of this individual substance, even in the midst of many other substances.

If while examining our sodium flame through the spectroscope we were to hold the flame between the poles of a powerful electromagnet, we should observe that the sodium lines which before appeared single are now split in two and separated. This phenomenon is called the Zeeman effect, in honor of its discoverer, Professor Peter Zeeman, of Amsterdam. It is a phenomenon of vast importance from the physicist's standpoint, inasmuch as it gives interesting clues to the activities of the atomic forces and to the character of light.

This phenomenon of the splitting-up of spectral lines has been observed by Professor George E. Hale, Director of the Mount Wilson Observatory, in connection with the light emanating from spots on the surface of the sun. The observation shows that sunspots are powerful magnetic fields. Thus, the sunspot gives a demonstration on a magnificent scale of physical laws that may be tested, changed only in degree and not in kind, in the laboratory. Incidentally, Professor Hale's observation explains the relation that had previously been observed between outbursts of sunspots—which are in reality gigantic volcanoes of gaseous matter—and the phenomena of terrestrial magnetism.

A further interest attaches to the Zeeman effect (whether manifested in the laboratory or in the sun) from the fact that it demonstrates the close relationship between magnetism and light. In Professor Zeeman's words, it shows that light is an electrical phenomenon. In the meantime, our experiment with the sodium flame demonstrated, obviously enough, a close relation between the activities of molecules or atoms of matter and the origin of light itself.

A single experiment thus suffices to show curious and interesting relationships between the ultimate particles of matter and those manifestations of energy which we term light, electricity, and magnetism. In fact, it is a matter of everyday observation that there is ordinarily the closest relationship between light and that other manifestation of energy termed heat.

It is no matter for great surprise, then, to be told that the different portions of the spectrum into which a beam of light is spread out show different degrees of temperature when tested by an apparatus of sufficient delicacy. It appears, in point of fact, that the dark lines in the spectrum are also areas of relative coolness, and that the spectrum may be charted by moving a sufficiently delicate heat measurer along it.

22. The main purpose of this passage is to
    (A) explain phenomena that show a connection between matter and manifestations of energy
    (B) describe the relative impact of spectral lines compared to older technologies
    (C) demonstrate that any element can be made into a form of energy
    (D) prove that scientists now have the tools to understand things that were previously invisible
    (E) present a new interpretation of the Zeeman effect

23. The word "impalpable" in line 3 most likely means
    (A) invisible
    (B) too subtle to understand
    (C) completely untouchable
    (D) nearly untouchable
    (E) white

24. According to the passage, salt powder in water results in a transparent solution because
    (A) the powder dissolves and essentially disappears
    (B) the salt is first crushed
    (C) lone salt molecules do not block light waves
    (D) the flame burns green to the naked eye
    (E) salt in solution gives off spectral lines, which are transparent

25. The word "rendered" in line 34 most likely means
    (A) interpreted
    (B) translated
    (C) caused to be
    (D) restored
    (E) given

26. According to the passage, the signature of the sodium spectrum
    (A) appears only under laboratory conditions
    (B) can be duplicated by related elements on the sun
    (C) is the green flame produced by a Bunsen burner
    (D) is unique to sodium alone
    (E) is identical to the spectrum of other elements

27. The effect of a powerful magnet on the spectral lines
    (A) produces a phenomenon that gives clues about atomic forces and light
    (B) will produce a phenomenon named after Professor Hale
    (C) is to bring separate lines into one
    (D) has not been of much import to physicists
    (E) shows that dark lines in the spectrum are relatively cool

28. According to the passage, Professor Hale's work with sunspots shows that
    (A) sunspots are remarkably like volcanoes on earth
    (B) the Zeeman effect happens outside the laboratory
    (C) Zeeman was not the first to identify the spectral splitting phenomenon
    (D) scientists have been negligent in picking up on critical clues in the environment
    (E) sodium has a spectrum all its own

29. According to the passage, the Zeeman experiment shows that
    (A) sodium burns green when in a flame
    (B) light is related to magnetism
    (C) magnetism and electricity are basically the same
    (D) sunspots are powerful magnetic fields
    (E) each element has its own spectral signature

30. The phrase "single experiment" in line 95 most likely refers to
    (A) dissolving salt in water
    (B) viewing sunspots through a spectrometer
    (C) viewing spectral lines influenced by a magnetic field
    (D) noting everyday observations
    (E) measuring the heat of dark spectral lines

31. According to the passage, which of the following would be *least* likely to demonstrate the relationship between heat and light?
    (A) A camp fire
    (B) The sun
    (C) A light bulb
    (D) A radiant moon
    (E) A burning candle

32. From the passage, one can infer that the dark lines of the spectrum
    (A) can be measured for temperature
    (B) are less interesting to scientists than light parts
    (C) are dark because they are cooler
    (D) are bands where light converges
    (E) are warmer than other parts of the spectrum

33. Which of the following would be the most appropriate title for this passage?
    (A) Salt and Science
    (B) Why Scientists Think Energy and Matter Are Related
    (C) Sunspots: Celestial Volcanoes
    (D) Remembering Professor Zeeman
    (E) The Spectrum of Elements: Why Every Element Has Its Own Signature

Quick Answer Guide

Test 1, Section 4: Verbal

1. E	11. C	21. A	31. D
2. D	12. B	22. A	32. A
3. C	13. B	23. D	33. B
4. D	14. B	24. C	
5. C	15. C	25. C	
6. B	16. C	26. D	
7. E	17. A	27. A	
8. A	18. B	28. B	
9. E	19. D	29. B	
10. E	20. C	30. C	

For explanations to these questions see Day 16.

Test 1, Section 4: Verbal

Explanations and Strategies

Assignment for Today:

Review the explanations for the test you just took. See which answer is right, and learn what makes each wrong answer wrong.

1. Correct choice (E) spawned..frightening

As you read, the word "merger" probably made you think of "has created a monster" or "has made a monster." *Spawned* is close. So is *engineered. Terrorized* and *unleashed* could fit, too.

And there are no obvious flags. It's tough to anticipate choices in two-blank sentences. So the best strategy may be to plug in choices and eliminate the ones that don't work.

The second blank settles the issue. Only choice (E) fits with the imagery and tone of the sentence and makes sense. *Spawned* means "to produce" and is normally used with fish and frogs, but monsters will do. And *frightening* goes with monsters and intrusions. Read the sentence with the choices plugged in:

The biggest merger ever in the communications industry has *spawned* a monster that will make *frightening* intrusions into our privacy.

(A) *Informed* means "told," not formed. A merger isn't going to *tell* a monster.

(B) *Terrorized* starts to make a weird fairy-tale sense, especially if the second word were "indig*nant*." But *indigent* means "poor" and doesn't make sense in this sentence.

(C) *Engineered* can mean "created" and sounds good with communications industry and mergers. But *genetic* means "pertaining to genes," and the communications industry has nothing to do with *genetics*.

(D) *Unleashed* means "let loose." But *trivial* means "unimportant." Wouldn't you expect a newly released communications monster to make *important* or *unpredictable* intrusions?

2. Correct choice (D) vortex..maneuvers

Can't anticipate unless you know planes and flying. No flags here. Plug in the choices, and reason it out.

Only choices (D) and (E) make sense in the second blank. The others don't go with "sharp." And (E) doesn't fit in the first blank. That leaves (D), which makes good sense.

The fins of a plane generate a *vortex* or whirling airflow like a small tornado on each side of the aircraft and control spinning during sharp *maneuvers.*

A *vortex* is a whirling mass, so "vortex or whirling airflow" makes sense. A *maneuver* is a move, especially skillful vehicular moves like those made by Luke Skywalker in *Star Wars*.

(A) The fins of a plane generate a "swirling or whirling airflow . . ."

Swirling is the same as whirling, so you can eliminate this choice. *Vortex* in (D) means a *swirling mass,* which at least creates a picture of a whirlpool.

You make *sharp turns* or *maneuvers,* but *steep* ascents or *descents.*

(B) An *updraft* is not a "whirling airflow like a small tornado." It's just the upward movement of air.

(C) A *whirligig* is a merry-go-round or anything that goes round in circles. It's barely okay. Anyway, "sharp ascents" doesn't work. You make *sharp turns* or *maneuvers,* but *steep* climbs or *descents.*

(E) An orthogonal airflow would be perpendicular or right-angled, not like a small tornado. If you're not sure of a word meaning, skip it and work with those words you do know.

3. Correct choice (C) lambasted..insular

Here's what the sentence tells you: A movie star gets annoyed at the press and moves far away. Because the words in the choices are fairly difficult, the best way to solve this problem is to read through the choices and eliminate the ones that don't work. Using this process, you'll find that (C) works the best. *Lambasted* means scolded. *Insular* means isolated.

After the movie star had been *lambasted* by the press, she yearned to make herself more *insular,* so she moved out to the desert where no one could find her.

(A) *Pursued* fits the meaning of the sentence, but *accessible* is the complete opposite of what works here. The movie star wants to get away from things, wants to be *in*accessible.

(B) *Ignored* really doesn't fit. What movie star wants to be ignored? And would being ignored make her move away? *Infamous* means being famous for the wrong reasons, like robbing a bank. This choice doesn't fit.

(D) *Slandered,* having her reputation damaged, is a good choice for the first blank. This would make the movie star want to hide. However, *vulnerable,* which means open to harm, doesn't fit at all. She wants to become invulnerable, unapproachable, separate.

(E) *Followed* is okay, though a more dramatic word would probably better account for the movie star's actions. *Discreet* means careful, which again is okay but not great.

4. Correct choice (D) list..academician

The easiest way to find the right choice here is to eliminate the choices that are obviously wrong: (A),(B), and (E). These three just don't make sense in the sentence. Of the remaining choices, (C) also is problematic: a *pagan* (one who holds no belief in a god) might not be able to recite scholarly books, but a conductor *should* be able to *articulate* (say) the names of Verdi's operas. Finally, choice (D) is left—the correct answer. An *academician* is a scholar, someone who studies.

The famed conductor can *list* the titles of Verdi's operas as deftly as a(n) *academician* can enumerate the works of the great scholars.

(A) Why would a conductor *destroy* Verdi's titles? This doesn't make sense.

(B) Why would a conductor *write* the titles of Verdi's operas? Question-mark this choice and look for a better one.

(C) *Articulate* fits well here, but a *pagan* (one who worships no particular god) would not necessarily know about scholarly works.

(E) Neither word in this answer works at all.

5. Correct choice (C) futuristic..revolutionary

You can't anticipate the first blank. *Instead* is a flag but not much help. It just implies that the dumbwaiter helped in replacing kitchens. So, try to understand what the sentence means. Then plug in the choices and start zapping.

The blanks are adjectives. They describe the nouns *architects* and *invention.* So they should reflect the sense of the sentence.

Building apartments without kitchens is pretty zany. The architects felt creative people didn't need drudgery. So they eliminated kitchens.

That's not *unimaginative*, nor is it *lethargic*. It could be *irresponsible*, but they did supply a replacement: dumbwaiter connections. So it's *futuristic* or *innovative*.

Check out the second blanks. Both *revolutionary* and *hackneyed* make sense. *Revolutionary* is "overthrowing established ideas." *Hackneyed* is "stale or commonplace." Assume the dumbwaiter is a commonplace invention. The architects are doing something new with it. So the sentence should say, "through a(n) *until then thought of as hackneyed* invention called the dumbwaiter." It doesn't, so *revolutionary* wins.

Futuristic implies hostility to and violation of traditional actions. *Innovative* implies changing established forms. *Futuristic* wins because it's more radical. Like tossing out kitchens.

The *futuristic* architects of twentieth-century Manhattan sought to relieve creative people of the drudgery of cooking by designing apartment buildings without kitchens, instead connecting each apartment to a restaurant below through a *revolutionary* invention called the dumbwaiter.

(A) It takes imagination to throw out kitchens and to connect apartments with restaurants below by means of dumbwaiters.

(B) *Lethargic* means "drowsy or sluggish." Do those architects really sound drowsy? Also, they used dumbwaiters not to save space but to eliminate drudgery by eliminating kitchens. Drudgery is menial and uninspiring, routine work.

(D) The architects might be considered *irresponsible if* they hadn't provided a kitchen substitute: dumbwaiter connections to restaurants. A different kind of room service.

(E) The architects were definitely *innovative*. They changed established forms. But *futuristic* is the best choice because it's more radical. Also, a *revolutionary* invention makes more sense than a *hackneyed* (banal, ordinary) invention. This was tricky.

6. Correct choice (B) suspected..decency

By reading the sentence you should get the impression that these women are suspicious of men—that they don't think men give them a fair shake on things. With this in mind you can see that choice (B) makes the most sense here. Women *suspect*, and men don't have common *decency*.

Strong, independent women have long *suspected* that men have been paying mere lip service to feminist ideas or, for that matter, have rarely manifested common *decency*.

(A) *Anticipated* doesn't work well here. *Anticipate* has a sense of looking toward the future, while this sentence has women looking back in time. *Courtesy*, however, works quite well.

(C) These independent women are not likely to *conceal* anything bad about men. Common *ground* doesn't make sense in the overall sense of the sentence.

(D) These independent women are not likely to *deny* anything bad about men, although common *sense* works well here.

(E) *Asserted* works well here because that's what you expect independent people to do. In contrast, common *roots* does not work with the rest of the sentence.

7. Correct choice (E) resilience..belied

This is such a long-winded sentence, it's almost impossible to figure out what best goes in the blanks. So the best strategy may be to read in each of the choices to see which makes sense. What's going on is the clash of traditional cultures versus Westernization (Western cultures taking over the traditional ones). Choice (A) doesn't make sense: If traditional cultures *disappeared*, then expectations of Westernization wouldn't be *frustrated*; they would be enhanced. Likewise, choice (B) also makes no sense: if traditional cultures *spread*, then Westernization wouldn't be *confirmed*, but rather hampered. Same with (C): If traditional cultures were *preserved*, expectations of Westernization would *not* be *fulfilled*. Finally if traditional cultures *disintegrated* (broke down), then expectations of Westernization would not be *confounded*; they would be confirmed

Finally (phew!), choice (E) works: The *resilience* of traditional cultures (or their ability to recover from shock and hardship) *belied* (or proved false) expectations that the entire world would come to look like the modern West.

The *resilience* of traditional cultures through the twentieth century has *belied* early expectations that the colonial and post-colonial expansions of the West could lead only to an inevitable Westernization of the world.

This was a time-consuming question, if not a difficult one.

(A) *Disappearance* is a possibility for the first blank in the sentence. However, if we insert *disappearance* then we need a word meaning "confirmed." What we have instead is *frustrated*. Doesn't work.

(B) *Spread* is a possible choice for the first blank in the sentence—although we might think it unlikely that someone would speak of the *spread* of traditional cultures in the twentieth century. However, *confirmed* doesn't work in the sentence with *spread*.

(C) While *preservation* is a possibility for the first blank, it needs a word meaning "contradicted" to go with it in the second blank. Instead, we have *fulfilled*. That doesn't work.

(D) The *disintegration* of traditional cultures would have *confirmed* early expectations of Westernization, not *confounded* them.

8. Correct choice (A) captious..repudiated

The clues in the sentence should lead you to expect the first blank to be filled by a word that means "critical." The second blank needs a word that means "rejected." Choice (A) gives you the best pair of words. *Captious* means overly critical about petty things. To *repudiate* means to reject.

The *captious* woman criticized her family about so many petty things that they eventually *repudiated* any overtures she made toward them.

(B) *Sagacious* means wise. Why would a wise woman be so critical? *Considered* is also wrong because you would expect the family to stop taking the woman seriously.

(C) *Acrimonious* means bitter, which works well for the first blank. But *endorsed* is not logical for the second blank. To *endorse* means to support, the opposite of what you would expect from her family.

(D) *Implacable* means impossible to please, which is an excellent choice here. But to say the family eventually began to *embrace* her overtures doesn't make sense, since you know she had criticized them.

(E) *Conciliatory* means inclined to make peace. You should realize that *conciliatory* behavior is just the opposite of the behavior that this woman has demonstrated. However, *rejected* works well.

9. Correct choice (E) Pleistocene

Anticipating this is impossible. Even if you're familiar with biology, plug in and see which one works. All you need are good reasoning skills to zap the bad answers.

Okay. She's succeeding a paleontologist. That's someone who studies fossilized organisms. So, (A) and (B) are out. She's "in the modest field of —— *animal development*." *Coniferous* is plant-related. (D) is out.

The choice is between (C) *prehistoric* and (D) *Pleistocene*. Plug in both. You wonder what Pleistocene is. You don't need to know.

When you can't figure out a word, check the sentence for clues.

She's "in the *modest field* of —— animal development." *Modest* means "not huge." *Prehistoric* means "before recorded history." That's several billion years. Not *modest*, is it?

Ms. Gerber, who will succeed the ailing paleontologist, is widely recognized as the leading authority in the modest field of *Pleistocene* animal development.

(A) *Geological* means "pertaining to earth's composition and change." Minerals and earthquakes and the like. What does *geological* animal development mean? It's nonsense.

(B) *Abiotic* means "characterized by the absence of life." That's non-living things. Not just dead or fossilized. ". . . *non-living things* animal development . . . " is impossible.

(C) You probably worried: prehistoric or *Pleistocene?* What is *Pleistocene?* You don't need to know. You only need to realize that *prehistoric* means "before recorded history." That's several billion years; so it can't be called *modest*.

(D) *Coniferous* is plant stuff; pines, spruce, Christmas trees. It has nothing to do with animal development.

10. Correct choice (E) scholar:academy

teller—someone who works with customers at a bank

bank—a place that offers financial services

A *teller* works in a *bank*.

(A) Does a sheriff work in a badge? No.

(B) Does a nurse work in a needle? Hardly.

(C) Does an *ophthalmologist* work in a *cataract?* No. However, ophthalmologists *remove cataracts*.

(D) Does an *epidemiologist* work in a *hatchery?* No. (Unless he lost his job at the hospital.)

(E) Does a *scholar* work in an *academy?* Often, yes. An *academy* is a university or college. Therefore, *teller* is to *bank* in the same way that *scholar* is to *academy*. **Correct choice**.

11. Correct choice (C) small:microscopic

amusing—to be pleasant

hilarious—marked by boisterous laughter

If something is *hilarious*, it is very *amusing*.

(A) If something is *clever*, is it very *sad?* No.

(B) If something is *unclear*, is it very *unfair?* No.

(C) If something is *microscopic*, is it very *small?* Yes. *Small* has the same relationship to *microscopic* as *amusing* does to *hilarious*. **Correct choice**.

(D) If something is *frustrating*, is it very *painful?* Not necessarily.

(E) If something is *furious*, is it very *cold?* Nonsense.

12. Correct choice (B) bard:epic

novelist—a person who writes novels

novel—a fictitious prose narrative of considerable length portraying characters and presenting a sequential organization

A novelist creates *novels*.

(A) Does a *troubadour* create *doggerel?* No. A *troubadour* writes courtly love songs. *Doggerel* is comic or crude verse.

(B) Does a *bard* create *epics?* Yes. A *bard* is a person who composes and recites *epics*. An *epic* is a poetic composition that narrates the numerous achievements of a hero, usually in sequence. **Correct choice**.

(C) Does a *litterateur* create *literature?* Yes. But literature is too broad. It embraces all forms of writing, unlike novels or epics, which are specific forms.

(D) Does a *pedagogue* create *essays?* No. A *pedagogue* is a teacher, not an essayist.

(E) Does a *minstrel* create *psalms?* No. A *minstrel* is a musician who sings accompanied by instruments. A *psalm* is a sacred song or hymn and is not written or sung by *minstrels*.

13. Correct choice (B) morass:quagmire

surfeit—an overabundant supply, excess

excess—an overabundant supply, surfeit

Surfeit means the same as *excess*.

(A) Does *dearth* mean the same as *glut?* No. *Dearth*, a lack of something, means the *opposite* of *glut*, which is to have too much of something.

(B) Does *morass* mean the same as *quagmire?* Yes. They both refer to something that traps, confuses, or impedes. **Correct choice**.

(C) Does *zenith* mean the same as *nadir?* No. They are opposites. The *zenith* is the highest point whereas the *nadir* is the lowest point.

(D) Does *synonym* mean the same as *homonym?* No. *Synonyms* are words that share a common meaning, while *homonyms* are words that share a common sound.

(E) Does *forfeit* mean the same as *savings?* No. When you *forfeit*, you concede without a struggle; *savings* are what you end up with when you have a surplus.

14. Correct choice (B) italic:typeface

contusion—a bruise to the tissue without laceration or cut *injury*—a general category of harm to the body

A *contusion* is a type of *injury*.

The correct choice has to do with the first word belonging to the category described by the second word. In this case a *contusion* is a type of *injury*.

The correct choice here, (B), is quite difficult, not only because two of the other choices have to do with cutting the body, but also because the relationship between *italic* and *typeface* is not general knowledge to many people.

(A) Is *amputation* a type of *tourniquet?* No, an *amputation* may be treated by a *tourniquet*, but it is not a type of *tourniquet*.

(B) Is *italic* a type of *typeface?* Yes, it is. **Correct choice**.

(C) Is a *zipper* a kind of *snap?* Not really. Had the choice read zipper:closure device, then this would be a good choice.

(D) Is *suture* a type of *surgeon?* No. This answer probably tripped you up because it deals with cuts and injuries. ***Remember:*** look for *relationships* between terms, not similar subject matter.

(E) Is *leaf* a type of *photosynthesis?* No.

15. Correct choice (C) philanthropic:misanthropic

sympathy—mutual affection or understanding

antipathy—revulsion or aversion

Sympathetic is very nearly the opposite of *antipathetic*.

The stem words, SYMPATHETIC:ANTIPATHETIC, are a pair of opposites. The trick here is not only knowing that they are opposites, but which of the choices are also opposites. This is a difficult question because the stem words and choices are not everyday, simple words.

(A) Is *sympatric* the opposite of *antiquarian? Sympatric* means occurring in the same place. *Antiquarian* means dealing in old or rare books. They certainly are not opposites.

(B) Are *consecrated* and *sanctified* opposites. No, *consecrated* and *sanctified* both mean "sacred."

(C) *Philanthropic* means "reaching out to help others" and *misanthropic* means "distrusting or hating others." *Philanthropic* and *misanthropic* are near opposites in the same way as *sympathetic* and *antipathetic*. **Correct choice**.

(D) *Choleric* means "hot-tempered." *Anthropic* means "relating to human beings." They are not near antonyms.

(E) Are *truculent* and *antiseptic* opposites? No. *Truculent* means "ferocious or harsh," and *antiseptic* means "protecting." They are almost opposites, but not antonyms like *sympathetic* and *antipathetic*.

16. Correct choice (C)

The author hopes to change people's opinions about dictionaries. The author admits that most people think dictionaries are no fun, but goes on to give examples of how dictionaries can be interesting.

(A) Not addressed—The author may *feel* that people don't use dictionaries enough, but this is never mentioned in the passage.

(B) Too specific—The author does point out that dictionaries have interesting and useful drawings, but this idea is simply one small part of the passage. It is not the main idea.

(D) Too specific—The author discusses the use of word origins as indicators of history, but this idea is just one part of the passage. It is not the main idea.

(E) Contradiction—The author argues pretty much the opposite point in this passage, hoping to get people to see dictionaries as an endless source of fascination.

17. Correct choice (A)

In the context of the passage, "heavy" refers to something that is intricate, complicated, or labored. It is not meant for "light reading" and is "cumbersome." Only choice (A), "ponderous," fits this definition and, as such, is the best response.

(B) *Massive* refers to something that has a lot of weight, something that is impressively large. Athough dictionaries may look large, this is not the meaning referred to in the passage.

(C) *Profound* refers to something that has a lot of intellectual depth and is difficult to fathom or understand. This is not the context in which "heavy" is used.

(D) *Depressive* refers to something that is sad or discouraging. It also means something that causes something else to sink to a lower position. This is not the context in which "heavy" is used.

(E) *Crushing* refers to squeezing or forcing by pressure. This is not the context in which "heavy" appears.

18. Correct choice (B)

Although this answer does not sound right at first, the last sentence of the second paragraph shows that the author is arguing that dictionary artwork is indeed imaginative, or "a work of fancy."

(A) True, but—The author does not try to prove that dictionaries can teach a lot about nature.

(C) Too general—Although the author seems to enjoy the drawings in dictionaries, there is no mention that the drawings belong in an art gallery.

(D) Too specific—The author does call the woodcuts preposterous, but does not think they are unsuitable for use in the dictionary. The two examples cited indicate that the author enjoys such whimsical portrayals.

(E) Too general—The author may agree that the drawings are not precisely accurate, but would hardly call such inaccuracy "unfortunate."

19. Correct choice (D)

The topic sentence in the third paragraph is somewhat misleading, but a careful reader will notice that the author has stopped discussing illustrations in dictionaries and has moved on to discussing quotations. The line about Milton and Billingsgate refers to the varied quotes the dictionary will list as samples of how words are used by the masters.

(A) Contradiction—This answer is a tricky one because the word "illustration" appears in the same sentence; however, the author is talking about how the dictionary uses quotations to illustrate how words have been used.

(B) Not addressed—If you read the third paragraph carefully, you'll see that the author is not talking about who wrote the definitions.

(C) Not addressed—If you read the third paragraph carefully, you'll see that the author is not talking about who edited the dictionary.

(E) Not addressed—If you read the third paragraph carefully, you'll see that the author does not mention who published the dictionary.

20. Correct choice (C)

Even if you don't know what "etymology" means, the context of the paragraph should make it fairly clear. The author is talking about word origins and word histories, citing an example of where our word "war" came from.

(A) Contradiction—The author uses the words "literary examples" here to make a transition from the preceding paragraph.

(B) Not addressed—*Etymology* does not mean synonym list. Take a closer look at the context cues for more help.

(D) Not addressed—The pronunciation guide is not part of this passage. To find out what *etymology* means, examine the context cues in the paragraph.

(E) Not addressed—The word *etymology* does not mean "diacritical makings." Check the context cues for more help.

21. Correct choice (A)

The author would likely agree with all the statements given except the statement about dictionaries being cumbersome. The tone of the passage indicates that dictionaries are enlivening, not burdening. Note that in the second paragraph the author refers to dictionaries as a source of "unlimited delight."

(B) The author supports this idea in paragraphs four and five.

(C) The author obviously understands that words go from one language to another and that word meanings change over time. From this, we can infer that the author believes that language evolves.

(D) The author makes this point in paragraph four.

(E) The author never uses the word "fun," but certainly comes close: note the use of "unlimited delight" in paragraph two.

22. Correct choice (A)

This passage takes three paragraphs to really get going, but by paragraph four, you see that the author is mostly concerned with showing that matter and energy are related in some way. The passage does not say exactly what this relationship is, but it does describe an experiment and other observations that support this point. The second-to-last paragraph makes it clear that matter is somehow related to light, electricity, and magnetism. Knowing this, you can look back over the rest of the passage and say, "Yeah, that's what the author is really getting at here."

(B) True, but—The passage mentions spectral lines and Bunsen burners, but no direct comparisons are made.

(C) Not addressed—The passage gives only the vaguest hint that matter can be transformed into forms of energy. If you picked this answer, you probably know too much about Einstein's theory of relativity. Remember that correct answers are derived *only* from what is stated or implied in the passage.

(D) True, but—The author wants the readers to know about certain tools, but the passage doesn't "prove" anything. It's an explanation. Can you see the difference?

(E) Not addressed—The passage mentions the Zeeman effect, but gives no new interpretation.

23. Correct choice (D)

The word "impalpable" usually refers to something that cannot be touched. However, in this case the powder would be there, and you could touch it. This makes choice (D) the best response. Think about it: The powder could be extremely fine, but you could still touch it. The powder hasn't disappeared. The author is using this word here to exaggerate.

(A) *Impalpable* does not mean "invisible" in this context. The grains themselves might be invisible to the naked eye, but you could still see the powder.

(B) This is a possible meaning of *impalpable*, but it is not the meaning called for here.

(C) Technically speaking, *impalpable* usually refers to something that cannot be touched. However, you would be able to touch the powder.

(E) Although the powder would be white, this is not what *impalpable* means. The test maker is trying to trick you into a familiar word association: white powder.

24. Correct choice (C)

The passage says that when salt dissolves in water, it separates into individual molecules. These molecules are so small that they do not block light waves, which makes the solution transparent. See paragraph three for reference.

(A) True, but—This may be true, but it does not provide the explanation from paragraph three of the passage.

(B) True, but—The fact that the salt is crushed isn't enough of an explanation. That's only the beginning of the process.

(D) True, but—Paragraph four says that a salt solution burns green, but this doesn't explain why the solution is clear to begin with.

(E) Contradiction—The salt solution gives off spectral lines only when placed in a flame, but this doesn't tell us why the solution is clear to begin with.

25. Correct choice (C)

"Render" has many meanings in the dictionary. If you know French, you should recognize its cognate *rendre* (which can mean "to throw up" as well as "to give up"). However, this is of little help here. The context of the sentence makes choice (C) the best choice: The flame has caused the salt solution to give off a green light.

(A) This is a common meaning of *rendered*, but it's not the one the author is using here.

(B) This is a common meaning of *rendered*, but it's not the one the author is using here. How could particles of salt be "translated" luminous?

(D) This is a common meaning of *rendered*, but it's not the one the author is using here. Would particles of salt be "restored" luminous?

(E) "Given" is a common meaning of *rendered,* but it's not the one the author is using here.

26. Correct choice (D)

Paragraph five contains the answer to this question. Notice that the passage refers to the sodium spectral lines as something unique to sodium. No other element will give off the same pattern of lines. That's why the author calls it a "signature"—it's a one-of-a-kind occurrence.

(A) True, but—The passage shows that the lines can be viewed in the lab, which makes this answer partly true. But the passage also says that the sun or a star provides the right conditions as well.

(B) Contradiction—This choice is a bit tricky. The sodium spectral lines indicate sodium and nothing else. No related elements, on the sun or elsewhere, will give the same pattern of lines.

(C) Nope—The green flame is not the same as the spectral lines. Only when you view the green flame with the special scope will you see the spectral lines.

(E) Contradiction—The sodium spectral lines indicate sodium and nothing else. No related elements, on the sun or a star 50 billion miles away, will produce the same pattern of lines.

27. Correct choice (A)

The author gets excited about the fact that a magnet has an effect on spectral lines. According to the passage, this shows that atomic forces and light are somehow related.

(B) Not addressed—If there is an phenomenon named after Hale, it's not in this passage. You may have been thinking of the Zeeman effect. Different person!

(C) Contradiction—The passage says a magnet has just the opposite effect. Single lines separate into two.

(D) Contradiction—You didn't really think this was the right answer, did you? The passage says just the opposite.

(E) True, but—The passage does mention that the dark lines are cooler, but this has nothing to do with magnets.

28. Correct choice (B)

The author states that what Zeeman demonstrated in the laboratory is a small display of what happens on the sun in a very large way. The sunspots produce electromagnetic fields, which are analogous to the powerful magnet used in a lab setting.

(A) Too general—The passage uses "volcano" to indicate the motion of the gases. We don't have any gas volcanoes here on earth.

(C) Not addressed—The passage doesn't tell us who was first and who was second. The order of the passage implies that Zeeman was first, but we can't be sure.

(D) Not addressed—The author doesn't say anyone has been negligent, although this may or may not be true.

(E) True, but—This isn't the reason the author cites Hale's work, which has to do with the splitting up of spectral lines.

29. Correct choice (B)

The passage pinpoints the answer pretty clearly: The Zeeman effect indicates that light and magnetism are related. The passage even gives you Zeeman's words without using quote marks. The trick in answering this question correctly is finding the information in time or being sure of what you've already read.

(A) True, but—Sodium does burn green, but this is not the point of the Zeeman experiment.

(C) Not addressed—While the passage implies a strong relationship between electricity and magnetism, it never says that these are one and the same. Certainly, this was not the point of the Zeeman experiment, which shows the relationship between light and magnetism.

(D) True, but—It was Hale, not Zeeman, who concluded that sunspots are magnetic fields. Always mark proper nouns when you read the passages. It can make finding the answer a little easier.

(E) True, but—The passage implies that by the time of the Zeeman experiment, scientists already knew that elements had their own spectrums.

30. Correct choice (C)

The "single experiment" referred to here is the experiment that produces the Zeeman effect. This includes dissolving salt in water, burning the solution, exposing the flame to a magnetic force, and viewing it through a special instrument that detects spectral lines.

(A) Too specific—The experiment is more complicated. This is just the first step.

(B) Too specific—Just viewing sunspots does not give scientists all the information they need to draw conclusions about the relationship between matter and energy forms. Look for a more comprehensive experiment.

(D) Everyday observation is not an experiment.

(E) Measuring heat of the spectral lines is not the "single experiment" referred to here.

31. Correct choice (D)

All of the choices except (D) have light and heat related in an ordinary observation. A radiant moon does not show this light–heat relationship because we don't feel any heat coming from the moon, even when it's a full moon.

(A) A camp fire emits both light and heat together. This is not the exception you needed to find.

(B) The sun, though far away, presents both light and heat together. That's why we go to the beach.

(C) A light bulb, though not a natural phenomenon, nevertheless demonstrates the relationship between light and heat. This is not the exception the questions asks for.

(E) A burning candle gives both light and heat together. This is not the exception you needed to find.

32. Correct choice (A)

The last paragraph of the passage makes it clear that scientists can measure the relative temperature of the dark lines in a spectrum. This is an easy inference to make, especially since the paragraph says this same thing in different words.

(B) Contradiction—The passage discusses the importance of the dark lines in great detail and says almost nothing about the lighter parts.

(C) Not addressed—One would think that the lines are cooler because they are dark and not the other way around. But the passage never really says whether the light causes the heat or vice versa.

(D) Not addressed—If light is converging, wouldn't you expect to see a lot of light and not a dark line? The passage, though, never explains this point.

(E) Contradiction—The passage says the dark lines are cooler, not warmer, than other parts of the spectrum.

33. Correct choice (B)

Choice (B) gives the clearest indication of what the overall passage is about. This title also gives a brief indication about the main point of the article—the relationship between matter and energy. Furthermore, this title makes a promise: The article will explain some of the evidence scientists have gathered.

(A) Too general and too specific—This title wins the award for short and sweet, but it doesn't summarize the article very well. You might think the passage was about scientists swimming in the Dead Sea or the Great Salt Lake.

(C) Too specific—Sunspots are discussed only in one part of the article.

(D) Too specific—Zeeman's work does play an important part in the passage, but this passage is not about remembering him.

(E) Too general—This title promises more than the article delivers. To explain the spectrum of elements in details this thorough would likely take at least a semester.

Day 17

Test 1, Section 5: Math and Section 6: Verbal

Questions and Answers

Assignment for Today:

Take a sample SAT Math Test and a sample SAT Verbal Test under actual test conditions. Allow yourself only 15 minutes to complete the 10-question Math Test. Then allow yourself another 15 minutes to complete the 13-question Verbal Test.

SECTION 5: MATH

Directions: *Solve each problem, and circle the appropriate answer choice, A–E.*

1. Anita's parents have agreed to pay 25 percent of the cost of a new stereo. The stereo that Anita wants costs \$200. If Anita finds a job that pays \$3 per hour, for how many hours will Anita have to work in order to have enough money to pay the remaining 75 percent of the cost of the stereo?

   (A) 30
   (B) 50
   (C) 58.33
   (D) 66.66
   (E) 150

2. In the figure below, the area of the trapezoid *ABCD* is equal to the area of the triangle *PQR*. Sides *AB* and *CD* are of equal length. What is *x*?

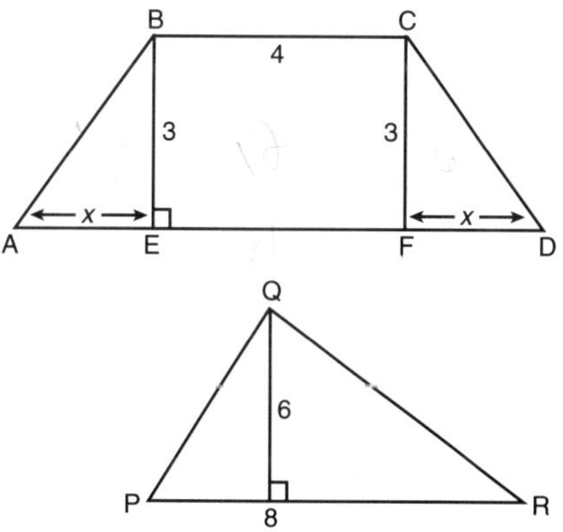

Note: Figure not drawn to scale.

   (A) 2
   (B) 4
   (C) 8
   (D) 12
   (E) 24

3. In the figure below, OAB is a quarter circle with radius 1. If point P lies at the center of arc AB, what is the y-coordinate of point P?

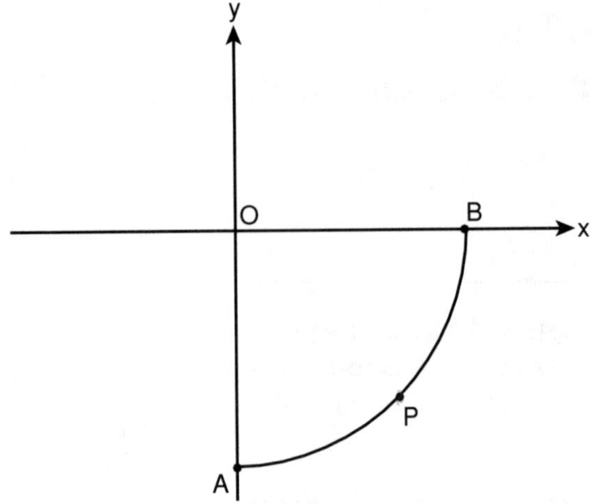

(A) -1

(B) $-\frac{\sqrt{2}}{2}$

(C) $\frac{1}{2}$

(D) $\frac{\sqrt{2}}{2}$

(E) 1

4. The smallest of three cubes has edge of side 2, the largest cube has edge of side 4, and the third cube has edge of side 3. What is the average volume of the 3 cubes?

(A) 9
(B) 9.67
(C) 18
(D) 27
(E) 33

5. In the figure below, ABC is an isosceles triangle with base AC and BDE is an equilateral triangle. If $y = 20$, what is the value of x ?

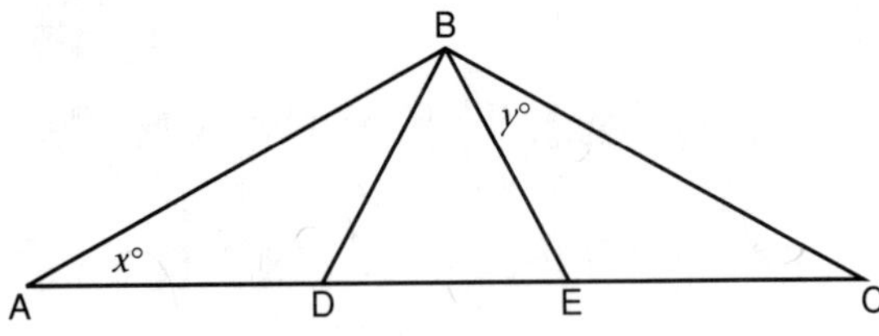

Note: Figure not drawn to scale.

(A) 20
(B) 30
(C) 40
(D) 45
(E) 60

6. If 1 megaböte = 1 MB = 10^6 bötes, and
1 kiloböte = 1 KB = 10^3 bötes, then
5,313.3 KB = $5.3133 \times n$ MB

According to the rules above, what is the value of n?

(A) 0
(B) 1
(C) 10
(D) 100
(E) 1000

7. In a store, the combined price of 4 shirts and 6 ties is \$56 and the combined price of 3 shirts and 5 ties is \$44. What is the price of each shirt?

(A) \$3.00
(B) \$4.00
(C) \$5.50
(D) \$8.00
(E) \$13.00

8. If one number is 15, and the sum of two other numbers is 21, what is the average (arithmetic mean) of the three numbers?

(A) 12
(B) 18

(C) 19
(D) 21
(E) 36

9. From a certain airport, flights to Chicago leave every 36 minutes, flights to Los Angeles leave every 40 minutes, and flights to New York leave every 60 minutes. At 12 noon, all three flights left at the same time. When will all three flights leave at the same time again?
(A) 12:04 P.M.
(B) 1:36 P.M.
(C) 2:16 P.M.
(D) 4:00 P.M.
(E) 6:00 P.M.

10. Store X sells p packs of chewing gum for $3d$ dollars. Each pack has $2g$ sticks of gum. Store Y, where a different brand of gum is sold, sells p packs of gum for $2d$ dollars. Each pack has $5g$ sticks of gum. With d dollars, how many more sticks of gum can you get at Store Y than at Store X?

(A) $\frac{7}{12}gp$

(B) $\frac{13pd}{10g}$

(C) $\frac{15}{8}gp$

(D) $\frac{2pg}{3d}$

(E) $\frac{5pg}{4d}$

SECTION 6: VERBAL

***Directions:** Read the two passages below. Then answer questions 1–13, basing your answers only on what is stated or implied in the passages.*

Passage 1

One of the strangest facts in literary criticism is that, after more than forty years of intense and occasionally even feverish activity on the part of scholars of Beckman, the question of what is Beckman's "Song to Me" is still a legitimate one. If the poem were a brief and much-mutilated fragment containing part of a single episode, the present state of criticism would be understandable and excusable. But of this poem we have nearly all that was written or planned by the author. Though incomplete, the extant copy contains 21,258 lines, and it obviously could never have been intended to contain much more. We have, therefore, in the present version, nearly all that he intended to write.

Moreover, we have, as an indication of the meaning of the poem, the title given by the author himself. And we have a positive and definite statement not only of the main features of the narrative as far as it is preserved to us, but also of the principal incident of the unwritten portion.

Why, then, are not the purpose and meaning of the poem clear and well recognized? Several reasons may be suggested.

In the first place, much of the study devoted to this poem has been concerned not with the interpretation of the author's meaning, but with the discovery of the sources of his materials. What suggested the temple? And the figures on the walls? And the treeless desert? Did the eagle come from Ovid, or from Dante, or from folklore? Whence came the ice-capped mountain and the revolving house? Correct answers to these questions would be interesting. If rightly used, they might be important. But they could hardly, in any event, contribute largely to the interpretation of the poem, for an author's meaning depends not upon where he got his materials, but upon what use he makes of them.

That students of Beckman should persist in interpreting him allegorically is strange. As a matter of fact, his work is singularly free from allegory in the strict sense of the term. The mere presence of nonhuman actors, whether animal or mythological or even personified abstractions, does not create allegory. For this, there must be symbolism of action or of character. But a debate between two girls concerning their lover is not allegory, even if birds take sides and debate and fight, and the decision is left to the god of love or his representative.

Passage 2

In "Song to Me," Beckman has given the world a stirring, spiritual autobiographical treatise. Born and educated in the Orthodox Church of Russia, Beckman lost while still a mere boy all faith in the dogma of that church and hence grew up, like the vast majority of educated Russians, without definitely formulated religious belief. But questions of personal conduct never ceased to occupy him. The moral law was present with him as a potent, if not always a controlling, factor in his personal life. At last, in his mature years, doubts and questionings on religious and moral problems began to present themselves to him with ever increasing vividness. What is the aim of life? What profits it a man to toil upon earth not knowing the purpose of his labors? These questions Beckman could neither solve nor forget. The "riddle of fate" would not let him rest, and at age forty-six, rich and famous, surrounded by a family whom he loved and who loved him, he found himself on the verge of suicide. He must solve the riddle or perish.

Beckman first sought an answer in science, but could find none; science would answer questions of the chemical constitution of matter, or of the laws of light, but of man's destiny it knew nothing. Rather, it confirmed his belief that life is void and meaningless; reason taught him that life is contrary to reason. Distrusting his own powers, Beckman turned for help to the sages of different times and nations, to Solomon, Socrates, Buddha, and Schopenhauer, and in them found answers that later he would explicate in "Song to Me." But he saw that the ideas of these writers applied only to people of his own class in society; that the millions of toiling peasants belonged to no one of his immediate social stratum. His colleagues recognize the problem of life with surprising clarity. They regard suicide as a fearful crime. Their solution of the riddle is the faith of the church, with its doctrines of reason and goodness. Yet their illogical faith justifies life for them, and gives to their existence a dignity utterly wanted in that of men of higher station. Beckman's course was clear; he set aside his reasoning powers and became a faithful member of the Orthodox Church, cheating himself into believing, or professing that he believed, doctrines that were repugnant to his intellect. And so he created "Song to Me."

1. In line 5 of passage 1, the word "legitimate" most nearly means
   (A) justifiable
   (B) conforming to established rules
   (C) sanctioned by custom
   (D) important yet difficult
   (E) unanswered

2. According to passage 1, Beckman scholars benefit from all of the following *except*
   (A) the extant copy of the poem has 21,258 lines
   (B) "Song to Me" has always been published as the author intended
   (C) Beckman himself gave the work a title
   (D) the principal incident surrounding the poem is clear
   (E) the present version of the poem is faithful to Beckman's intention

3. In passage 1, paragraph four lists a series of questions in order to
   (A) indicate these as the questions for the future work of Beckman scholars
   (B) list issues that have yet to be addressed about "Song to Me"
   (C) show the misguided research efforts of past scholars
   (D) illuminate "Song to Me" as an extended allegory
   (E) argue that the poem's meaning resides in questions that delve into the poem's interpretation

4. The author of passage 1 implies that an allegorical reading of Beckman's work is "strange" because
   (A) allegories are common in the Bible, and Beckman was not religious when he wrote this poem
   (B) the poem lacks personified abstractions
   (C) "Song to Me" does not suggest that the plot or the characters are symbolic of anything
   (D) Beckman used other works to explore allegory
   (E) birds and other animals are the actors instead of people

5. According to passage 1, in order to understand "Song to Me" more fully, scholars should
   (A) examine the competing editions of the text to see what Beckman's intended meaning was
   (B) discover the sources for the elements of Beckman's work
   (C) view the poem as an extended allegory of opposing forces
   (D) abandon current lines of scholarship and further explore basic questions about meaning and purpose
   (E) balance their research between criticism and interpretation

6. According to passage 2, Beckman was on the verge of suicide because
   (A) the riddle of Russian Orthodoxy was too difficult to solve to his satisfaction
   (B) he could not satisfy his questions about the purpose of life
   (C) he found emptiness in his great wealth
   (D) his family, although loving, could not understand his moral dilemma
   (E) science could not offer him hope for living

7. From passage 2 we can infer that Beckman was dissatisfied with the wisdom of the sages because
   (A) the sages lived in a time that was too different from his own to have any relevance in his life
   (B) the sages didn't account for the great bodies of knowledge that science had discovered
   (C) their wisdom applied only to people of a limited social category
   (D) their insights contradicted one another
   (E) the sages ultimately supported the views of the Church

8. Passage 2 implies that faith in the Church's teachings
   (A) is an admirable answer to life's riddles
   (B) can coincide with the words of the sages
   (C) allows one to recognize the problems of life with surprising clarity
   (D) does not make logical sense
   (E) is characteristic of men of higher stations

9. The phrase "utterly wanted" in line 96 most likely means
   (A) completely deficient
   (B) intensely desired
   (C) surprisingly sought after
   (D) thoroughly needed
   (E) slightly short of

10. The author of passage 2 most likely feels that Beckman
    (A) found both enlightenment and peace in his final religious conviction
    (B) is a role model of philosophical inquiry for later writers and scholars
    (C) ultimately left his deepest questions unanswered
    (D) created "Song to Me" to explain why religion is deficient in answering philosophical questions
    (E) finally reconciled his intellect with his religion

11. The two passages differ markedly in the way they discuss
    (A) Beckman's motivation for writing works other than "Song to Me"
    (B) the meaning and purpose of "Song to Me"
    (C) the economic hardships that followed the Bolshevik Revolution
    (D) how human actors eventually find their ways into literary works
    (E) Beckman's eventual failing in reverting to the faith of the Church

12. The two passages are similar with respect to
    (A) the apparent admiration for Beckman's abilities as a writer
    (B) the tone of the writing
    (C) the approach each author takes in discussing Beckman's work
    (D) the apparent purpose for writing the passage
    (E) the acknowledgment of serious shortcomings in past Beckman scholarship

13. The passages suggest that the two authors would most likely *disagree* with each other about which statement?
    (A) Beckman's work is worthy of continued study.
    (B) "Song to Me" should not be included in college-level literary anthologies.
    (C) Religion has played a formative role in creating "Song to Me."
    (D) "Song to Me" is best viewed as an autobiographical allegory.
    (E) Beckman scholarship is on the verge of resurgence.

Quick Answer Guide

Test 1, Section 5: Math

1. B
2. B
3. B
4. E
5. C
6. B
7. D
8. A
9. E
10. A

Test 1, Section 6: Verbal

1. A
2. B
3. C
4. C
5. D
6. B
7. C
8. D
9. D
10. C
11. B
12. A
13. D

For explanations to these questions see Day 18.

Day 18

Test 1, Section 5: Math and Section 6: Verbal

Explanations and Strategies

Assignment for Today:

Review the explanations for the tests you just took. See which answer is right, and learn what makes each wrong answer wrong.

SECTION 5: MATH

1. Correct choice (B) 50

To solve this problem, first figure out how much Anita's parents are contributing. They have agreed to pay 25 percent of the cost. If the stereo costs \$200, then Anita's parents will pay \$50 (because 25 percent of \$200 = \$50). This means Anita needs to earn \$200 – \$50 = \$150.

At \$3 an hour, Anita will have to work for $150 \div 3 = 50$ hours to earn \$150.

(A) Miscalc—Did you divide 150 by 3 and get 30? Check your work again.

(C) Miscalc—Looks like you figured that 25 percent of \$200 was \$25. No, 25 percent of \$200 is \$50, not \$25.

(D) Oversight—You need to subtract the \$50 from the \$200 before you divide by 3.

(E) Misread—Looks like you figured out how much money Anita has to earn. But, the question asked you to find how many hours she has to work to earn the \$150 she needs.

2. Correct choice (B) 4

$$\text{Area of triangle PQR} = \left(\frac{1}{2}\right)\text{base} \times \text{height} = \left(\frac{1}{2}\right) 8 \times 6 = 24$$

To find the area of the trapezoid, first find the area of the rectangle BCFE.

Area of rectangle BCFE $= 4 \times 3 = 12$

Then, area of trapezoid ABCD is the sum of the area of rectangle BCFE and two equal triangles BEA and CFD.

So, area of trapezoid ABCD = 12 + 2(area of BEA)

$$= 12 + 2\left(\left(\frac{1}{2}\right)3x\right)$$

$$= 12 + 3x$$

But, we know that the area of trapezoid ABCD is equal to the area of triangle PQR. Let's equate these two quantities.

Then, $24 = 12 + 3x$

Or, $12 = 3x$

So, $4 = x$

(A) Oversight—Did you use the formula for area of a rectangle instead of a triangle for the two triangle shapes in the trapezoid?

(C) Oversight—You probably forgot to consider one of the triangles in the trapezoid. Notice that two triangles of equal area and one rectangle form the trapezoid. Or, you may have thought the question asked for the value of $2x$.

(D) Miscalc—Looks like you found the area of triangle *PQR* to be 48, instead of 24. Check your work again.

(E) Misread—This is the area of the triangle. But we want the length of side x. Do you see that *ABCD* is really a rectangle and two equal triangles?

3. Correct choice (B) $-\frac{\sqrt{2}}{2}$

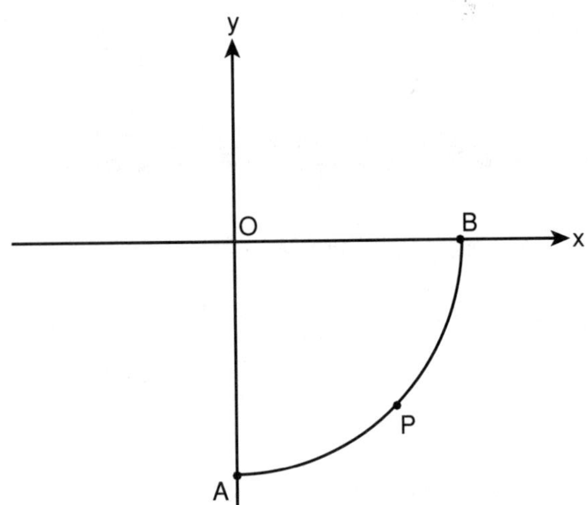

The smartest way to answer this question is to look at the answer choices. You know that point P is below the x-axis, which means its y-coordinate must be negative. Only two of the answer choices have a negative y-value, choices (A) and (B). You can rule out choice (A) –1 because the y-coordinate of *point A* is –1, which means P cannot have –1 as its y-coordinate. There's only one answer choice remaining. Now here's the long way of doing the problem.

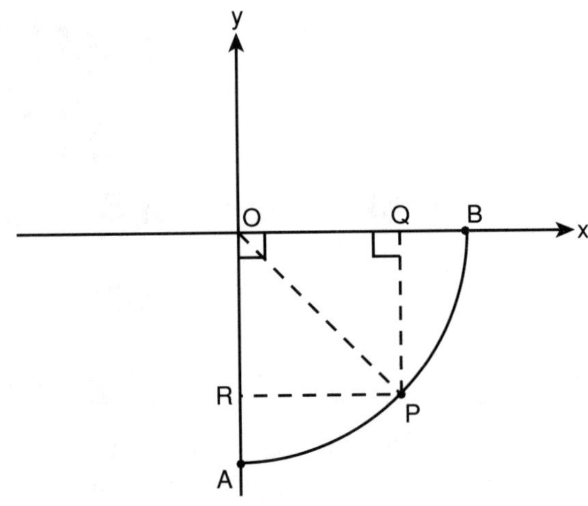

Let's drop 2 perpendiculars from point P: one to point Q on the x-axis and the other to point R on the y-axis. Then, we need to find QP.

We know that OP is the radius and is equal to 1. Notice that the semicircle has center at the origin which means OB (a radius) is equal to OA (another radius). So we know that $QP = PR$.

Now let's look at the right triangle OQP. The hypotenuse is OP and the two perpendicular sides are OQ and QP. But we know that $OQ = PR = QP$.

So, $OP^2 = OQ^2 + QP^2$

Or, $1 = QP^2 + QP^2$

Or, $1 = 2QP^2$

Or, $\frac{1}{2} = QP^2$

Then, $\sqrt{\frac{1}{2}} = QP =$

$$\frac{1}{\sqrt{2}} = \frac{1}{\sqrt{2}}\,\frac{\sqrt{2}}{\sqrt{2}} = \frac{\sqrt{2}}{2}$$

So, the distance from Q to P is $\frac{\sqrt{2}}{2}$. Since P lies *below* the x-axis, its y-coordinate must be negative. Therefore, the y-coordinate is $-\frac{\sqrt{2}}{2}$.

(A) Missing key insight—You probably took 1 as the radius and took its negative value because P is below the x-axis. But a y-value of –1 is at point A, not point P. To solve this problem, first draw a perpendicular from P to OB. Then work with the radius, OP, and PO to find PO.

(C) Missing key insight—Perhaps you figured that because P is in the center of the arc, its y-value is half the radius. Half the radius is the midpoint of OP. To solve this problem, first draw a perpendicular from P to OB. Then work with the radius, OP, and PQ to find PQ.

(D) Careless—You did everything correctly, except you forgot that P is *below* the x-axis. This means it should have a negative y-coordinate.

(E) Missing key insight—This is the radius of the circle. P cannot have a y-value of 1 because, first of all, it is *below* the x-axis, and, secondly, point A has a y-coordinate of –1, which tells you that the y-coordinate of P cannot be 1 or –1.

4. Correct choice (E) 33

Volume of a cube is the length of an edge cubed. So:

Volume of the smallest cube	$= 2 \times 2 \times 2 = 8$	
Volume of the largest cube	$= 4 \times 4 \times 4 = 64$	
Volume of the third cube	$= 3 \times 3 \times 3 = 27$	
The sum of the three volumes		$= 99$
Then, the average volume	$= \frac{99}{3}$	$= 33$

(A) Missing key insight—Looks like you took the average of the three edges: average of 2, 3, and 4 = 3. And then perhaps you found the area: $3 \times 3 = 9$. But this is a "volume" problem. Remember, the volume of a cube is the length of an edge cubed. You have to find the individual volumes first. And then find the average.

(B) Missing key insight—Perhaps you found the average of 2^2, 3^2, and 4^2. But this is a "volume" problem, which means you have to first find the volume of each cube (volume = edge^3) and then take the average of the three volumes.

(C) Careless—Looks like you found the average of (2×6), (3×6), and (4×6). But the volume of each cube is not 6 times the length of the side. It is the length of the side cubed (raised to the power of 3).

(D) Oversight—Perhaps you first found the average of 2, 3, and 4 and then cubed this amount. You did it in reverse. You should first find the volume of each cube and then only take the average.

5. Correct choice (C) 40

For this problem, we need to know that an equilateral triangle always has three 60-degree angles. An isosceles triangle, on the other hand, has two equal sides and equal angles opposite these sides. The best strategy is to try to find all the angles for triangle ABD.

We want to find x. We know that all the angles in triangle BDE are 60° (because this triangle is equilateral). We can use this information to find angle ADB. Angle ADB and angle BDE form a straight line which is always 180°. Since we know angle BDE is 60°, angle ADB will be 180 – 60 = 120°.

To find x, let us first find angle ABD. Once we know angle ABD, we will add it to angle ADB and subtract the total from 180 to find x.

We know that angle ABD will be the same as y. This is so because, when an equilateral triangle is placed within an isosceles triangle and the vertices of both converge on the same point, the smaller triangle will divide the larger triangle proportionately. So, if y is 20°, angle ABD is also 20°. Then, to find x, we just subtract from 180 the sum of angle ABD and angle ADB. That is,

$x = 180 - (\text{Angle } ABD + \text{Angle } ADB)$

Or, $x = 180 - (20 + 120) = 180 - 140$

So, $x = 40°$

(A) Grabbing numbers—If you got 20, you probably didn't know how to solve this and just picked 20 because you saw that it was one angle and hoped that it might pop up again as the answer.

(B) Miscalc—If you wound up with 30, you probably made a calculation mistake. Or, maybe angle A and angle C looked like they might be 30° each. Don't be fooled by looks.

(D) Missing key insight—Perhaps you thought that because triangle ABC is an isosceles triangle, each angle at the base might be 45°. No. This would be true only if angle B were 90°. But, we're not told that it is.

(E) Missing key insight—Did you get isosceles and equilateral confused? If you did, you might have wound up with angle x as 60°. But, remember, an equilateral triangle has all angles 60°. An isosceles triangle has two angles at the base equal.

6. Correct choice (B) 1

If there are 10^3 (1 thousand) bötes in 1 kiloböte, and 10^6 (1 million) bötes in 1 megaböte, then there must be 10^3 (1000) kilobötes in 1 megaböte.

In other words 1,000 kilobötes = 1 megaböte.

So 5,000 kilobötes = 5 megabötes.

And 5,313.3 kilobötes = 5.3133 megabötes.

So 5313.3 Kb = 5.3133×1 M = 5.3133 M

In other words, n should be equal to 1.

(A) Oversight—This would have been the right answer if the question had asked for the power to which 10 must be raised. The answer cannot be zero because if you multiply by zero, the quantity on the right side of the equation will be zero.

(C) Miscalc—If you multiply the right side of the equation by 10, then you'll get $5.3133 \times 10 = 53.133$. This is incorrect because there are 1000 kilobötes in 1 megaböte.

(D) Miscalc—If you multiply the right side of the equation by 100, then you'll get $5.3133 \times 100 = 531.33$. This is incorrect because there are 1000 kilobötes in 1 megaböte.

(E) Missing key insight—You probably chose this answer because you knew that there are 1000 kilobötes in 1 megaböte. But you overlooked the fact that the quantity on the right side has already been divided by 1000.

7. Correct choice (D) $8.00

First, set up the two equations, using S for the price of shirts and T for the price of ties.

4 shirts and 6 ties is $56. Then, $4S + 6T = 56$.

3 shirts and 5 ties is $44. Then, $3S + 5T = 44$.

We want the price of each shirt. This means we should find a way to cancel the "T" terms. We can do this if we multiply the first equation by 5 and the second equation by 6.

So, the first equation × 5 is: $20S + 30T = 280$

The second equation × 6 is: $18S + 30T = 264$

Subtract these two equations:

$$(20S - 18S) + (30T - 30T) = 280 - 264$$

$$\text{Or, } 2S = 16$$

$$\text{So, } S = 8$$

This means the price of each shirt is $8.00.

(A) Miscalc—Looks like you didn't multiply the right side of the equations. For example, did you get the equation: $20S + 30T = 56$? The correct equation should be: $20S + 30T = 280$. In other words, if you multiply terms on the left side of the equation by 5, then you should also multiply terms on the right side by 5.

(B) Misread—You found the price of each tie. But the question asked you to find the price of each *shirt*.

(C) Missing key insight—Looks like you subtracted the dollar amounts and took the average. This is incorrect because the shirt and the tie don't cost the same. You should cancel the price of ties so that you're left only with shirts in your equation. What if you multiplied the first equation by 5 and the second equation by 6?

(E) Miscalc—You made a mistake in subtraction. Did you subtract 264 from 280 (the dollar amounts after you multiplied one equation by 5 and the other by 6) and get 26, instead of 16, which you then divided by 2 to get 13? Check your math again.

8. Correct choice (A) 12

We're told that 1 number is 15 and the other 2 numbers add up to 21. Then the total of all 3 numbers is 36.

Let's work from the choices. As always, let's start from choice (C) 19. If 19 is the average of 3 numbers, then the sum of the three numbers = $19 \times 3 = 57$ (because sum = average × number of items). But this is too high because the sum is supposed to be 36. If choice (C) is too high, so are choices (D) and (E).

Let's try (B) 18. If the average of 3 numbers is 18, their sum must be $18 \times 3 = 54$. Too high. At this point, we can be sure the answer is choice (A). Let's see if it works.

Choice (A) says the average is 12. Then the sum must be $3 \times 12 = 36$.

(B) Careless—You probably just computed the average of 15 and 21, which is not what the question asked for. You did not take into account the third number and divided the total by 2, instead of by 3.

(C) Misread—Perhaps you thought you had to find the average of the numbers 15, 21, and 21. Read the question again.

(D) Grabbing numbers—You may have just grabbed the number 21 from the problem statement.

(E) Oversight—You probably just added 15 and 21 together and found the sum. You forgot to divide by 3 to get the average.

9. Correct choice (E) 6:00 P.M.

Here we need to find the common multiple of 36, 40, and 60 because that will tell us how much time passes before all three flights leave at the same time. To find the common multiple, take the largest number, 60, and see which multiple of 60 is also a multiple of the other two numbers.

60 × 1 = 60: not a multiple of 36, not a multiple of 40

60 × 2 = 120: multiple of 40 (40 × 3), not a multiple of 36

60 × 3 = 180: multiple of 36 (36 × 5), not a multiple of 40

60 × 4 = 240: multiple of 40 (40 × 6), not a multiple of 36

60 × 5 = 300: not a multiple of 36, not a multiple of 40.

60 × 6 = 360: multiple of 40 (40 × 9) and a multiple of 36 (36 × 10)

So, the flights will leave at the same time 360 minutes after 12 noon, which is 6 hours (360 ÷ 60 = 6) later. So the correct answer is 6:00 P.M.

(A) Oversight—Looks like you took the highest common factor of 36, 40, and 60. You were on the right track. This is actually a "common multiple" problem.

(B) Missing key insight—Looks like you added 36, 40, and 60 to get 136 minutes, which you then converted to 1 hour 36 minutes. Actually 136 minutes is 136 ÷ 60 = 2 hours and 16 minutes. At any rate, you cannot just add the three time periods. This is actually a "common multiple" problem.

(C) Missing key insight—Looks like you added 36, 40, and 60 to get 136 minutes, which you then converted to 2 hours and 16 minutes. You cannot just add the three time periods because this is a "common multiple" problem.

Actually, you can zap choices (A), (B) and (C) because planes have to leave on the hour. Do you see why?

(D) Oversight—You were definitely on the right track. You took the common multiple of the 3 flight times but then you made a mistake in converting 360 minutes. How many hours is 360 minutes? You have to divide by 60.

10. Correct choice (A) $\frac{7}{12}gp$

This problem is a killer—if you do it the old fashioned way. Our way, of course, is to simply plug in numbers for the unknowns.

For example, let's say $p = 1$, $g = 1$, and $d = 1$. Now let's solve the problem with these values and see which answer choice works.

At store X, we can get 1 pack with 2 sticks of gum per pack for \$3. That means 2 sticks cost \$3. Or, for \$1, we can get $\frac{2}{3}$ stick.

At store Y, we get half of a pack with 5 sticks of gum per pack for \$2. Or, $\frac{5}{2}$ sticks for 2 dollars. Then, for \$1, we can get $\frac{5}{4}$ sticks.

So, for \$1, we get $\frac{2}{3}$ stick in store X and $\frac{5}{4}$ sticks in store Y.

With a budget of \$1, the difference between the stores is $\left(\frac{5}{4} - \frac{2}{3}\right) = \frac{7}{12}$

So, if we substitute the values of $p = 1$, $d = 1$, and $g = 1$, our answer should be $\frac{7}{12}$. Let's see which choice gives us $\frac{7}{12}$. Notice that p, d, and g are all 1's, which means we can scan the answer choices and not worry about these unknowns (they will cancel out). Only choice (A) will give us the value of $\frac{7}{12}$ and so it's the right answer.

(B) Missing key insight—If you chose this answer, then you were probably confused about how to set up the problem. Remember that in a phrase like "p packs of chewing gum *for* 3d dollars." *for* generally means a ratio, so you should get an expression with a $\frac{p}{d}$ term. But the best way to solve this problem is to assign values to p, d, and g and see which answer choice works.

(C) Oversight—If you chose this answer, you correctly figured out how much gum you could buy at each store, but you calculated the *ratio* of the amounts at the two stores instead of their *difference*, which is what the problem asked for.

(D) Misread—This is the correct number of sticks of gum you can get in store X. But, this isn't what the problem asked for.

(E) Misread—This is the correct number of sticks of gum you can get in store Y. But, this isn't what the problem asked for.

SECTION 6: VERBAL

1. Correct choice (A)

The author's use of "legitimate" here most nearly means justifiable. The point is that "Song to Me" is not yet a clearly understood work and that the most basic questions about it still need to be asked. The author then uses the rest of the passage to explain why that question is justifiable.

(B) Although this is a common definition for "legitimate," it is not the best meaning of the word used in this context.

(C) Although a common definition for "legitimate," there's another choice which better reflects the meaning used in the sentence.

(D) Although this meaning may work here, "important yet difficult" is not the definition of "legitimate" as used in this sentence.

(E) Although the passage states that the question is yet unanswered, this is not the meaning of "legitimate."

2. Correct choice (B)

According to the passage, all the statements given are helpful to Beckman scholars except (B). The passage says nothing about the publication history of the poem. Furthermore, the publication history would be less beneficial to these specific scholars than the other facts, which deal with Beckman's idea about what the poem should be and mean.

(A) The passage states that having such a complete version of Beckman's work is indeed helpful. Find something that the passage does *not* state as being helpful.

(C) The passage clearly states that Beckman titled his own poem, which should be very helpful. Find an answer that the passage does not say is beneficial.

(D) The passage notes that the principal incident surrounding the unwritten portion of the poem is clear, which is very beneficial.

(E) The passage implies that the current version of the poem is faithful to what Beckman intended. This should help scholars understand it.

3. Correct choice (C)

The author lists the series of questions in paragraph four as a criticism of past research. The author says that these questions might be interesting to a degree, but they are not the key to understanding "Song to Me." The author hopes that future scholarship will get away from studying the sources of Beckman's work and instead examine what the author really meant in his poem.

(A) Contradiction—The author implies that future scholars should not study the sources of Beckman's work (the questions posed), but the author's meaning instead.

(B) Contradiction—The author's point is that marginally useful questions have been studied too much already. The author wants to know, "What's the heart of the issue?"

(D) Too specific—These questions do indicate that some allegorical readings have been done on "Song to Me," but the author had a better reason than that for asking these questions.

(E) True, but—The author would agree with (E), but this choice does not match up to the questions in this paragraph. ***Hint:*** the author does *not* like these kinds of research questions. Read the paragraph again to find out why.

4. Correct choice (C)

In order to have allegory, the author states, "there must be symbolism of action or of character." Because the author argues against reading "Song to Me" as an allegory, we can safely conclude that the poem does not suggest this kind of symbolism.

(A) True, but—While choice (A) may well be true, it does not answer the question.

(B) Contradiction—The passage implies that "Song to Me" has personified abstractions, which is exactly the reason that so many scholars want to read the poem as an allegory.

(D) Contradiction—The passage points out that Beckman almost never uses allegory in the strict sense of the word.

(E) Too specific—The passage implies that nonhuman actors may well be present in Beckman's work, but this is not the reason the author calls an allegorical reading "strange."

5. Correct choice (D)

It should be clear that the author wants scholars to get away from two current lines of research: sources of materials and allegorical criticism. In many ways, the author is asking colleagues to get back to the basic questions of purpose and meaning without wandering off into more alluring (and, according to the author, less productive) scholarship. The author here is still eager to see more attention devoted to meaning and purpose.

(A) Not addressed—The passage doesn't mention competing editions of the text.

(B) Contradiction—The author wants other scholars to stop pursuing research into Beckman's sources for his work, implying that this research is not as helpful as another kind would be.

(C) Contradiction—The author wants other scholars to stop pursuing an allegorical reading of Beckman's work, implying that this research is not as helpful as another kind would be.

(E) Not addressed—The passage never talks about the need to balance different kinds of scholarship. Find an answer the author would support (and one that is contained in the passage).

6. Correct choice (B)

Passage 2 states that Beckman was on the verge of suicide because he had intense questions about the meaning and purpose of life that he could not answer to his own satisfaction. Passage 2 calls these questions the "riddle of fate."

(A) Not addressed—Passage 2 never talks about Russian Orthodoxy as a riddle that was difficult to solve. The author, in fact, leads us to believe that religion was too simple for Beckman, not too complex.

(C) Too narrow—The passage implies that wealth did not satisfy Beckman, but we have no reason to believe that this dissatisfaction led him to consider suicide.

(D) Not addressed—Passage 2 gives no information about how Beckman's family responded to his moral dilemma.

(E) True, but—Although passage 2 implies that Beckman could not find hope for living in science, it does not give this as the reason for almost committing suicide.

7. Correct choice (C)

The passage implies that the wisdom of the sages provided answers for Beckman, but these ideas applied only to people of his own class, which would be educated rich folks. From this we can infer that Beckman realized that such wisdom was limited because it excluded the great mass of humanity.

(A) Not addressed—Passage 2 does not make the difference in time into an issue; in fact, we are led to believe that Beckman didn't care that the sages lived centuries earlier.

(B) True, but—Of course, the sages didn't have access to the science of Beckman's time, but this wasn't the reason Beckman couldn't fully endorse the sages' ideas.

(D) True, but—It's logical to conclude that the sages gave contradictory explanations for the meaning of life, but we don't have any reason to conclude that these contradictions bothered Beckman.

(E) Contradiction—Passage 2 implies that the wisdom of the sages is not the same as the faith of the Church; therefore, the sages did not support the views of the Church.

8. Correct choice (D)

The author of passage 2 conveys the idea that faith in the Church is not an acceptable answer to life's questions, especially not for people with a high level of education. The final paragraph of passage 2 describes faith as "illogical." The author writes critically of Beckman's colleagues who embraced religion as an explanation for life's questions.

(A) Contradiction—The author writes harshly of Beckman's colleagues who embraced religion as an explanation for life's questions.

(B) Not addressed—The author doesn't say how much religious faith can coincide with the words of the sages, although we are led to believe that the author would say the various views are, for the most part, incompatible.

(C) Too specific—Passage 2 states that Beckman's colleagues recognized the "problems of life with surprising clarity." The author does not imply, however, that this is an effect of having faith. Instead, the recognition of life's problems has driven them to accept religion.

(E) Too general—Passage 2 implies that some "men of higher station" have faith, but there is no evidence to suggest this characteristic of such people.

9. Correct choice (D)

The author uses "want" in a way that is not common in our normal speech and means "to need." For example, "He wants for money" means "he needs money." Therefore, *utterly wanted* means "needed to a great degree," so (D), thoroughly needed, is the best choice.

(A) Although a want can be a deficiency, "completely deficient" is not the best choice for this context. Part of the problem with this choice is the word "completely"; it's just too extreme.

(B) Although most people think of desire when they hear the word "want," there's a better answer than this choice.

(C) When we want something, we sometimes seek after it, but this is not the meaning of *utterly wanted* in this sentence.

(E) In this sentence, "wanted" could well mean "to be short of." However, *utterly* is a word that intensifies things; it makes the want even stronger. Therefore, "slightly" is not correct here.

10. Correct choice (C)

The author makes it clear that Beckman sold out in the end—he didn't adequately answer his questions about the meaning and purpose of life; instead, he adopted the standard answers that religion provided. The author is not happy about this, as is shown by the use of the word "cheating" in the second-to-last sentence.

(A) Too general—The passage hints that Beckman found some sort of peace in finally reverting to religious views, but the passage does not say that Beckman found enlightenment.

(B) Not addressed—Passage 2 doesn't address how well Beckman acts as a role model for later intellectuals. The best guess we can make from the passage is that the author is disappointed in Beckman's final resolution to his questions, and he would therefore not be much of a role model.

(D) Contradiction—This answer is just the opposite of what passage 2 implies. Instead, passage 2 indicates that "Song to Me" is some sort of poem that highlights religion at the expense of intellect.

(E) Contradiction—The end of passage 2 makes it clear that Beckman ultimately abandoned his intellectual quest and adopted the mainstream religious answers to his questions about the purpose and meaning of life.

11. Correct choice (B)

Perhaps the most notable difference between the two passages is the authors' different approaches to Beckman. The author of passage 1 takes a traditional literary criticism approach, posing the question "What does 'Song to Me' mean?" The author of passage 2 takes a biographical approach, concluding in the final sentence that "Song to Me" is a reflection of Beckman's spiritual wanderings. The second author assumes that the meaning of the poem is clear, while the first author says we need to keep probing to find Beckman's real intent.

(A) Too general—The authors don't say why Beckman wrote works other than "Song to Me." This answer isn't the best choice because it addresses an issue the authors never make fully clear.

(C) Not addressed—Passage 2 briefly describes Beckman's wealth, but neither passage discusses the economic conditions following the Bolshevik Revolution.

(D) Not addressed—Passage 1 mentions human actors, but passage 2 does not. This choice is not correct because it implies that both authors wrote about human actors emerging in Beckman's work, a topic neither author addresses very well.

(E) Too specific—Passage 2 talks quite a lot about Beckman's relationship to religion, but passage 1 does not. Find an answer that reflects the content of both passages.

12. Correct choice (A)

About the only thing these authors have in common is that they both seem to really admire Beckman. So we can safely infer that both authors think Beckman was a great writer, worthy of serious study. Other than their admiration for Beckman, these authors have very little overlap in their passages. Of course, they may agree with each other quite a bit in real life, but from the passages alone we can't be sure.

(B) Contradiction—If you reread the passages carefully, you'll see that the author of passage 1 is critical and sort of hostile; however, the author of passage 2 is quite pleased with what he can tell us about Beckman's life.

(C) Contradiction—Passage 1 takes a different approach to Beckman's work than does passage 2. The first passage is more a statement on others' scholarship of Beckman, while the second passage describes Beckman's life.

(D) Too general—Although it's difficult to know the exact purpose for writing the passage, we can probably infer that the author of passage 1 wanted to critique what had happened in the field of Beckman scholarship. In contrast, the author of passage 2 probably wrote to help people gain insight into Beckman's life and work.

(E) Too specific—Only passage 1 addresses the issue of shortcomings in the work of Beckman scholars. The author of passage 2 never mentions it.

13. Correct choice (D)

The authors take very different approaches—so different that identifying areas of overlap and conflict is somewhat challenging. However, choice (D) would divide the two authors. The author of passage 1 would object to viewing the work only as an allegory; the author of passage 2 would likely endorse viewing "Song to Me" as a biographical allegory. As far as the passages suggest, these authors would argue over this issue.

(A) Both authors would likely agree with this statement. You should be able to tell from the tone of both pieces that they admire Beckman's work. Find a statement the authors would argue over.

(B) Both authors would likely disagree with this statement, but they would not argue with each other over this point. They would both assert that a college-level literature book should have Beckman included.

(C) While the author of passage 2 discusses the religious influence in Beckman's work, the author of passage 1 does not deny the influence of religion. Find a statement the authors would argue over.

(E) Neither passage gives a strong indication whether Beckman scholarship is going to get more popular soon. You might be able to guess that both authors would like to see a resurgence, but it's not clear if the authors feel a resurgence is likely. Find another choice that is clearly an area for argument.

Test 2

Questions and Answers

Explanations and Strategies

Test 2, Section 1: Math

Questions and Answers

Assignment for Today:

Take a sample SAT Math Test under actual test conditions. Allow yourself exactly 30 minutes to complete the 25 questions in this test.

Directions: *For questions 1–15, each question contains two quantities—one on the left (Column A) and one on the right (Column B). Compare the quantities and answer*

(A) if Column A is greater than Column B
(B) if Column B is greater than Column A
(C) if the two columns are equal
(D) if you cannot determine a definite relationship from the information given
Never answer E.

In some questions, information appears centered between the two columns. Centered information concerns each of the columns for that question only. For each question, any symbol used in one column represents the same value if it appears in the other column.

	Column A	Column B
1.	$\frac{1}{8} - \frac{-3}{4}$	$\frac{1}{8} - \frac{-1}{2}$

n is an integer greater than zero

2.	$\frac{0.000036}{2n}$	$\frac{0.00018}{n}$

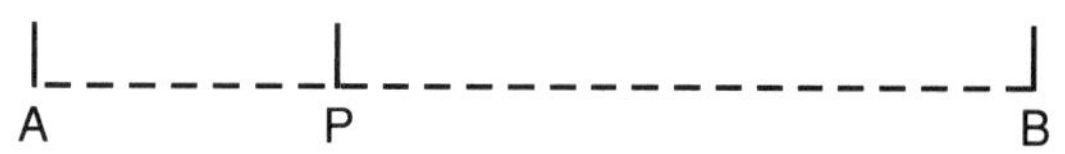

Point P divides line segment AB in the ratio 3:4 and $AP < PB$.

3.	$AP + PB$	7

Column A	Column B

For integers q, r, s, and t, their "Motor" is defined by the following relationship:

"motor" of $\{q,r,s,t\} = s$ if $q > r$ and
"motor" of $\{q,r,s,t\} = t$ if $q < r$

	Column A	Column B
4.	the "motor" of {2,4,1,3}	1

$$p + q + r = 15$$

p, q, and r are positive integers

$$p < q < r$$

	Column A	Column B
5.	The greatest value of $(p) \times (q) \times (r)$	$1 \times 8 \times 15$

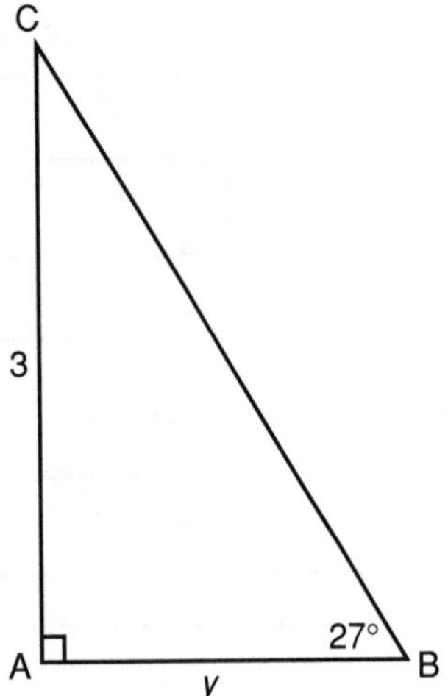

	Column A	Column B
6.	y	$3\sqrt{3}$

Column A	Column B

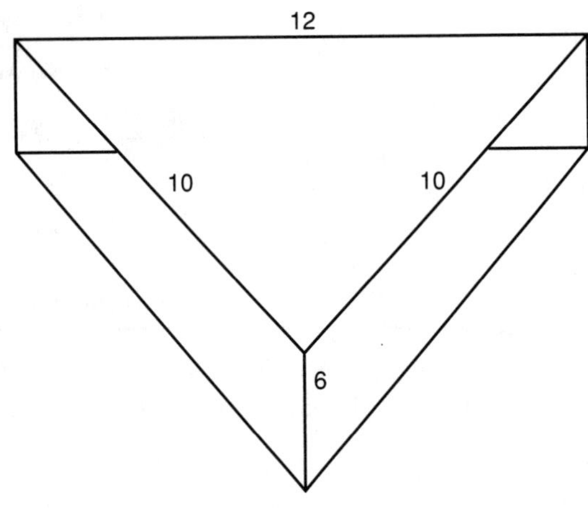

	Column A	Column B
7.	Volume of right triangular prism P	360

Box A and box B have 6 cards each. Each card in box A is marked with 1 integer from 1 through 3. Each card in box B is marked with 1 integer from 2 through 6. The sum of all integers in each box must be 18.

	Column A	Column B
8.	Smallest possible number of cards marked "3" in box A	Greatest possible number of cards marked "4" in box B

	Column A	Column B
9.	$(t - 3)^2$	$(t + 3)^2$

$$2.2 \div a = 220$$

	Column A	Column B
10.	$220 \div \sqrt{a}$	2200

Column A	Column B

It takes 300 operations to assemble a computer in a factory. Each operation takes 9 seconds.

11.

Number of computers that can be assembled in 3 hours	$\frac{300 \times 9}{3 \times 60 \times 60}$

Clarence drives his car to the zoo, a distance of 120 miles, at an average speed of 40 miles per hour. He returns home at an average speed of 30 miles per hour.

12.

Clarence's average speed for the entire trip	35 miles per hour

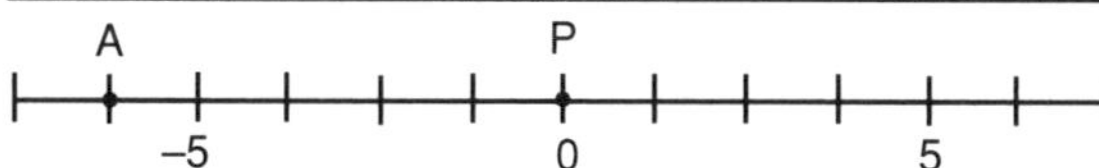

Tick marks in the figure above are equally spaced.

13.

–2(A)	12

Let $a \oplus b$ denote the distance between the point (a,b) and the point (3,1) in a coordinate plane.

14.

$1 \oplus 1$	$4 \oplus 0$

During a weekend sale, all items in a warehouse were discounted 15 percent. At the end of the weekend, all prices were increased x percent so that all items had their original, pre-sale prices.

15.

15	x

Directions: *For questions 16–25, solve each problem, and enter your answer in the grid provided.*

16. If $t - p = 7$ and $u - p = 10$, what is the value of t when $u = 10$?

17. The average (arithmetic mean) of three consecutive odd integers k, l, and m is 13. What is m?

18. Jerry has \$56 to spend on ties. With tax, brand X ties cost \$7 and brand Y ties cost \$6. Jerry bought two brand X ties, a certain number of brand Y ties, and had \$6 remaining. How many ties did he buy altogether?

16.

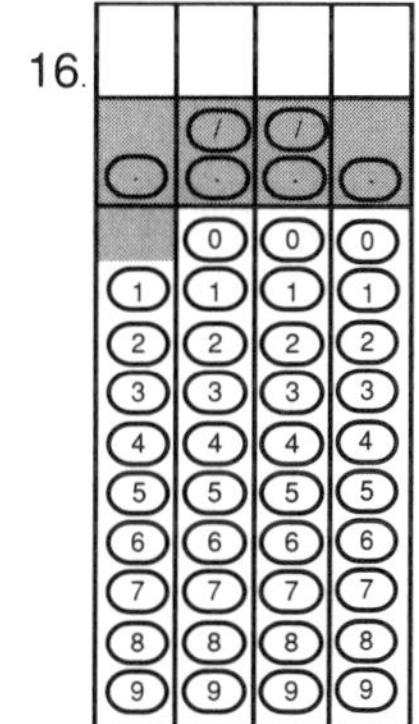

17.

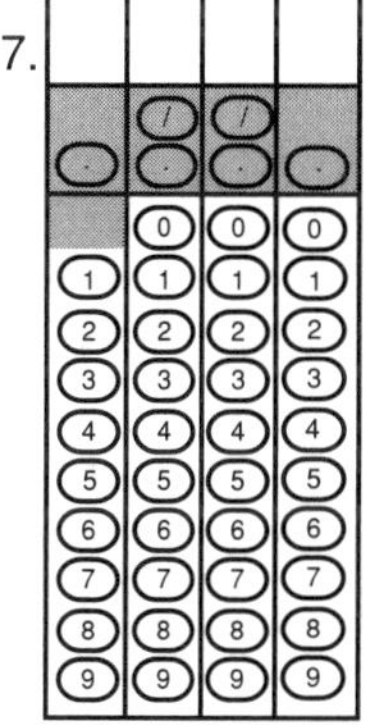

18.

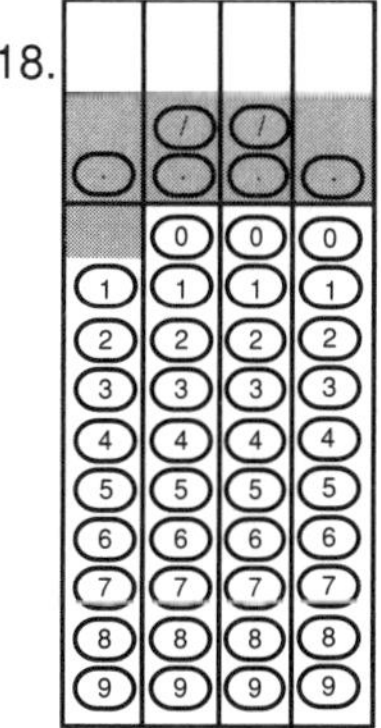

19. In the figure below, point $P(4,3)$ is the center of line segment OB. What is the perimeter of triangle OAB?

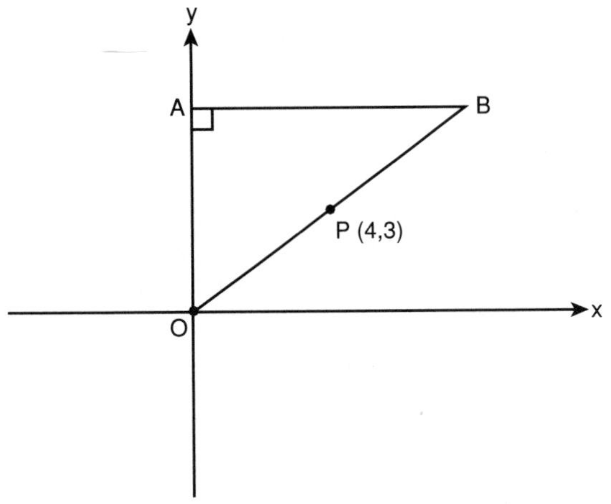

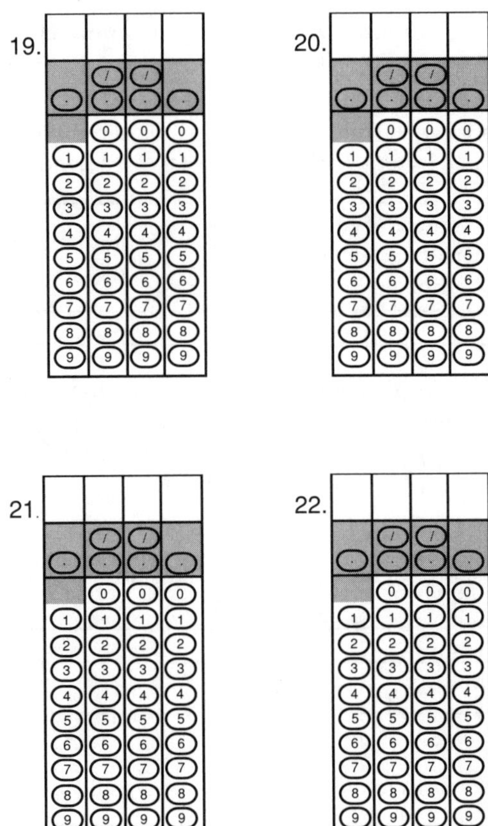

20. Linda bought a box containing 3 dozen pens, out of which 6 were defective. Linda's cost per usable pen was $0.60. How many dollars did Linda pay for the box of 36 pens? (Disregard the dollar sign when gridding your answer.)

21. The number of points Sue received on the second test was $1\frac{1}{2}$ times the number of points she received on the first test. The number of points she received on the third test was $1\frac{1}{2}$ times the number of points she received on the second test. If her total sum over three tests was 475, how many points did Sue receive on the first test?

22. A company distributes 20 percent of its profit among its shareholders and invests the rest. If the company invests $100, how many dollars does it distribute to its shareholders?

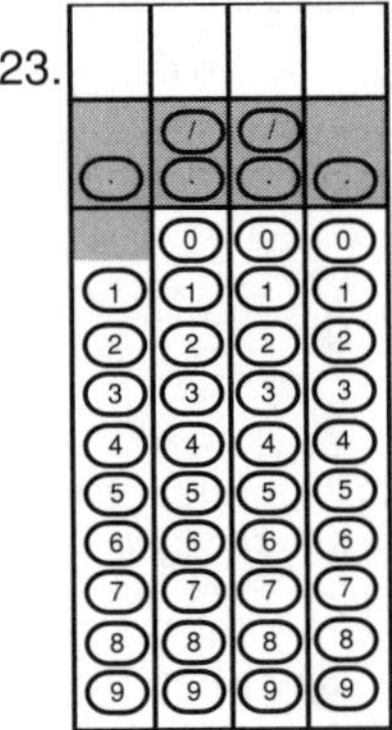

23. The average (arithmetic mean) test score of 10 students in a class is 80. If the test scores of 2 of the students are not included, the average drops to 78. What is the *sum* of the 2 scores that are not included?

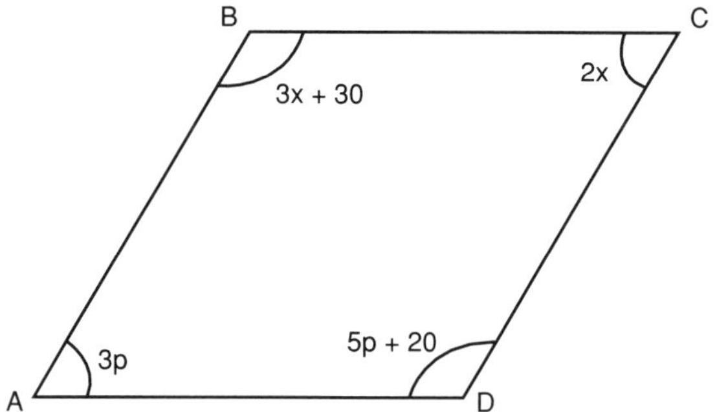

Note: Figure not drawn to scale.

24. In the figure above, *ABCD* is a parallelogram. What is the value of *x?* (Disregard the "degree" symbol when gridding your answer.)

25. The number of Bacteria A in a jar doubles every hour, and the number of Bacteria B triples every hour. At noon, the number of Bacteria A in the jar is 4 million, and the number of Bacteria B is one-third million. How many *million* more Bacteria A than Bacteria B will the jar contain at 4:00 P.M. that same day?

24.

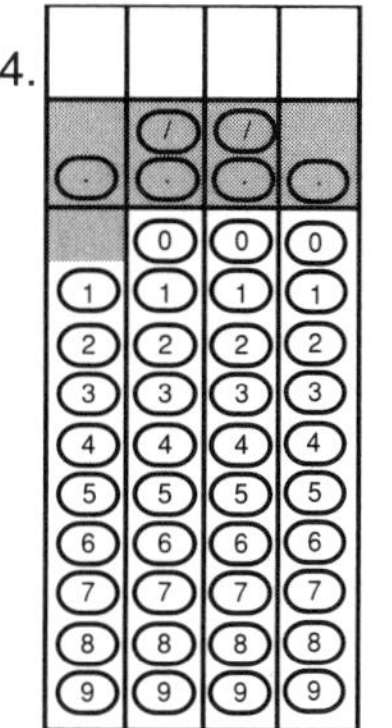

25.

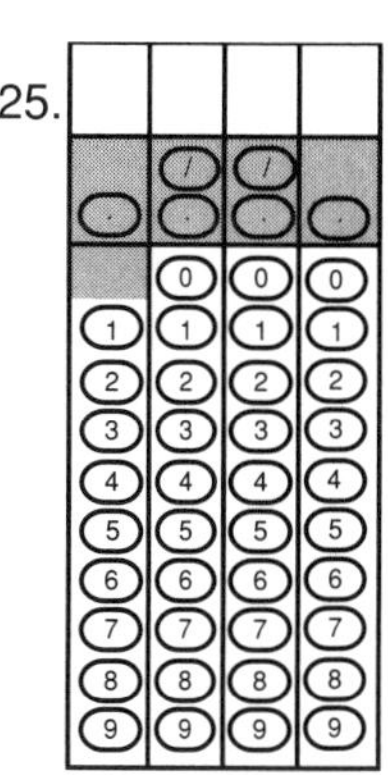

Quick Answer Guide

Test 2, Section 1: Math

1. A
2. B
3. D
4. A
5. C
6. A
7. B
8. A
9. D
10. C
11. A
12. B
13. A
14. A
15. B
16. 7
17. 15
18. 8
19. 24
20. 18
21. 100
22. 25
23. 176
24. 30
25. 37

For explanations to these questions, see Day 20.

Day 20

Test 2, Section 1: Math

Explanations and Strategies

Assignment for Today:

Review the explanations for the test you just took.

1. Correct choice (A)

Cancel common terms from both columns. Notice that $\frac{1}{8}$ is common to both columns and so we can get rid of it.

Then, Column A is: $-\frac{-3}{4}$, which is really $\frac{3}{4}$.
And, Column B is $-\frac{-1}{2}$, which is really $\frac{1}{2}$, or $\frac{2}{4}$.
So, Column A is greater than Column B.

2. Correct choice (B)

We can simplify Column A by dividing by 2:

$$\frac{0.000036}{2n} = \frac{0.000018}{n}$$

Notice that the numerator in Column A has 4 zeros before the "18" and the numerator in Column B has only 3 zeros. This indicates that the quantity in Column B is greater than the quantity in Column A. To confirm this, let's plug in values for n . Let $n = 1$.

Then, Column A = $\frac{0.000018}{n} = \frac{0.000018}{1} = 0.000018$

and Column B = $\frac{0.00018}{n} = \frac{0.00018}{1} = 0.00018$

Here, Column B is greater than Column A. Now, to make the difference between the two columns large, let's try $n = 100$.

For $n = 100$, Column A = $\frac{0.000018}{n}$

$\frac{0.000018}{100} = 0.00000018$

Column B = $\frac{0.00018}{n} = \frac{0.00018}{100} = 0.0000018$

For both cases, (n = 1 and n = 100), Column B is greater than Column A. So, the answer is choice (B).

3. Correct choice (D)

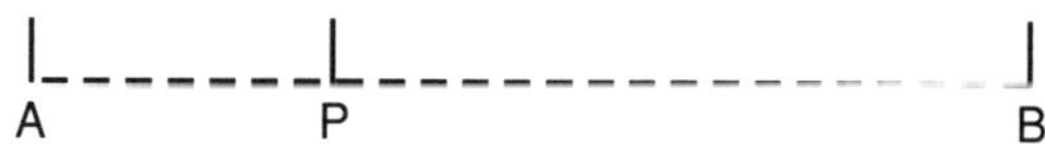

Let's draw a figure. As shown above, $\frac{AP}{PB} = \frac{3}{4}$.

Notice, this doesn't mean that $AP = 3$ and $PB = 4$. It only means that AP and PB are in the ratio 3:4. In other words, AP could be 15 and PB could be 20 so that their ratio is still 3:4. In this case, $AP + PB$ would be 35.

So, the exact value of $AP + PB$ is impossible to tell.

4. Correct choice (A)

We find the quantity in column A by following the pattern in the definition of a "motor":

The "motor" of {q,r,s,t} is s (the third element) if q (the first element) is more than r (the second element). If q is less than r, then the "motor" is t (the last element).

The "motor" of {2,4,1,3} is 1 if 2 is more than 4 and 3 if 2 is less than 4.

Well, we know that 2 is less than 4 and so the "motor" is the last element of {2,4,1,3}, which is 3.

So, Column A is 3 and Column B is 1 and so Column A is greater than Column B.

5. Correct choice (C)

To find the greatest value of $(p) \times (q) \times (r)$, note that we want the highest possible values for p, q, and r. That is to say, p, q, and r have to be closest to each other (and, don't forget, they have to add up to 15). Then, the highest value of $(p) \times (q) \times (r)$ will be obtained if $p = 4$, $q = 5$, and $r = 6$. Then their product is $4 \times 5 \times 6 = 120$.

The value of Column B is $1 \times 8 \times 15 = 120$

Then, both columns are equal and the answer is (C).

6. Correct choice (A)

Let's suppose for a second that angle B is really 30 degrees. Then, we get a 30–60–90 triangle (because if angle B is 30 degrees, angle C has to be 60 degrees so that the 3 angles add up to 180 degrees). We know that a 30–60–90 triangle has sides in the ratio 1 (opposite the smallest angle), $\sqrt{3}$, and 2 (the hypotenuse).

In our problem, the smallest side is 3 (because it is opposite the smallest angle), which means we should multiply each side by 3. So, if our triangle were a 30–60–90 triangle, y would be 3 times $\sqrt{3}$, that is $3\sqrt{3}$. But, angle B is less than 30 degrees, which means that angle C must be more than 60 degrees (only then will the three angles add up to 180 degrees). If angle C is more than 60 degrees, y is more than $3\sqrt{3}$. So, Column A is greater.

For this problem, we had to remember that when an angle increases, the length of the opposite side also increases.

7. Correct choice (B)

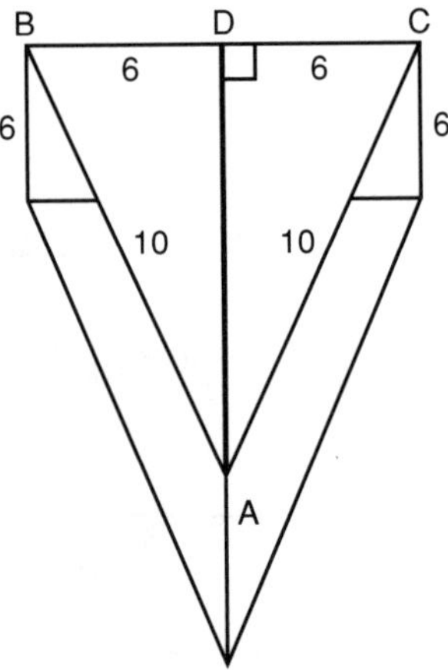

The formula for the volume of a triangular prism is:

volume = area × height

To find the volume, we first need to find the area of the triangular base. The area of the base is the same as the area of the top. To find the area of the top, we need to know the height, AD (drawn in the figure) of triangle ABC. Note that side BD and side AD form the two sides of a right triangle with side AB as the hypotenuse. BD is 6 and AB is 10, which means that the triangle is a 6–8–10 triangle and so AD is 8. If AD is 8, the area of the triangle is $\frac{1}{2} \times 12 \times 8 = 48$.

So, the volume of the prism = area × height

$= 48 \times 6 = 288$.

Column A is 288 and Column B is 360, which means that the correct answer is choice (B).

8. Correct choice (A)

Let's see what the smallest possible number of cards marked "3" in box A is. We know that the total of 6 cards is 18 and the largest number on any card is 3. This means all six cards must be 3s. Otherwise it's not possible to get a sum of 18. So, Column A = 6.

Now Column B. Is it possible to have six 4s in box B? No. Otherwise the 6 cards would add up to 24. So right away we know that Column A is greater than Column B. We don't need to find the exact value.

9. Correct choice (D)

The best way to solve this kind of question is to plug in values for t.

If $t = 0$, Column A = $(-3)^2 = 9$, and Column B = $(3)^2 = 9$. Both are equal.

If $t = 1$, Column A = 4 and Column B = 16; Column B is larger.

Because we get two different results, the correct choice is D.

10. Correct choice (C)

If $2.2 \div a = 220$, then we can write: $\frac{2.2}{a} = 220$

Or, $2.2 = 220a$

So, $a = \frac{2.2}{220} = 0.01$

If $a = 0.01$, then $\sqrt{a} = 0.1$ (because $0.1 \times 0.1 = 0.01$).

Now we need to find the value of $220 \div \sqrt{a}$ in Column A.

If $\sqrt{a} = 0.1$, $220 \div \sqrt{a} = \frac{222}{.1} = \frac{2200}{1} = 2200$

So, the two columns are equal.

11. Correct choice (A)

It takes 300 operations to assemble 1 computer. And each operation takes 9 seconds. So, to assemble each computer, it takes $9 \times 300 = 2700$ seconds.

Now let's look at Column A. The number of seconds in 3 hours is: $3 \times 60 \times 60$ (because there are 60 minutes in 1 hour and 60 seconds in 1 minute) = $3 \times 3600 = 10{,}800$.

If it takes 2,700 seconds to assemble 1 computer, in 10,800 seconds, it's possible to assemble $\frac{10{,}800}{2{,}700} = \frac{108}{27} = 4$ computers. So, Column A = 4

Now let's look at Column B. We can see that the number at the top ($300 \times 9 = 2700$) is less than the number at the bottom ($3 \times 60 \times 60 = 10{,}800$) and so Column B is less than 1.

In fact, Column B is $\frac{1}{4}$, just the opposite of 4. So, Column A is greater than Column B.

12. Correct choice (B)

The common and incorrect answer is to say that both columns are equal because the average of 40 and 30 is 35. To find the average speed for the entire trip, we have to divide the total distance by the total amount of time taken for the two trips.

To go to the zoo, Clarence traveled at a speed of 40 miles per hour. Then, the time it took him is $120 \div 40 = 3$ hours. (Remember, distance ÷ speed = time).

Returning from the zoo, Clarence traveled at 30 miles per hour. So, the time it took him is $120 \div 30 = 4$ hours.

So, the total amount of time is $3 + 4 = 7$ hours. The total distance traveled is $120 + 120 = 240$ miles. So, the average speed for the entire trip = total distance ÷ total time = $\frac{240}{7} = 34\frac{2}{7}$.

As you can see, this is not equal to 35, but is slightly less than 35. So, Column B is greater than Column A.

13. Correct choice (A)

The trick here is to realize that there are only 4 (not 5) tick marks from 0 to –5 (and only 4 tick marks from 0 to 5).

So, 4 tick marks = 5 units

Then, 1 tick mark = $\frac{5}{4} = 1.25$ units

Point A is 5 tick marks to the left of point P at the center. So, A is a negative quantity.

So, $A = -1.25 \times 5 = -6.25$

Then, $-2A = -2 \times -6.25 = 12.50$

So, Column A = 12.5 and Column B = 12, which means the correct answer is choice (A).

14. Correct choice (A)

We can calculate the quantity in columns A and B by applying the definition of the ⊕ operator:

$a \oplus b$ is the distance between the point (a,b) and the point (3,1).

So, Column A, ⊕, is the distance between the point (1,1) and the point (3,1). Let's sketch a diagram.

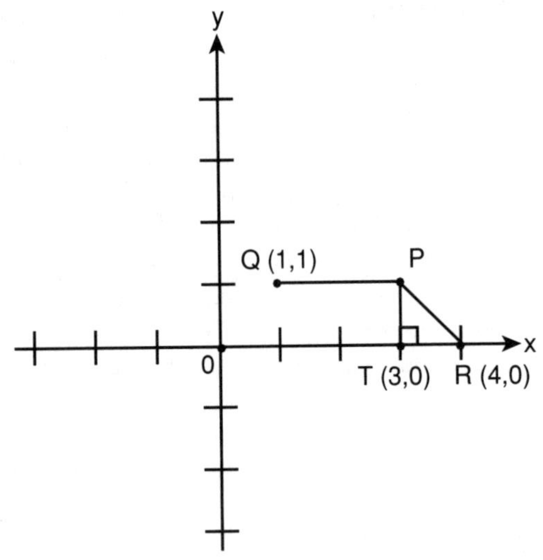

We need to find the length of line QP. As you can see, this line is $3 - 1 = 2$ units long. So, Column A is 2.

Now Column B. $4 \oplus 0$ means we have to find the distance between the point (4,0), which is shown as point R, and (3,1), which is still point P. Notice that PR is not $4 - 3 = 1$.

To find PR, first let's drop a perpendicular from P to T. Then, $PT = 1 - 0 = 1$. Also, $TR = 4 - 3 = 1$. Now PR is the hypotenuse of a triangle of lengths 1 (PT) and 1 (TR). Then, we can write:

$$PR^2 = PT^2 + TR^2$$

Or, $PR^2 = 1^2 + 1^2 = 2$

Then, $PR = \sqrt{2}$.

So, Column B $= \sqrt{2}$ and Column A $= 2$. Then we know that Column A is greater than Column B and the right answer is choice (A).

15. Correct choice (B)

To solve this problem, we can pick \$100 as a starting price of one of the items in the warehouse (you can pick any number, but we pick 100 because it's an easy number to work with). During the sale, all items were discounted 15 percent. This \$100 item was marked down to \$85.

At the end of the sale, this \$85 item was increased by x percent so that its new price was back to the original \$100. This is a \$15 increase. So now we need to figure out \$15 is what percent of \$85 (notice it's no longer a percent of \$100 because the new starting price now is \$85, not \$100). Or, let's see if 15% is more or less than \$15.

Well, 10% of \$85 is \$8.50 and 5% is \$4.25, which means 15% is 8.50 + 4.25 = \$12.75. This tells us that 15% of \$85 is only \$12.75, which means that \$15 is going to be more than 15%. So, x is more than 15% and Column B is greater than Column A.

16. Correct answer 7

If $u = 10$, we can write the second equation:

$$\begin{aligned} u - p &= 10 \text{ as:} \\ 10 - p &= 10 \\ \text{This means } 10 - 10 &= p \\ \text{So, } p &= 0 \end{aligned}$$

If $p = 0$, we can write the first equation:

$$\begin{aligned} t - p &= 7 \text{ as:} \\ t - 0 &= 7 \end{aligned}$$

17. Correct answer 15

The average of three consecutive integers (whether they are odd or even) is always the middle integer. For example, the average of 2, 3, and 4 is 3, and the average of 3, 5, and 7 is 5.

So, if the average of k, l, and m is 13, then the middle integer must be 13. Because the three integers are odd and consecutive, the other two integers must be 11 and 15. So, the three integers are 11, 13, and 15, which means m must be 15.

18. Correct answer 8

After the purchase, Jerry had \$6 remaining. This means he spent 56 – 6 = \$50 on ties. We know that he bought 2 brand X ties. Each brand X tie costs \$7, so 2 of them cost \$14. This means he spent 50 – 14 = \$36 on brand Y ties. Each brand Y tie costs \$6, which means the number of brand Y ties he could've bought for \$36 is 36 ÷ 6 = 6.

So, Jerry bought 6 brand Y ties and 2 brand X ties for a total of 8 ties.

19. Correct answer 24

We're told that point $P(4,3)$ is the center of OB. The x–coordinate of point P is 4, which means the x–coordinate of point B is $4 \times 2 = 8$. Similarly, the y–coordinate of point P is 3, which means the y–coordinate of point B is $3 \times 2 = 6$.

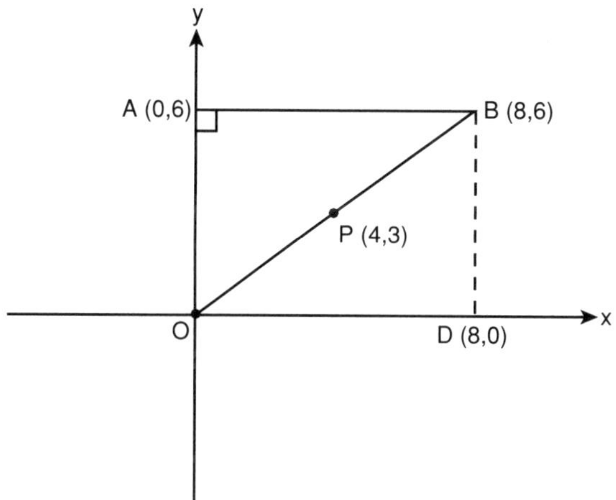

To find the perimeter of the triangle, we need the lengths of the three sides OA, AB, and OB. From B, we can drop a perpendicular BD on the x–axis. Then, the x–coordinate of point D is 8. And, if the y–coordinate of point B is 6, the y–coordinate of point A is also 6.

Then, $OA = 6$. And $AB = OD = 8$. Now we need to find OB. Notice that if $OA = 6$ an $OD = 8$, we have a 6–8–10 right triangle, which means OB must be 10.

(If you have a right triangle with perpendiculars of lengths 3 and 4, then the hypotenuse must be of length 5. This is called a 3–4–5 right triangle. In fact, the two perpendiculars can be any multiples of 3 and 4 and the hypotenuse will be the same multiple of 5. In other words, if the two perpendiculars are 9 (which is *three* times 3) and 12 (which is *three* times 4), then the hypotenuse is 15 (*three* times 5). In this example, the two sides were 6 (*two* times 3) and 8 (*two* times 4), which means the hypotenuse must be *two* times 5, or 10.)

So now we know the three sides of the triangle: 6, 8, and 10. Then, the perimeter of the triangle is $6 + 8 + 10 = 24$.

20. Correct answer 18

The box that Linda bought contained 3 dozen, or 36, pens. Of these, 6 were defective. Then, the number of usable pens was $36 - 6 = 30$. We're told that the cost per usable pen was 60 cents. This means the total cost for 36 pens was $.60 \times 30 = 18$ dollars.

Notice that the total cost is *not* $.60 \times 36$ because 6 pens were unusable, and the given cost of \$0.60 was for each *usable* pen.

21. Correct answer 100

Let's assume that x is the number of points Sue received on the first test. Then, the number of points she received on the second test was one and a half times x. So, the number of points she received on the second test was $1.5x$. On the third test, she received 1.5 times the number of points she received on the second test. So, the number of points she received on the third test must be 1.5 times $1.5x$.

So, points on first test $= x$

points on second test $= 1.5x$

points on third test $= 1.5(1.5x) = 2.25x$

We know that the sum of these three tests was 475.

So, $x + 1.5x + 2.25x = 475$

Or, $4.75x = 475$

Or, $x = \frac{475}{4.75} = \frac{47500}{475} = 100$

22. Correct answer 25

We know that the company distributes 20 percent of its profit. This means the company invests the remaining 80 percent. If the company invests \$100, then 80 percent of its profits is equal to \$100. We now need to find 100 percent of the profits.

Well, if $80\% = 100$,

then $1\% = \frac{100}{80} = \frac{10}{8} = \frac{5}{4}$

And, $100\% = \frac{5}{4} \times 100 = 5 \times 25 = 125$

So, the total profit is \$125. Now we need to know how much the company distributes to its shareholders. We know that it distributes 20 percent of its profit. So we need to find 20 percent of 125, which is $.2 \times 125 = 25$.

23. Correct answer 176

For questions like this, it's best to work with sums, not averages, because averages have to be added with caution.

We know that the average is the sum divided by the number of items. So, the sum is the average times the number of items. If the average of 10 scores is 80, the sum must be $10 \times 80 = 800$.

When 2 scores are removed, the average drops to 78. So now, the average of 8 scores (not 10) is 78. The sum then must be $8 \times 78 = 624$. In other words, the sum dropped from 800 to 624. This means the sum dropped by $800 - 624 = 176$.

So, the sum of the two scores = 176.

24. Correct answer 30

The key here is to know that, in a parallelogram, opposite angles are equal. This means angle *B* is equal to angle *D*, and angle *C* is equal to angle *A*. So let's write the two equations:

$\angle A = \angle C$ ====> $3p = 2x$, and

$\angle B = \angle D$ ====> $3x + 30 = 5p + 20$

We're looking for the value of *x*, which means we should get rid of the values of *p* from the two equations. So let's find the value of *p* in the first equation and plug it into the second equation.

From the first equation, $3p = 2x$, we get:

$$p = \frac{2}{3}x$$

Let's plug this value of *p* into the second equation.

$3x + 30 = 5(\frac{2}{3}x) + 20$

Or, $3x + 10 = 5(\frac{2}{3}x)$

Multiplying by 3: $9x + 30 = 10x$

Or, $30 = 10x - 9x = x$

So, the value of *x* is 30

25. Correct answer 37

At noon, the number of Bacteria A is 4 million. The bacteria double every hour. Also at noon, the number of Bacteria B was $\frac{1}{3}$ million and they triple every hour. So let's make a chart that shows the number of Bacteria A and Bacteria B at various times:

Bacteria	*Noon*	*1:00 P.M.*	*2:00 P.M.*	*3:00 P.M.*	*4:00 P.M.*
A	4 mil.	8 mil.	16 mil.	32 mil.	64 mil.
B	$\frac{1}{3}$ mil.	1 mil.	3 mil.	9 mil.	27 mil.

So, at 4:00 P.M., there are 64 million Bacteria B and 27 million Bacteria A. The difference is: $64 - 27 = 37$.

Day 21

Test 2, Section 1: Verbal

Questions and Answers

Assignment for Today:

Take a sample SAT Verbal Reasoning Test under actual test conditions. Allow yourself exactly 30 minutes to complete the 35 questions in this test.

Directions: *For questions 1–10, one or more words have been left out of each sentence. Circle the answer, A–E, which contains the word or words which best fit the meaning of the entire sentence.*

1. Clyde was on a diet, but when he walked past the donut shop, he couldn't help but —— to his desires.
   (A) forbear
   (B) abstain
   (C) rant
   (D) skulk
   (E) succumb

2. The —— of American culture, according to Tylor, lies in the fact that our yearning for normalcy is matched only by our desire to be special.
   (A) comfort
   (B) caprice
   (C) epitome
   (D) drama
   (E) paradox

3. While —— through the library stacks, the professor —— a manuscript that had been misplaced.
   (A) stomping..browsed
   (B) wandering..hid
   (C) meandering..discovered
   (D) getting..revealed
   (E) walking..reviewed

4. Unfortunately, neither housing reform nor new —— for the poor will do anything to bring housing —— under control.
   (A) regulations..bureaucracy
   (B) clothing..construction
   (C) handouts..affiliates
   (D) subsidies..costs
   (E) labyrinths..authorities

5. —— rose and cornflower extracts moisturize the fragile areas that encircle the eye, promoting a more —— skin texture.
   (A) Precious..compliant
   (B) Aromatic..soothing
   (C) Emollient..supple
   (D) Gelatinous..limpid
   (E) Colorless..burnished

6. For those burdened by that —— legacy of a liberal education and more taste than money, the back roads of New England with their overflowing antique shops lead to a chamber of torment, especially when the acquisitive streak —— reason.
   (A) inescapable..elucidates
   (B) unwonted..suborns
   (C) impoverished..subverts
   (D) material..overwhelms
   (E) eccentric..flaunts

7. Unlike a diverse native community in which at least one plant is green and appealing to cattle, cheat-grass —— most often present cattle only with dry, barbed and almost inedible ——.
   (A) plants..cud
   (B) families..provender
   (C) pastures..nourishment
   (D) monocultures..forage
   (E) species..rumination

8. Although most psychologists now —— some notion of an unconscious mind, many reject the other theories of Sigmund Freud, who first —— subliminal consciousness in the late nineteenth century.
   (A) mitigate..transmogrified
   (B) repudiate..predicted
   (C) augur..entertained
   (D) accept..hypothesized
   (E) espouse..assuaged

9. While intelligence is a characteristic essential to wisdom, certain other qualities —— with greater accuracy who will be wise; the most essential characteristic may be ——, a general concern for mankind's well-being.
   (A) apprehend..kindliness
   (B) indicate..harmlessness
   (C) infer..sociability
   (D) predict..benignity
   (E) imply..salubrity

10. The Chrysler Building is a —— structure of glass and cement with a vast entryway, designed by corporate —— to overwhelm visitors and make them feel insignificant.
   (A) contemporary..infidels
   (B) monolithic..commissaries
   (C) vestibular..tycoons
   (D) gargantuan..savants
   (E) monumental..strategists

Directions: *For questions 10–23, determine the relationship between the two words given in capital letters. Then, from the choices listed A–E, select the one pair that has a relationship most similar to that of the capitalized pair. Circle the letter of that pair.*

---

11. JUDGE:COURTROOM::
   (A) mortician:mortuary
   (B) cowhand:spurs
   (C) butcher:beef
   (D) author:pen
   (E) lapidary:stones

12. INCISION:GASH::
   (A) scab:wound
   (B) toy:purchase
   (C) button:elevator
   (D) breeze:gale
   (E) cloth:rag

13. DOCUMENTARY:FILM::
   (A) child:mother
   (B) highway:state
   (C) negative:strip
   (D) treatise:print
   (E) portico:mansion

14. SANCTUARY:DANGER::
   (A) battlefield:aggression
   (B) village:seclusion

(C) sty:cleanliness
(D) prison:incentive
(E) lounge:relief

15. GARBLED:COHERENCE::
(A) impertinent:shame
(B) ingenuous:guile
(C) decadent:sanity
(D) paradoxical:truth
(E) humorous:wit

16. BELLICOSE:PUGNACIOUS::
(A) comical:serious
(B) sagacious:wise
(C) brilliant:colorless
(D) complex:benign
(E) lewd:repentant

17. ANEMIA:VITALITY::
(A) blatancy:contrition
(B) kettle:hole
(C) tenuousness:solidity
(D) hussy:ingenuity
(E) amputation:leg

18. PUB:IMBIBE::
(A) rink:skate
(B) restaurant:cook
(C) garage:dissemble
(D) party:crash
(E) church:enter

19. TEPID:TORRID::
(A) germane:relevant
(B) vapid:brilliant
(C) moist:sodden
(D) hot:dry
(E) sleepy:sleeping

20. PENCHANT:PROCLIVITY::
(A) respect:liberty
(B) enjoyment:ability
(C) retirement:security
(D) pendant:beauty
(E) trepidation:anxiety

21. EQUANIMITY:ANXIETY::
(A) imbroglio:brawl
(B) penury:wealth
(C) equality:parity
(D) generosity:charity
(E) apprehension:dread

22. PREHENSILE:GRASP::
(A) shrewd:bully
(B) loquacious:mute
(C) sanguine:feign
(D) mutable:change
(E) sensible:fool

23. VITIATE:INCORRUPTIBLE::
(A) protect:absent
(B) wake:deceased
(C) bribe:venal
(D) laud:indomitable
(E) outrage:moral

Directions: *Answer each question based only on what is stated or implied in the passage and any introductory material given.*

Questions 24–35 are based on the following passage.

Nerve cells play a critical role in the functioning of our bodies. While much remains unknown about neurons, we have learned a considerable amount, enough to cause some to marvel at their remarkable qualities.

The neuron, or nerve cell, besides possessing the powers of absorption and growth common to all the cells of the body, also has three special duties or functions: sensitivity, conductivity, and modifiability.

The first of these functions is sensitivity or impressibility. All matter is influenced by what happens to it; all living matter is especially so, and the nerve cells are the parts of living animals which carry this trait to the extreme. If we compare a person's body to a building, calling the steel framework the skeleton and the heating/air-conditioning unit and ventilation shafts the lungs and circulatory system, the nervous system would include with other things the thermometers, heat regulators, electric buttons, door bells, valve openers, fire alarms, smoke detectors, etc.—the parts of the building which are specially designed to respond to influences of the environment.

Just how the nerve cell conducts or transmits is not known. But the fact itself is sure. As a copper wire at one end of which an electric current is excited is so influenced that the current appears at the other end; as the air so acts that a vibration in any part spreads to other parts, so too the neuron when stimulated at one end acts so as to produce a corresponding activity at the other end. It then produces, under certain conditions, activity in an adjoining neuron and in the synapse connecting them.

The activity or disturbance which is transmitted is called the nervous impulse. When such an impulse is started in a nerve cell, we say that the nerve cell is stimulated and call the agency by which the impulse is begotten the stimulus. The conduction or transmission is commonly over a series of nerve cells. For instance, when the stimulus of pain at the finger's end makes us rub the injured spot, the impulse does not go from the skin to the muscles via a single cell or set of cells, but traverses at least three: one set running from the skin to the spinal cord, one from the spinal cord to the muscles and one or more sets in the spinal cord connecting these. The transmission is, in any given neuron, usually in the same direction—toward the extremities of the neuraxon. A cell carrying impulses from the brain to a muscle does not, so to speak, carry return messages. For that, another route is used. A nerve cell may receive impulses from several nerve cells. It may and commonly does transmit its impulses to many nerve cells.

As might be expected, the two functions of sensitivity and conductivity are aided by such an arrangement of the nerve cells that stimuli are received at important points in the body and conducted to appropriate muscles. The constituents of the nervous system are not arranged at random. They are not like the chance tangle of a billion little threads which would receive stimuli hit or miss and conduct them nowhere in particular, but are, like the wires of the telephone system of a major city or the railroads of this nation, definitely placed for transmission between important points, and are so arranged at central offices as to permit a great number of useful connections. For instance, the neurons receiving the stimuli of light in the retina have definite connections with the neurons that carry impulses to the muscles that open and close the eyes, also to the muscles that move the eyes in turning to and focusing for objects, and to the muscles that move the head.

The analogy with a telephone system fails when we come to the third function, characteristic of many of the nerve cells of the human brain, their power of modification of use. Unlike any system of wires or machines, the human nervous system possesses the power, at least in many of its parts, to be so altered by whatever happens to it as to enable the body on the next occasion to meet the situation more successfully. The same nervous system which causes at a child's early sight of the fire the reaction of reaching for it becomes a nervous system that causes in later trials the reaction of avoidance. The connection between the impression and the former motor discharge has been weakened and an opposite one formed. The neurons learn, so to speak, to form, break, and modify their interconnections. If a telephone system possessed within itself the power by which the connections between the wires to certain houses would, with successful use, become more and more easily made while other connections would become increasingly more difficult, the analogy would be complete. But of course no mere machine has such a power to modify its workings, to make or break connections in accordance with the frequency of their use and the desirability or discomfort of the results to which they lead.

These are the three major functions of the neuron, the basic element of the human nervous system. While comparisons with a building or telephone system or national railway system may be convenient and illustrative, the analogy ends there. For our nervous system is in many ways a remarkably unique and complex miracle, unfathomable if it were not to exist, and barely comprehensible that it does.

24. The primary purpose of this passage is to
   (A) show how the body is like familiar mechanical objects
   (B) demonstrate how extraordinary the human nervous system is
   (C) challenge misconceptions about the neurons
   (D) explain the main functions of the basic element of the nervous system
   (E) argue for new kinds of machines that are modeled after the body

25. The extended analogy in paragraph two primarily serves the purpose of
   (A) showing how complex modern buildings have become
   (B) illustrating the relationship between the nervous system and other body systems
   (C) describing how the nervous system works
   (D) arguing that even biological complexities can be made familiar
   (E) explaining the function of building parts

26. The author uses the term "agency" in line 35 to mean
   (A) an outside force that causes the stimulus
   (B) a cooperative organization
   (C) a neuron's ability to choose various pathways
   (D) a decision-making structure within the nervous system
   (E) an impulse that is transmitted along the neuron

27. According to the passage, the transmission of a nerve impulse to the brain
   (A) is largely a random process
   (B) requires more than one neuron
   (C) uses the same pathway as reflexive impulses traveling from the brain
   (D) is analogous to a flock of birds
   (E) causes the neuron to degenerate

28. If the author were to create an analogy to describe the transmission path of an impulse (see the middle of paragraph four), which analogy would be best?
   (A) Tag team wrestling
   (B) Track team relay
   (C) Elevator
   (D) Cross-country skiing
   (E) Pogo stick

29. The best definition of constituents in line 58 is
   (A) those having power to elect
   (B) evolutionary manifestations
   (C) parts that make up a whole
   (D) individual subsystems of the neurons
   (E) member of an elected group

30. According to the passage, which is *not* the best metaphor for either neurons or the nervous system?
   (A) Copper wire
   (B) Railroads
   (C) Little threads
   (D) Telephone system
   (E) Building

31. In discussing the abilities of neurons, the passage does *not* mention
   (A) impressibility
   (B) growth
   (C) modifiability
   (D) absorption
   (E) regeneration

32. Which phrase best describes the tone of the passage?
    (A) Supportively pedagogical
    (B) Unqualified admiration
    (C) Reluctant condescension
    (D) Pedantically rigid
    (E) Undeniably banal

33. The author would *disagree* with which of the following statements?
    (A) Our nervous system responds to influences of the environment.
    (B) Analogies are useful in explaining biological phenomena.
    (C) How nerve cells conduct nervous impulses is well known.
    (D) Neurons can learn to some extent.
    (E) The human body is amazing.

34. The word "unfathomable" in line 110 means
    (A) shameful
    (B) not in keeping with current science
    (C) lamentable
    (D) disastrous
    (E) not fully understandable

35. The most appropriate title for this passage would be
    (A) Neurons: Three Amazing Abilities
    (B) Why Your Body Is Like a Building
    (C) Human Beings: Machines After All
    (D) An Anatomy of Analogies
    (E) Stimulation from End to End

Quick Answer Guide

Test 2, Section 2: Verbal

1. E
2. E
3. C
4. D
5. C
6. C
7. D
8. D
9. D
10. E
11. A
12. D
13. D
14. C
15. B
16. B
17. C
18. A
19. C
20. E
21. B
22. D
23. B
24. D
25. B
26. A
27. B
28. B
29. C
30. C
31. E
32. A
33. C
34. E
35. A

For explanations to these questions, see Day 22.

Day 22

Test 2, Section 2: Verbal

Explanations and Strategies

Assignment for Today:

Review the explanations for the test you just took.

1. Correct choice (E) succumb

Flag word: "but." Because of the "but" in this sentence, you should expect Clyde to break his diet and buy a donut, right? So look for a word that has him giving in to the temptation. *Succumb*, to give in, is the only choice that fits well.

Clyde was on a diet, but when he walked past the donut shop, he couldn't help but *succumb* to his desires.

2. Correct choice (E) paradox

To complete this sentence, we have to understand its meaning. The middle part of the sentence ("our yearning for normalcy") is compared to the last part of the sentence ("our desire to be special"). These are two opposite wishes: to be normal *and* to be special. So what's going on here is a "contradiction."

Working through the answer choices, we find choice (E) is close to "contradiction." A *paradox* is something that seems to be self-contradictory.

The *paradox* of American culture, according to Tylor, lies in the fact that our yearning for normalcy is matched only by our desire to be special.

3. Correct choice (C) meandering..discovered

The sentence itself is not difficult, but the choices might be because a few make at least some sense. The challenge is to find the choice that makes the best sense. Choice (C) fits best because professors are prone to *meander* (walk aimlessly) and because misplaced manuscripts are more likely to be *discovered* than any of the other four choices.

While *meandering* through the library stacks, the professor *discovered* a manuscript that had been misplaced.

4. Correct choice (D) subsidies..costs

You can find the right answer to this question by using a different strategy for each blank. First, think of what word you might use for the second blank. The sentence has an economic twist to it, so you should look for a choice that deals with money. Next, to find a good choice for the first blank, read through the choices. A few work okay in the first blank, but only one choice makes sense in the context of the entire sentence.

Unfortunately, neither housing reform nor *subsidies* for the poor will do anything to bring housing *costs* under control.

5. Correct choice (C) Emollient..supple

If you don't see an obvious choice, then plug in choices and eliminate the ones that don't work. This strategy takes time, so consider leaving this question, and other difficult ones, until the end of the section. Do the easier ones first.

The sentence says that plant extracts are used to add moisture to the skin. Probably makes it less dry, more soft, right? Question is, what kind of extracts? Something that moisturizes and makes skin soft. So there must be a functional relationship between the two blanks. Like *glue* is used to make things *stick*.

Emollient means "softening" or "to make supple." *Supple* means "yielding," "pliant" or "soft." Plug them in. This gives:

Softening rose and cornflower extracts moisturize the fragile areas that encircle the eye, promoting a softer skin texture.

Unlike the other choices, (C) works. It's easy when you know the meaning of *emollient*. If you weren't sure, check the other choices and eliminate the ones that don't work. Then guess from the remaining choices, if necessary.

Emollient rose and cornflower extracts moisturize the fragile areas that encircle the eye, promoting a more *supple* skin texture.

6. Correct choice (C) impoverished..subverts

Long sentence. The blanks are close to the beginning and near the end. Your best bet is read in all choices and see which make sense.

Note the clues: (a) The legacy is called a burden; (b) "more taste than money" refers to the legacy. This isn't a normal legacy like the Kennedy millions. It could be *unwonted* (unusual), *eccentric* (peculiar or not customary), or *impoverished* (poor).

So, we have people with more taste than money. When would they have a problem with antique shops? Only when they want to buy everything in the store but can't. And when this acquisitive streak defeats the voice of reason that says, "You can't have it," then *subverts* or *overwhelms* might work.

For those burdened by that *impoverished* legacy of a liberal education and more taste than money, the back roads of New England with their overflowing antique shops lead to a chamber of torment, especially when the acquisitive streak *subverts* reason.

7. Correct choice (D) monocultures..forage

Not your daily conversation. So, it's tough to anticipate blanks. But there's a flag: "unlike." It tells us the second half of the sentence is opposite to the first.

Break the first half into two parts: "diverse native community" and "at least one plant is green and appealing to cattle."

Break the second half into two parts: "cheatgrass ——" and "only with dry, barbed and almost inedible ——."

Look for opposites: "Green and appealing to cattle" is opposite to "dry, barbed and . . . inedible." "Diverse native community" could be opposite to "cheat-grass ——" Only (D) fits. A monoculture is one culture, the opposite of a diverse community.

Read the sentence. Sound OK with *forage?* Yes. *Forage* is fodder, provender, or food for cattle.

Unlike a diverse native community in which at least one plant is green and appealing to cattle, cheat-grass *monocultures* most often present cattle only with dry, barbed and almost inedible *forage*.

8. Correct choice (D) accept..hypothesized

The word "although" is a flag. It suggests that the verb in the first clause will be an opposite of or contrast with the verb in the second clause. (Notice that both the first and second clauses share the same subject—contemporary psychologists.) So you want to look for a verb that contrasts with the verb *reject*, such as *accept* or *espouse*. Looks like choices (D) and (E) might work.

In the third clause of the sentence, the word "first" is also a flag. The sentence tells us, in so many words, that the theory of the unconscious originated with Sigmund Freud in the nineteenth century. So we need a verb that means brought into existence or identified, such as *predicted*, *entertained*, or *hypothesized*. Looks like choices (B), (C), or (D) might work.

But we can rule out choices (B) and (C) because they don't contain a first verb that contrasts with the verb *reject*. So we know that choice (D), the only choice remaining, is the one that works.

Although most psychologists now *accept* some notion of an unconscious mind, many reject the other theories of Sigmund Freud, who first *hypothesized* subliminal consciousness in the late nineteenth century.

9. Correct choice (D) predict..benignity

Long, complex sentence. Similar choices. Examine the choices carefully.

Break the sentence in two. The second part says " . . . the most essential characteristic may be ——, a general concern for mankind's well-being.

Obviously, "a general concern for mankind's well-being" refers to the blank. Only (A) and (D) come close to meaning that. Now try (A) and (D) in the first blank. Here's (A): " . . . certain personal qualities *apprehend* with greater accuracy . . ." And here's (D): " . . . certain personal qualities *predict* with greater accuracy . . ."

Apprehend means "arrest, understand or perceive." *Predict* means "foretell with precision." We need *accuracy*, not general understanding. Choice (D) wins.

While intelligence is a characteristic essential to wisdom, certain other qualities *predict* with greater accuracy who will be wise; the most essential characteristic may be *benignity*, a general concern for mankind's well-being.

10. Correct choice (E) monumental..strategists

No flags here. Work your way through the choices until you find one that works.

There's one clue. Ask yourself, "What sort of corporate people would most likely want *to overwhelm visitors and make them feel insignificant*?" Maybe people who want to put visitors at a disadvantage, awe them, or impress them?

A *strategist* is expert at tricks or plans that gain an advantage over people. *Monumental* means "massive, or imposing, or historic."

Both choices fit the sense of the sentence. Read it back:

The Chrysler Building is a *monumental* structure of glass and cement with a vast entryway, designed by corporate *strategists* to overwhelm visitors and make them feel insignificant.

11. Correct choice (A) mortician:mortuary

judge—someone who makes a living presiding over cases of law.

courtroom—a place where a judge works.

A *judge* works in a *courtroom*.

Does a *mortician* work in a *mortuary?* Yes. Therefore *judge* is to *courtroom* in the same way as *mortician* is to *mortuary*.

12. Correct choice (D) breeze:gale

incision—a cut

gash—a very large cut

A *gash* is an overly large *incision*.

Is a *gale* an overly large *breeze?* Yes, whereas a *gale* is a powerful wind, a *breeze* is a gentle wind. Therefore, *incision* is to *gash* as *breeze* is to *gale*. This is not a great choice, but it is clearly the best choice.

13. Correct choice (D) treatise:print

documentary—a dramatically structured film of an actual event

film—a visual medium

A *documentary* uses the *film* medium.

Does a *treatise* use the *print* medium? Yes. A *treatise* consists of writing that systematically exposes a particular subject in *print*.

14. Correct choice (C) sty:cleanliness

sanctuary—a place of safety

danger—a threat to safety

A *sanctuary* is a place free from *danger*.

Is a *sty* a place free from *cleanliness?* Yes, *sties* are filthy, which makes them free from *cleanliness*. So *sanctuary* is to *danger* as *sty* is to *cleanliness*.

15. Correct choice (B) ingenuous:guile

garbled—distorted, confused, jumbled

coherence—consistent, logical, connected, a natural agreement of parts

If something is *garbled*, it lacks *coherence*.

Does something *ingenuous* lack *guile?* Yes. *Ingenuous* means innocent or free of artful deceit. So, free of *guile*.

16. Correct choice (B) sagacious:wise

bellicose—ready to fight

pugnacious—ready to fight

Bellicose means the same thing as *pugnacious*.

Does *sagacious* mean the same thing as *wise?* Yes, *sagacious* means *wise*. So *bellicose* is to *pugnacious* in the same way that *sagacious* is to *wise*.

17. Correct choice (C) tenuousness:solidity

anemia—lack of power or vitality arising from red blood cell depletion

vitality—remarkable energy or liveliness

Anemia is characterized by a lack of *vitality*.

Is *tenuousness* characterized by a lack of *solidity?* Yes. *Tenuous* means "flimsiness or lack of *solidity*." *Solidity* means "substantialness; firmness and strength."

18. Correct choice (A) rink:skate

pub—a place where alcoholic drinks are served

imbibe—to drink

A *pub* is a place where people (customers) *imbibe*.

Is a *rink* a place where people *skate?* Yes, it is; both ice skating and roller skating. So you can see that *pub* is to *imbibe* as *rink* is to *skate*.

19. Correct choice (C) moist:sodden

tepid—lukewarm, unenthusiastic

torrid—scorchingly hot, intensely emotional

Tepid is a mild quality and *torrid* an extreme quality.

Is *moist* a mild quality and *sodden* an extreme quality? Yes. A *moist* cloth is only slightly wet, whereas a *sodden* cloth is completely soaked.

20. Correct choice (E) trepidation:anxiety

penchant—inclination, strong leaning

proclivity—inclination or predisposition

Penchant means the same as *proclivity*.

Does *trepidation* mean the same as *anxiety?* Yes. *Trepidation* and *anxiety* both mean fear.

21. Correct choice (B) penury:wealth

equanimity—balance or calm, especially under stress

anxiety—apprehension or worry

Equanimity is the absence of *anxiety*.

Is penury the absense of wealth? Yes! P*enury* is poverty. And poverty is the absence of *wealth*.

22. Correct choice (D) mutable:change

prehensile—able to grasp

grasp—to hold or control

Prehensile means able to grasp.

Does *mutable* mean able to *change?* Yes, that's exactly what it means.

23. Correct choice (B) wake:deceased

vitiate—to corrupt or seduce

incorruptible—not corruptible; cannot be perverted or bribed

You cannot *vitiate* someone who is *incorruptible*.

Can you *wake* someone who is *deceased?* No. So *vitiate* is to *incorruptible* as *wake* is to *deceased*.

24. Correct choice (D)

Unlike many writers, the author clarifies the primary purpose of this passage in both the introduction and the conclusion: to explain three main functions of neurons, the basic element of the nervous system. The author outlines the purposes and then follows the outline step by step. When it comes to reading passages on exams, it doesn't get much clearer than this.

25. Correct choice (B)

The extended analogy in paragraph two serves various useful purposes, but the primary purpose is to illustrate how the nervous system relates to other body systems. The author effectively shows this relationship by comparing the nervous system to a large building, an everyday object that most people already understand.

26. Correct choice (A)

The sentence containing the word "agency" gives some indication of how this word is being used. The agency is whatever caused the neuron to respond. This could be a hot stove, a kiss on the cheek, or a pat on the back.

27. Correct choice (B)

In paragraph four, the author makes the point that a single nerve impulse with a corresponding reflex will use at least three neurons to get to the brain: from sense organ to spinal cord, from spinal cord to brain, and from brain to muscle. Getting to the brain, according to the author, would take at least two neurons.

28. Correct choice (B)

The best analogy to describe how a nervous impulse travels from a finger to the brain would be a track team relay. The author states that the impulse (which would be the baton each runner carries at various times in the race) travels through different channels (which would be the runners) until it reaches its destination (which would be the finish line). The other analogies listed have some merit, but none of them work quite as well.

29. Correct choice (C)

In this sentence, the word "constituents" refers to all the parts that make up the nervous system. This would include the various kinds of neurons, the synapses, the chemical transmitters, and even the brain. Although the author does not mention all these constituents, the meaning of the word is fairly clear from the clues given in the sentence that follows.

30. Correct choice (C)

This question is tricky. The best choice is (C) because the author explicitly states that the parts of the nervous system are *not* like random little threads (see paragraph five). However, the author uses the telephone analogy two ways: like the nervous system and not like the nervous system (see next-to-last paragraph). If you didn't fall for this trick, congratulations.

31. Correct choice (E)

Nowhere in the passage does the author mention the regenerative powers of the neuron. The power to modify itself is called "modifiability" and is given as one of the options. The other choices listed are also mentioned by name at some point in the passage. In fact, a common characteristic of this question type is for the answers that are stated explicitly to appear in the same paragraph or close to one another.

32. Correct choice (A)

The best phrase given to describe this passage is "supportively pedagogical," which means the author is something like a very nice teacher who really wants you to learn this stuff. Didn't you get that feeling when you read this? Here is a teacher who presents information in a logical order and with lots of examples.

33. Correct choice (C)

The author would disagree with this statement because he clearly states in paragraph three that no one knows how nerve cells conduct impulses. However, modern science has since discovered how this works. In fact, if you are really savvy about biology, you likely could teach this author a thing or two. If you got this answer wrong because you were smarter than the author, then let this be a lesson to you: You must take each passage for what it is, not for what you know.

34. Correct choice (E)

If our nervous system did not exist, we would have to create it. "Unfathomable" in this context means "cannot be understood."

35. Correct choice (A)

The title that best represents this piece would be "Neurons: Three Amazing Abilities." This title states the topic clearly, hints at the structure, and conveys the author's attitude toward the subject. If all titles were this informative, we would have a much easier time choosing what to read.

Test 2, Section 3: Math Questions and Answers

Assignment for Today:

Take a sample SAT Math Test under actual test conditions. Allow yourself exactly 30 minutes to complete the 25 questions in this test.

Directions: *Solve each problem, and select the appropriate answer choice, A–E.*

1. If $R \times S = -30$, then S is approximately

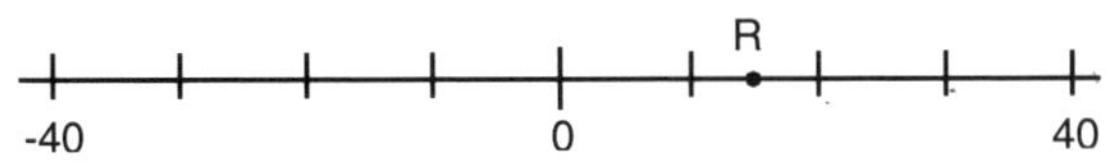

(A) –20
(B) –15
(C) –2
(D) 2
(E) 15

2. Which of the following is the closest value of 600.708?

(A) $600 + \frac{7}{1000}$

(B) $600 + \frac{70}{1000}$

(C) $600 + \frac{71}{1000}$

(D) $600 + \frac{71}{100}$

(E) $600 + \frac{708}{100}$

3. What is the value of $(p + p^2 + p^3 + p^5)$, when $p = -1$?

(A) –11
(B) –4
(C) –2
(D) –1
(E) 0

4. If $3x$, $3x + p$, $3x + 2p$, $3x + 3p$, ... represent consecutive multiples of 3 in increasing order, where x is an integer, which of the following is the *lowest* possible value of p ?

(A) 0

(B) $\frac{1}{3}$

(C) 1

(D) 2

(E) 3

5. The positive root of $\sqrt{4\left(x^2+y^2\right)\left(x^2+y^2\right)}$ is
   (A) 2
   (B) $2x^2+2y^2$
   (C) $2x^2+2\sqrt{2}xy+2y^2$
   (D) $2x^2+4xy+2y^2$
   (E) $4x^2+4y^2$

6. If k, $k + 1$, and $k + 2$ are three consecutive integers and k is divisible by 6, which of the following *must* be true?
   (A) k is divisible by 4
   (B) $k + 1$ is divisible by 2
   (C) $k + 1$ is divisible by 3
   (D) $k + 2$ is divisible by 2
   (E) $k + 2$ is divisible by 3

7.

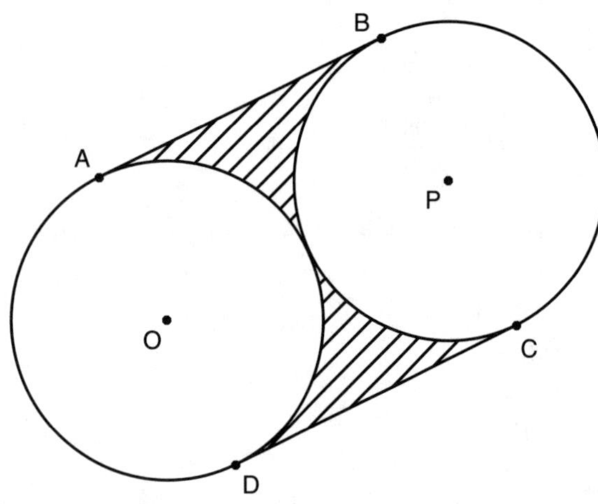

In the figure above, one circle has center at O and the other circle has center at P. Both circles have a radius of 1. The two circles are tangent at one point. Line segments AB and CD are tangent to both the circles. What is the area of the shaded region?
   (A) $1 - \pi$
   (B) $4 - \pi$
   (C) π
   (D) 4
   (B) $4 - 2\pi$

8. If $\left(\frac{a}{b}\right)\left(\frac{b}{c}\right)\left(\frac{c}{d}\right)=\left(\frac{1}{2}\right)\left(\frac{2}{3}\right)\left(\frac{3}{4}\right)$, then $\frac{d}{a}=$
   (A) $\frac{1}{4}$
   (B) $\frac{3}{8}$
   (C) $\frac{6}{9}$
   (D) $\frac{8}{3}$
   (E) $\frac{4}{1}$

9. A swimming pool is 1.5 times as long as it is wide. The depth of the pool is 2 meters. Every week, 5 percent of the water in the pool evaporates. When the pool is filled, 60 cubic meters of water evaporate every week. What is the *length* of the pool in meters?
   (A) 13
   (B) 15
   (C) 20
   (D) 30
   (E) 60

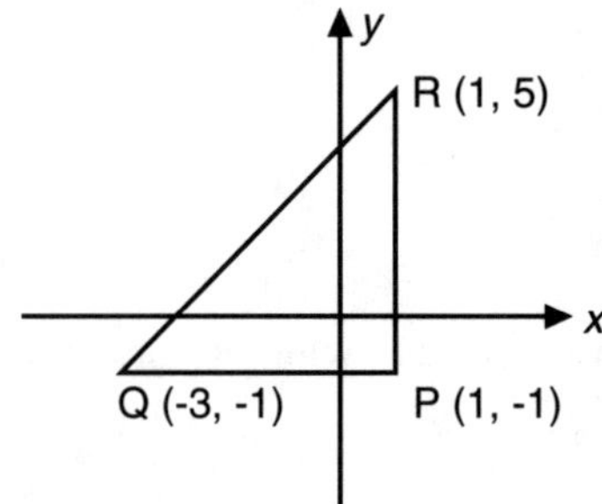

10. In the figure above, if PR is perpendicular to the x–axis and QP is perpendicular to the y–axis, what is the area of triangle PQR?

(A) –12
(B) 8
(C) 10
(D) 12
(E) 24

11. A class of 32 students has a male–to-female ratio of 3:5. What fraction of the class is female?

(A) $\frac{3}{8}$
(B) $\frac{2}{5}$
(C) $\frac{15}{32}$
(D) $\frac{5}{8}$
(E) $\frac{5}{3}$

12. If $a > b > c > d$ where a and b are the two highest factors of 12, and c and d are the two lowest positive factors of 12, what is the value of $a \times d$?

(A) 6
(B) 12
(C) 13
(D) 24
(E) 48

13. If $\frac{t-3}{12} = \frac{-1}{t+5}$, and $t < 0$, what is the value of $(t - 5)$?

(A) –10
(B) –8
(C) –4
(D) –3
(E) –2

14. At 2:00 P.M., Jack wants to bake some cookies for his party that starts later that afternoon at 5:00 P.M. If it takes 20 minutes to make a batch of 12 cookies, how many cookies can Jack make at this rate before the party begins?

(A) 36
(B) 60
(C) 108
(D) 300
(E) 720

15. A station wagon averages 15 miles per gallon while a small two–door car averages 25 miles per gallon. If gasoline costs $1.50 per gallon, how much more would the gasoline cost for a 900-mile trip in the station wagon than in the two-door car?

(A) $15
(B) $16
(C) $18
(D) $24
(E) $36

16. At 10 A.M., a parking lot has 14 cars. At 11:00 A.M., the number of cars in the parking lot increases to 21. At this rate, at what time will the parking lot be full if it can hold a maximum of 49 cars?

(A) 3:00 P.M.
(B) 4:00 P.M.
(C) 5:00 P.M.
(D) 6:00 P.M.
(E) 7:00 P.M.

17. The sum of one fifth of an odd integer and twice the next consecutive odd integer is 59. What is the least even integer greater than both of these odd integers?

(A) 8
(B) 24
(C) 26
(D) 28
(E) 29

lons is butane. Container B has 8 gallons of fuel, of which an unknown amount is butane. When fuel from container A is mixed with fuel from container B, the mixture has 18 percent butane by volume. What was the butane content in container B as a percentage of total volume of fuel in container B before mixing?

(A) 1.2%

(B) 12%

(C) 15%

(D) 18%

(E) 30%

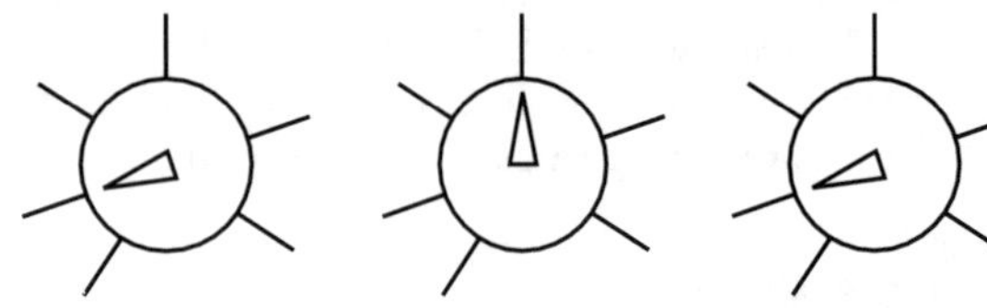

19. An audio technician has control of three dials, each with 6 settings, as shown in the figure above. If the rightmost dial is never to be set to its highest setting, how many possible settings are there?

(A) 17

(B) 180

(C) 216

(D) 665

(E) 729

20. Let the {} operator be defined by the following equation:

$$\{y\} = \begin{cases} 5-y & \text{if } y \leq 5 \\ y-5 & \text{if } y > 5 \end{cases}$$

The product of {6} and {3} is

(A) {–2}

(B) {2}

(C) {3}

(D) {9}

(E) {18}

21. When a rock is thrown into a pond, a circular wave is created such that its radius doubles every second. Two seconds after the rock hits the water, the radius of the wave is 10 feet. What is the surface area enclosed by the wave 5 seconds after the rock is thrown?

(A) 100π ft^2

(B) 160π ft^2

(C) $2{,}500\pi$ ft^2

(D) $3{,}600\pi$ ft^2

(E) $6{,}400\pi$ ft^2

22. Each page of a roster has cells formed by the intersection of horizontal and vertical lines. The first page has twice as many rows as columns. The second page has 3 times as many rows as columns and the third page has 4 times as many rows as columns. Which of the following could *not* be the total number of cells in the 3 pages of the roster?

(A) 9

(B) 18

(C) 36

(D) 81

(E) 441

23. There are two plants in Lani's living room. The first plant is 7 inches tall and grows at the rate of 1 inch per week. The second plant is 3 inches tall and grows 2 inches per week. In how many weeks will the second plant be 50 percent taller than the first plant?

(A) $\frac{1}{3}$

(B) $1\frac{1}{4}$

(C) 4

(D) 15

(E) 18

24. An army unit has 3 radars that beep at different intervals. Radar 1 beeps every 3 minutes, Radar 2 beeps every 7 minutes, and Radar 3 beeps every 13 minutes. All three radars beeped together at 11:00 A.M. When will the three radars beep together again?

(A) 11:23 A.M.

(B) 2:13 P.M.

(C) 3:33 P.M.

(D) 4:33 P.M.

(E) 5:33 P.M.

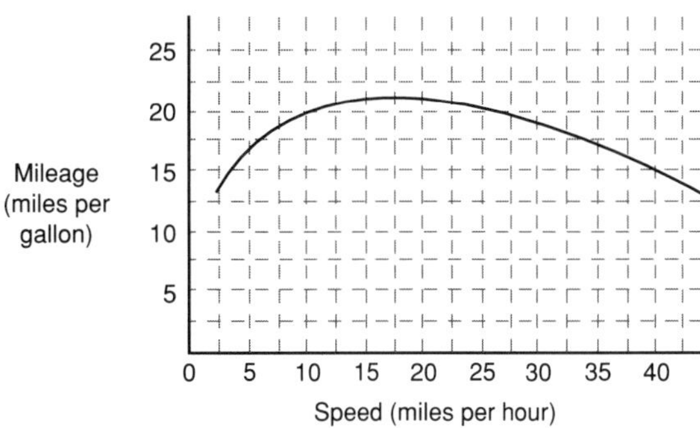

25. The figure above shows the mileage obtained by a vehicle traveling at various speeds. The vehicle leaves home, traveling at 40 miles per hour for 15 minutes. It then returns home, following the same route, at a speed of 10 miles per hour. The amount of gas consumed by the vehicle on the return trip is approximately what percent of the total amount of gas consumed by the vehicle on the entire trip?

(A) 43

(B) 50

(C) 53

(D) 63

(E) 67

Quick Answer Guide

Test 2, Section 3: Math

1. C
2. D
3. C
4. E
5. B
6. D
7. B
8. E
9. D
10. D
11. D
12. B
13. B
14. C
15. E
16. A
17. D
18. C
19. B
20. C
21. E
22. B
23. D
24. C
25. A

For explanations to these questions, see Day 24.

Day 24

Test 2, Section 3: Math

Explanations and Strategies

Assignment for Today:

Review the explanations for the test you just took.

1. Correct choice (C) –2

Notice there are 4 divisions from 0 to 40. This means each division is about 10. Point R is about 1.5 divisions, or 15. We want to find S such that $R \times S = -30$

$$R \times S = -30$$
$$15 \times S = -30$$
$$15S = -30$$
$$S = \frac{-30}{15}$$
$$S = -2$$

2. Correct choice (D) $600 + \frac{71}{100}$

The first number after the decimal point is in the tenth position, which means 0.7 is equal to 7/10. The second number after the decimal point is in the hundredth position, which means 0.07 is equal to 7/100. Note that 0.70 is the same as 0.7 and so 0.70 is equal to 70/100 or 7/10. In the same way, the third number after the decimal point is in the thousandth position, which means 0.007 is equal to 7/1000. Now, let's apply the same rules to the number 600.708.

The "7" is in the tenth position, so we should scan the answers for any choice that has 7/10. None. Let's keep going. We know that 0.70 is 70/100. Is there a choice that has 70/100 ? Well, choice (D) has 71/100, which is even closer than 70/100 because of the 8 in the last position. The only other possible choice is choice (E), but then, it has 708 at the top. For choice (E) to be the right answer, the number at the bottom should be 1,000, not 100. So, the correct answer is choice (D).

3. Correct choice (C) –2

If we plug in –1 for p, we get:

$$\begin{aligned} p + p^2 + p^3 + p^5 &= (-1) + (-1)^2 + (-1)^3 + (-1)^5 \\ &= -1 + 1 - 1 - 1 \\ &= -2 \end{aligned}$$

Don't forget, when –1 is raised to an even power (like 2, 4, 6, etc.), we get +1. When it's raised to an odd power (like 1, 3, 5, etc.), we get –1.

4. Correct choice (E) 3

Of the given terms, we know that $3x$ is the lowest multiple of 3. Think of x as 1. Then the lowest term is $3 \times 1 = 3$. If 3 is the lowest multiple of 3, then the next multiple should be 3 more than 3, which is 6.

Then, the term $3x + p$ should equal 6. If $x = 1$, then p has to equal 3 so that $3x + p$ can equal 6. The next higher term is $3x + 2p$, which then becomes $3 \times 1 + 2 \times 3 = 3 + 6 = 9$, which works. So, the lowest value of p is (E) 3.

Or, start from the choices. p cannot equal 0 because then all terms would be $3x$. If p equals $\frac{1}{3}$, then the second term, $3x + p$ would be only $\frac{1}{3}$ more than the first term, which means it cannot be a multiple of 3.

Similarly, p cannot equal 1 because the second term would then be only 1 more than the first. It is clear that each term has to increase by 3, which means p has to equal 3.

5. Correct choice (B) $2x^2 + 2y^2$

Notice that, within the radical sign, there are two perfect squares: 4 is a perfect square and $(x^2 + y^2)(x^2 + y^2)$ is a perfect square because it has the same two terms being multiplied by each other.

$$\sqrt{4(x^2+y^2)(x^2+y^2)} = \sqrt{2^2(x^2+y^2)^2}$$

To get rid of the radical sign, we just take the square root of both quantities.

$$\sqrt{4(x^2+y^2)(x^2+y^2)} = 2(x^2 + y^2)$$

As we scan the answers, we see that we need to get rid of the parentheses.

So, $\sqrt{4(x^2+y^2)(x^2+y^2)} = 2x^2 + 2y^2$

This is choice (B).

6. Correct choice (D) $k + 2$ is divisible by 2

We're told that k is divisible by 6. Let's plug in a real number for k. We can plug in 6 because 6 is divisible by 6. Then, the three consecutive numbers k, $k + 1$, and $k + 2$ are: 6, 7, and 8.

Now, let's look at the choices. Look at (A): Is 6 divisible by 4? No. Zap choice (A). How about(B)? Is 7 $(k + 1)$ divisible by 2? No. Zap choice (B). Next, (C): Is 7 divisible by 3? No. Zap choice (C).

So, look at (D): Is 8 $(k + 2)$ divisible by 2? Yes. This is it. Finally, (E): Is 8 divisible by 3? No. Zap it.

So, the correct answer is choice (D). Notice, if k is divisible by 6, it has to be an even number. If k is an even number, $k + 2$ must also be an even number. So $k + 2$ is always divisible by 2.

7. Correct choice (B) $4–\pi$

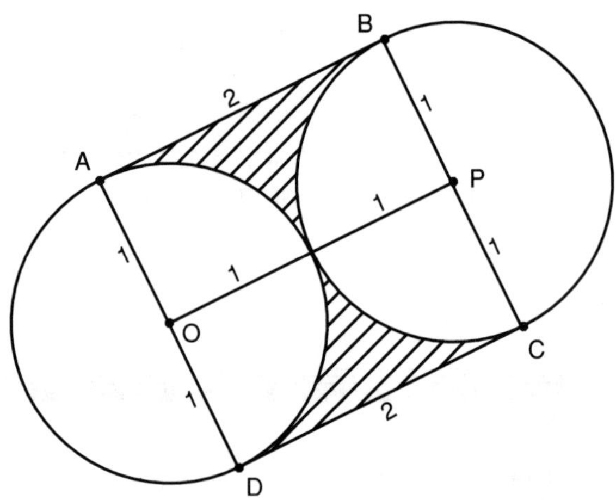

Let's mark on the given diagram. We know that the radius of each circle is 1. That means the diameters are 2. So $OP = 2$, $AB = 2$, and $CD = 2$. AD and BC are also diameters. So $AD = 2$ and $BC = 2$. Then, we can see that the shaded region is completely enclosed by a square of side 2. This square has an area of 4.

Area of one circle = $\pi r^2 = \pi(1)^2 = \pi$

How many circles are in the square region $ABCD$? $ABCD$ contains half of circle O and half of circle P. In other words, it contains 1 full circle, which has an area of π.

To find the area of the shaded region, we first find the area of the square $ABCD$ and then remove from it the area of one circle.

So, area of shaded region = area of $ABCD$ – area of 1 circle = $4 - \pi$

8. Correct choice (E) $\frac{4}{1}$

This is an easy problem—if we cancel. Notice that the b's and the c's cancel so that $\left(\frac{a}{b}\right)\left(\frac{b}{c}\right)\left(\frac{c}{d}\right)$ becomes $\frac{a}{d}$. On the right side of the equation, the 2's and the 3's cancel so that $\left(\frac{1}{2}\right)\left(\frac{2}{3}\right)\left(\frac{3}{4}\right)$ becomes $\frac{1}{4}$.

So, $\frac{a}{d} = \frac{1}{4}$. Then, if we invert both sides, we get $\frac{d}{a}=\frac{4}{1}$.

9. Correct choice (D) 30

We're told that 5 percent of the water evaporates. So, if 60 cubic meters evaporate, 5 percent of the volume is 60 cubic meters (we know it's volume and not area because the unit of water is *cubic* meters, not square meters).

If 5% is 60, 10% must be twice 60, or 120. And so 100% must be 12 × 10 = 1,200 meters, which is the volume of the pool.

But, volume = length × width × depth

So, 1,200 = length × width × 2

Or, 600 = length × width

Now, we can plug in values from the problem and see which one works. As usual, we start with choice (C) 20. Remember, we're looking for the length of the pool. So, let's plug in 20 as the length.

Then, 600 = 20 × width

This tells us that the width is 30. This is impossible, because the length is supposed to be 1.5 times the width. You can't have length as 20 and width as 30! So, the value of length we plugged in, choice (C), is too low. If choice (C) is too low, choices (A) and (B) are also too low. So, zap choices (A), (B), and (C).

Let's try choice (D) 30. If the length is 30,

then 600 = 30 × width

This tells us that the width is 20. So, the length (30) *is* 1.5 times the width (20). This is the right answer.

10. Correct choice (D) 12

The coordinate plane should not confuse us! It's really very easy. To find the area of a triangle, remember the good old formula "$\frac{1}{2}$ base times height"? Let's use the given coordinates to find the lengths of sides PQ and PR. PQ is 4—we start at Q and count over 4 to P. PR is 6—we start at P and count six moves to R. Now, we plug them into the formula and we're done!

$$\text{Area} = \frac{1}{2} \times PQ \times PR$$

That is,

$$\text{Area} = \frac{1}{2} \times 4 \times 6 = 12$$

Also, we could actually measure the length and width of the triangle and use the formula, $\frac{1}{2}$ base × height, to find the area.

11. Correct choice (D) $\frac{5}{8}$

To do ratio problems like this, first we should add the two ratios and make the sum the denominator. So, our denominator (number at the bottom of a fraction) is 3 + 5 = 8. The numerator (number at the top) is the number that goes with what we want to find. In this problem, we want the ratio for *girls*, which means 5 should go on top. So, the fraction of the class that is female is $\frac{5}{8}$.

In the same way, if we'd been asked to find the fraction that is male, our denominator would be the same (3 + 5 = 8), but our numerator would be the number that goes with the boys in the class, which is 3.

Notice we had no use for the total number of students in the class to solve this problem.

12. Correct choice (B) 12

We know that a is the largest factor of 12. Well, the largest factor of 12 is 12 itself (it is not 6, mind you). And d is the lowest positive factor of 12, which is 1. Then, finding out $a \times d$ is easy: 12 × 1 = 12, choice (B).

13. Correct choice (B) –8

Let's avoid what they tell us in grade school about cross–multiplying. We'll plug in values instead. Let's start with the number in the middle, choice (C) –4, and plug it in for the value of $t - 5$. If $-4 = t - 5$, then t has to equal 1. But t cannot equal 1 because we are told that t is less than 0. Well, if $t - 5$ cannot equal choice (C), it cannot equal (D) or (E) because all those choices are larger than –4. So zap (C), (D), and (E).

Then let's try (B) –8. If $t - 5 = -8$, then $t = -3$. Let's plug in the value of t in the given equation. We get

$$\frac{-3-3}{12} = \frac{-1}{-3+5}$$

That is, $$\frac{-6}{12} = \frac{-1}{2}$$

This works because the left side of the equation is equal to the right side, which is $-\frac{1}{2}$. So (B) is the correct answer.

14. Correct choice (C) 108

Jack has three hours before the party begins at 5:00 P.M. First, let's see how many cookies Jack can bake in 1 hour. In 20 minutes, he can bake 12 cookies. Then, in 60 minutes (which is 1 hour), he can bake 3 times as many, which is $12 \times 3 = 36$ cookies.

He has 3 hours to go. So he can make a total of $36 \times 3 = 108$ cookies, which is choice (C).

15. Correct choice (E) 36

Take this problem in steps and it should be no problem. First, we need to find out how many gallons each car will need for the trip. To do this, we divide the total miles of the trip by each car's gas mileage. Make two columns, one for each car.

Wagon	*Two-door*
$\frac{900}{15} = 60$	$\frac{900}{25} = 36$

Now, let's figure out the difference in the amount of gas the two cars used during the trip.

$60 - 36 = 24$. So, the station wagon used 24 gallons more for the trip than the small car. Now, we use the cost of gas to find the price difference. Let's multiply the cost per gallon by the difference in the number of miles. $1.5 \times 24 = 36$. The large car used \$36 more gasoline than the small car.

Notice how we didn't need to find the total cost of gas for each car before finding the difference.

16. Correct choice (A) 3:00 P.M.

Between 10 and 11:00 A.M., the number of cars in the lot increases from 14 to 21. This means that there are 7 cars entering the lot every hour.

At 11:00 A.M., there already are 21 cars. So, for the lot to be full (49 cars), the number of additional cars = 49 – 21 = 28. If there are 7 cars entering the lot every hour, the lot will be full in 28 ÷ 7 = 4 hours after 11:00 A.M., which is 3:00 P.M.

Or, you can work the problem this way, once you know that there are 7 cars entering the parking lot every hour. At 11, there are 21 cars. At 12, there will be 21 + 7 = 28 cars.

At 1, there will be 28 + 7 = 35 cars

At 2, there will be 35 + 7 = 42 cars

At 3, there will be 42 + 7 = 49 cars

17. Correct choice (D) 28

Let's start from the answers. As always, we start from choice (C) 26. If 26 is the least even integer greater than the other two consecutive odd integers, then, the two consecutive odd integers must be 25 (which is 1 less than 26) and 23 (which is the next smaller odd integer). Do these numbers work?

We're told that the sum of one-fifth of an odd integer (that is, $\frac{1}{5}$ of 23, which is 4 plus some) and twice the next consecutive odd integer (2×25, which is 50) is 59. This is not going to work because a bit more than 4 and 50 do not add up to 59. Too small. Well, if choice (C) is too small, so are choices (A) and (B). Zap them all.

Let's try choice (D) 28. If 28 is the least even integer greater than the other two consecutive odd integers, then, the other two consecutive odd integers must be 27 (which is 1 less than 28) and 25 (which is the next smaller odd integer). Do these numbers work?

We're told that the sum of one-fifth of an odd integer (that is, $\frac{1}{5}$ of 25, which is 5) and twice the next consecutive odd integer (2×27, which is 54) is 59. Well, 5 plus 54 *does* equal 59. Choice (D) 28 works, and so it's the right answer.

18. Correct choice (C) 15%

Let's work from our answer choices. As usual, we start from choice (C) 15%. This is the percentage of butane in container B before mixing fuel from the two containers.

We know that container B had 8 gallons. If it had 15% butane, its butane content would be $.15 \times 8 = 1.2$ gallons. So, if 1.2 gallons of butane came from container B and 0.6 gallons came from container A, the total butane content of the mixture should be $1.2 + 0.6 = 1.8$ gallons. Is this right? Well, the mixture had 18% butane and 10 gallons total volume, which means it had $.18 \times 10 = 1.8$ gallons of butane. Yes, it matches, and so this is the right answer.

19. Correct choice (B) 180

There are 6 possible settings for the first two dials, and 5 for the third one (since we cannot set the third dial to its highest setting). To count the number of ways that we can set all dials, we *multiply* the number of possible settings for each dial with the others. Doing this, we get:

6 settings for dial #1

6 settings for dial #2

$\times$ 5 settings for dial #3

180 total settings for all three dials

20. Correct choice (C) {3}

To use the {} operators, we simply follow the pattern described in the operator's definition.

$$\{y\} = \begin{cases} 5-y & \text{if } y \le 5 \\ y-5 & \text{if } y > 5 \end{cases}$$

Since 6 is more than 5, $\{6\} = 6-5 = 1$

And since 3 is less than 5, $\{3\} = 5-3 = 2$

So $\{6\} \times \{3\} = 1 \times 2 = 2$

So the answer to this problem should be 2. Let's look at the answer choices. Choice (A), –2 is less than 5. So, $\{-2\} = 5 - (-2) = 7$. Doesn't work, so zap this choice.

Choice (B), 2 is less than 5. So, $\{-2\} = 5 - (-2) = 7$. No. Zap choice (B), too. Choice (C), 3 is less than 5. So, $\{3\} = 5 - 3 = 2$. So, this choice works and it's our answer.

21. Correct choice (E) 6,400π ft^2

The key here is to find the radius of the wave 5 seconds after the rock is thrown. Then, the "surface area enclosed by the wave" simply means we have to find the area of a circle with that particular radius.

We know that the radius at 2 seconds is 10 feet. It doubles every second. So, the radius at 3 seconds is 20 feet (2×10). The radius at 4 seconds is 40 feet (2×20) and the radius at 5 seconds is 80 feet (2×40).

So, if the radius of the circle is 80 feet, then its surface area is $\pi r^2 = \pi(80)^2 = 6{,}400\pi$.

22. Correct choice (B) 18

Let's assume that the each page has C columns. Then, the first page is supposed to have twice as many rows as columns, which means the first page has $2C$ rows.

So, number of cells = number of rows $\times$ number of columns $= 2C \times C = 2C^2$.

If the second page has C columns, the number of rows is three times the number of columns. So, the number of rows $= 3C$.

Then, number of cells

$$= 3C \times C = 3C^2$$

For the third page, number of cells

$$= C \times 4C = 4C^2$$

Then, total number of cells

$$= 2C^2 + 3C^2 + 4C^2 = 9C^2$$

We see that the total number of cells is always a product of 9 and a perfect square. In other words, if C is 2, the total number of cells is $9 \times 4 = 36$, which is a product of 9 and a perfect square (4).

Now let's look at the answer choices and see which choice is not a product of 9 and a perfect square. Choice (A), $9 = 9 \times 1$ (1 is a perfect square). Choice (B), $18 = 9 \times 2$ (2 is *not* a perfect square).

Choice (C), $36 = 9 \times 4$ (4 is a perfect square). Choice (D), $81 = 9 \times 9$ (9 is a perfect square). Choice (E), $441 = 9 \times 49$ (49 is a perfect square).

Only choice (B) is not a perfect square, and so it is the correct answer.

23. Correct choice (D) 15

Let's start from the answer choices. As usual, we start from choice (C) 4. In 4 weeks, the first plant grows 4 inches (because it grows 1 inch per week). It was already 7 inches tall, so, at the end of 4 weeks, it is 7 + 4 = 11 inches tall.

In 4 weeks, the second plant grows 8 inches (because it grows 2 inches per week). It was 3 inches tall, so, at the end of 4 weeks, it is 3 + 8 = 11 inches tall. Notice that after 4 weeks, the two plants are equal in height. The second plant is catching up, but after 4 weeks, it has managed to be only as tall as the first plant. We need to know how long it takes to become 50% taller.

So, for the second plant to be taller than the first plant, we need more time. In other words, choice (C) isn't large enough. Well, if choice (C) is too low, choices (A) and (B) are also too low. Zap (A), (B), and (C).

Let's try choice (D), 15. In 15 weeks the height of the first plant is 7 + (15 × 1) = 22 inches. And, the height of the second plant is 3 + (15 × 2) = 33. Is 33 50% more than 22? Well, 50% of 22 is 11, and 11 plus 22 is 33. So, 33 *is* 50% more than 22 and choice (D) is the right answer.

24. Correct choice (C) 3:33 P.M.

Here we need to find the common multiple of 3, 7, and 13 to find how many minutes after 11:00 A.M. the three radars will beep together. Notice that 3, 7, and 13 are all prime numbers. To find the common multiple of 3 prime numbers, we just multiply them. So, the common multiple of 3, 7, and 13 is 3 × 7 × 13 = 273.

In other words, the 3 radars will beep together 273 minutes after 11:00 A.M. Dividing by 60, we get 4 hours and 33 minutes (because 4 × 60 + 33 = 273). What is 4 hours and 33 minutes after 11:00 A.M.? It is 3:33 P.M., which is choice (C).

25. Correct choice (A) 43

This is a tough problem. On the test, if you see a question like this, it's best to take a guess and bail out. But watch how we can take a smart guess. We're asked to find the amount of gas consumed on the return trip as a percent of the total amount of gas. Let's look at the chart.

We know that the return trip gives more miles per gallon (20 at 10 m.p.h.) than the first trip (15 miles per gallon at 40 m.p.h.). In other words, the return trip consumes less fuel than the first trip. So, if we want the gas consumed on the return trip as a percent of the total consumption, the answer has to be less than 50%. Know why? Because if the two trips consumed equal amounts, they would both be 50% of the total. But if one consumes less than the other, it will be less than 50% of the total. Look at the answers. Only one answer choice is less than 50%—choice (A). So, choice (A) has to be the answer.

If you wanted to solve the problem, here's how you'd do it.

For the first trip, the vehicle travels at 40 miles per hour for 15 minutes. That means it travels for one quarter of an hour. If it travels 40 miles in one hour, it travels one quarter of 40 = 10 miles in 15 minutes. Now let's look at the chart for 40 miles per hour. The miles per gallon is 15. So, the vehicle gives 15 miles per gallon. But it traveled only 10 miles. So, the amount of gas it consumed is: $10 \div 15 = \frac{2}{3}$ gallon.

We know that the first trip was 10 miles. So, the return trip was also 10 miles. The speed was 10 miles per hour. From the chart, at 10 miles per hour, the mileage is 20. In other words, the vehicle gives 20 miles per gallon. Since it traveled for only 10 miles, the amount of gas it consumed is $\frac{1}{2}$ gallon.

So, total gas consumed =

$$\frac{2}{3} + \frac{1}{2} = \frac{4+3}{6} = \frac{7}{6} \text{ gallons}$$

Then, percent gas consumed on the return trip as a percent of the total consumption is:

(gas on return trip) ÷ (total gas)

$$\frac{1}{2} \div \frac{7}{6} = \frac{1}{2} \times \frac{6}{7} = \frac{3}{7}$$

We need to express $\frac{3}{7}$ as a percentage, so we multiply by 100 to get $\frac{3}{7} \times 100$ = approximately 43%.

Test 2, Section 4: Verbal

Questions and Answers

Assignment for Today:

Take a sample SAT Verbal Test under actual test conditions. Allow yourself exactly 30 minutes to complete the 30 questions in this test.

Directions: *For questions 1–9, one or more words have been left out of each sentence. Circle the answer, A–E, which contains the word or words which best fit the meaning of the entire sentence.*

1. There is something in the American mindset that doesn't see something wrong with disposing of garbage, or anything else —— to carry, in a beautiful forest or along a scenic highway.

   (A) expedient
   (B) inadequate
   (C) exhilarating
   (D) inconsiderate
   (E) inconvenient

2. Most chemists believe that the course of a chemical reaction is ——, but some catalytic reactions in both inorganic and organic chemistry can behave in bizarre and —— ways.

   (A) corrosive..mundane
   (B) saturated..irrational
   (C) transient..premature
   (D) predictable..unruly
   (E) expendable..deviant

3. After exploring the desert south of Tucson for eight years, Rimal became —— the trials of desert life and eventually learned to subsist with the most —— requirements for life.

   (A) displeased with..lavish
   (B) inured to..rudimentary
   (C) hardened to..elaborate
   (D) enchanted with..fundamental
   (E) attracted to..scanty

4. The TV executive cancelled the popular soap opera last fall, but the —— of angry phone calls and letters convinced her to —— her decision.

   (A) decline..sustain
   (B) dearth..retract
   (C) flood..revive
   (D) spate..reverse
   (E) increase..execute

5. The oil industry's —— on the western Siberian plain is transmuting what once was a pristine environment into a ——landscape of almost unimaginable proportions.
   (A) entrenchment..fertile
   (B) drilling..luxurious
   (C) assault..blighted
   (D) irrigation..lush
   (E) operation..ravaged

6. Dr. Shilling was upset that the computer center was ——; furthermore, she felt that the computer support staff was ——.
   (A) advanced..inaccessible
   (B) locked..friendly
   (C) dirty..religious
   (D) damaged..agreeable
   (E) outdated..incompetent

7. The irrevocable fact about twins and triplets is that their brothers and sisters will always be their ——; they can't ever quite leave them.
   (A) enemies
   (B) contemporaries
   (C) cacophonies
   (D) personalities
   (E) absentees

8. Because Mann was a consummate ——, he often bristled at the way politicians —— the affairs of the day.
   (A) consumer..affected
   (B) chef..described
   (C) flatterer..overworked
   (D) physicist..recalled
   (E) patriot..mishandled

9. When the young boy wouldn't stop talking, his teacher decided he would make a good politician because he was so ——.
   (A) loquacious
   (B) ingenuous
   (C) pedantic
   (D) vacuous
   (E) taciturn

Directions: *For questions 10–15, determine the relationship between the two words given in capital letters. Then, from the choices listed A–E, select the one pair that has a relationship most similar to that of the capitalized pair. Circle the letter of that pair.*

---

10. PULSE:LIFE::
   (A) heart:beat
   (B) birth:blood
   (C) bloom:spring
   (D) love:death
   (E) breath:rhythm

11. BANKRUPT:ASSETS::
   (A) indecisive:alternatives
   (B) balding:hair
   (C) fatigued:desiccation
   (D) convicted:morality
   (E) comatose:consciousness

12. VINTNER:WINE::
   (A) professor:students
   (B) poet:anthologies
   (C) historian:artifacts
   (D) physicist:trees
   (E) baker:bread

13. RAUCOUS:STRIDENT::
   (A) turbid:cloudy
   (B) confused:penetrating
   (C) choleric:gloomy
   (D) preemptive:unusual
   (E) logical:emotional

14. SYLVAN:WOODS::
    (A) country:bumpkin
    (B) pine:conifer
    (C) sculpture:stone
    (D) branch:tree
    (E) pastor:parish

15. PULCHRITUDINOUS:REDOUBTABLE::
    (A) helpful:tyrannizing
    (B) painful:agonizing
    (C) mournful:raucous
    (D) careful:nonchalant
    (E) joyful:tantalizing

Directions: *Answer the questions that follow each passage. Base your answers only on what is stated or implied in the passage and any introductory material given.*

Questions 16–34 are based on the passage that follows.

What constitutes the vital in the literature of imagination? What is the indescribable power that makes one book great and another commonplace? Not style, not plot, not analysis. Neither Thackeray nor Dickens is a master of style; neither is strikingly original in plot; but both live. The answer to the question that has so often perplexed writer and reader who attempt to find the source of the mysterious power that eludes discovery but reveals itself in a great book is to be found in one word—creation.

The vital in literature—the literature of imagination—is originality. Not the meretricious originality of trick or dialect or forced contrast; not the sordid parade of vice or the refinement of virtue; not the flaunting of passion or the subjecting of emotion—these do not constitute originality as the test is applied to literature. Originality—creation—means something more than a mere catalog of motives; it means the power to create a reproductive type; to visualize life; to project on the screen of existence a figure that is immediately recognized.

The writer of fiction appeals to the imagination and emotions first, the intellect afterward. There is no person so dull or so unimaginative who has not at some time been vaguely conscious that some other person with whom he was brought in contact typified the primitive emotions of which the person had understanding. The more limited the power of imagination, the more stunted the power of expression, the more powerful that type becomes. The servant who believes he has been unjustly treated by a master will forever afterward measure all meanness and injustice by the standard his imagination has created. The child's teacher who has shown partiality or vindictiveness is for many years to that child the antitype of all objectionable teachers.

Human nature is controlled by symbolism; unconsciously, it is true, but the unconscious emotions, like the mechanical functions, are the most powerful. Deep-seated in every human understanding is an immanent and instinctive desire to find a symbol for expression. The power of expression is limited; expression is genius. But although the average person is denied the gift of expression, its desire is never absent; ceaselessly, it beats on the back of the brain like a prisoner pounding with naked hands on the stone walls of his cell. To every human being, at least once in a lifetime, there comes the illumination of symbolic understanding; not, of course, the same understanding to all persons, but graduated according to their intellect and power of imagination. To some, it is a flash so fleeting that, like the ripple of a moonbeam on a lake, it comes but to disappear, and is as intangible as the color it reflects; to other persons it is like the setting sun of tropical seas, when sky gives to wave its burnished gold, and ocean, molten in its riot of color, slowly fades into the blackness of night.

16. The primary purpose of the passage is to
    (A) instruct the reader in writing the literature of creation
    (B) describe the style of great writers such as Dickens
    (C) identify the chief characteristic of what makes truly great literature
    (D) compare the literary abilities of different classes of human beings
    (E) demonstrate that the literature of imagination is the same as the literature of creation

17. The author uses the word "vital" in lines 1 and 12 to mean
    (A) kernel of life
    (B) vibrant
    (C) very important
    (D) life giving
    (E) animated

18. The passage implies that "creation"
    (A) is a quality that Dickens lacked in his writing.
    (B) is a careful cataloging of emotions
    (C) is similar to imitation but works on a more ethereal level
    (D) is exactly the same as originality
    (E) is the immanent desire to find a symbol for expression

19. The author uses the example of the servant to show
    (A) how masters sometimes mistreat their servants and do them a great injustice
    (B) that slavery is wrong in all circumstances
    (C) how those with limited imagination form indelible impressions
    (D) that children remember vindictive teachers for a long time
    (E) that all people often form impressions that need to be modified later

20. The author would most likely *disagree* with which of the following statements?
    (A) Symbolism works on an unconscious level.
    (B) Fiction appeals strongly to the emotions.
    (C) People understand literature at different levels.
    (D) All people seek a way to express themselves.
    (E) Not all human beings have a moment of symbolic understanding.

21. The author ends the passage with two visual metaphors in order to
    (A) illustrate the varying levels of symbolic understanding
    (B) describe what it feels like for people to gain understanding in different contexts
    (C) demonstrate how vivid writing can lead to originality and creation
    (D) use language in new ways that will stimulate the reader's mind
    (E) help readers know how important visual metaphors are in the writing of creation

Questions 22–30 are based on the passage that follows.

The function of thoughts and feelings—the work they do, the service they perform, their share in the business of life—is to influence actions. While mental states may seem to be important, what we actually *do* to help or harm our fellow citizens is what counts. Only when a person's ideas and emotions have some effect on one's deeds, words, gestures, facial expression or other bodily acts, do they make any difference to anyone else. And though it would be a long task to explain why, it is only when such thoughts influence acts of body that they make any permanent difference. Unless mental states result in acts that alter the physical world or the bodies and minds of others, they are of no service, and would just as well be nonexistent.

But sooner or later, directly or indirectly, every mental state is expressed or worked off in causing or inhibiting bodily movements or brain changes. That is what we now see to be their reason for being. We feel the outside world in order that we may react to it. We remember and learn and reason in order that we may modify our reactions to it. The great majority of our feelings have as their function to change our behavior.

The great majority of our actions are done in response to and under the guidance of mental states. Getting up, dressing, eating breakfast, the work of business or study, what we say, where we go—the entire course of day's doings minus the merely physiological activities of digestion, circulation, and the like—represent the stimulation to and control of conduct by thought. The history of a person's life of action as a whole, is the history of the changes in his natural make-up which have been wrought by his mental life. The steel which always reacts uniformly to the magnet by approach—the acid and metal which always react by combining to form hydrogen and a salt—these give no sight that they possess feelings; but in the animal kingdom in proposition as we find the power to change the individual's responses to conditions, to adapt behavior to circumstances, in the same proposition we find evidences of conscious life.

It is a common mistake to speak of mental states as a means to knowledge as if that were their final goal. Mental states are not in all cases means to knowledge. Many of our emotions and impulses furnish us only with tendencies to act. For instance, love and envy do not enlighten our minds with respect to their objects but only change our dispositions toward them. When mental states are means to knowledge, the knowledge itself is really valuable chiefly as a means to action. It would be of little advantage to have sensations of cold or knowledge of the physiological effects of low temperature if one never was moved thereby to put on a coat or build a fire. The reasoning of the mathematician is profitless until it is expressed in words or diagrams or some other form of expression so as to influence the world's behavior. We learn so as to do. Thought aims at knowledge, but with the final aim of using the knowledge to guide action.

Intelligent behavior, it is said, consists of three factors: (1) being sensitive to one's environment, (2) action or making movements, and (3) connecting with each of the different situations by certain particular actions. We might say then that the function of mental life was to be impressed by the environment and to associate suitable actions with all our impressions. The work of education is to make those impressions from the environment, our resulting actions and the connections between them capable not only of suiting the actual world, but also of helping transform the imperfect world into some better world of the future. At least that should be, some argue, the aim of education.

That mental life in general serves to adapt conduct to environment in useful ways does not imply that in each and every case it does so. Feet are useful in general but they sometimes trip us up. The blood is useful in general but it serves at times as the medium for disease. So thought, though useful in general, at times leads us into blunders. That we can swallow food implies that we can also swallow poison, and that we can think wisely implies also that we can make mistakes. Moreover, just as the evolution of the body does not keep pace with the changes in the environment and manifests useless organs, so also the mind shows useless sensations such as those coming from tickling, useless emotions such as hysterical fear or joy.

22. The author of this passage apparently believes that mental life is
    - (A) impervious to emotions
    - (B) merely a means to knowledge
    - (C) primarily caused by behavior
    - (D) highly correlated with action
    - (E) typically associated with digestion and circulation

23. The reference to "acid and metal" line 39 is used in the passage to illustrate that
    (A) physiology is destiny
    (B) form follows function
    (C) intelligent thought can predict chemical reactions
    (D) hydrogen and salt are formed by chemical processes
    (E) animate life reacts differently from inanimate life

24. The reference to "intelligent behavior" in line 67 connotes all of the following *except* the
    (A) modification of demeanor
    (B) association of cause and effect
    (C) transformation of action through cognition
    (D) eradication of emotions
    (E) cognizance of external circumstances

25. The author would most likely agree that education
    (A) should strive to improve the world
    (B) could inhibit bodily movements or brain changes
    (C) could furnish students with tendencies to act
    (D) should strengthen the emotional capacities
    (E) should adapt circumstances to suit behavior

26. The word "manifests" in line 94 most nearly means
    (A) rejects
    (B) replicates
    (C) exhibits
    (D) misconstrues
    (E) vouchsafes

27. According to the passage, the most important function of mental life is to
    (A) counteract emotional influences
    (B) regulate physiological processes
    (C) provide the ability to reason
    (D) transform the imperfect world
    (E) adjust action to environment

28. In paragraphs five and seven, the author is wary of emotional impressions because they
    (A) demonstrate the futility of love and envy
    (B) produce worthless and ineffective sensations
    (C) impede our sense of social responsibility
    (D) are profitless until expressed in words or diagrams
    (E) disrupt the processes of mental life

29. Which of the following statements can be inferred from the passage?
    (A) Evolution deals primarily with cognition.
    (B) Thought changes reality.
    (C) The mind mirrors an imperfect world.
    (D) Conduct functions as a means to knowledge.
    (E) Knowledge consists of an end in itself.

30. Which of the following best describes the author's tone in the passage?
    (A) recalcitrant
    (B) obstreperous
    (C) equivocal
    (D) fallacious
    (E) erudite

Quick Answer Guide

Test 2, Section 4: Verbal

1. E
2. D
3. B
4. D
5. C
6. E
7. B
8. E
9. A
10. C
11. E
12. E
13. A
14. E
15. B
16. C
17. D
18. D
19. C
20. E
21. A
22. D
23. E
24. D
25. A
26. C
27. E
28. B
29. B
30. E

For explanations to these questions, see Day 26.

Day 26

Test 2, Section 4: Verbal

Explanations and Strategies

Assignment for Today:

Review the explanations for the test you just took.

1. Correct choice (E) inconvenient

You are looking for a word that describes what it is like to carry garbage. If you substitute *inconvenient* (which means causing trouble or annoyance) into the sentence, you can see that it makes sense. It's certainly *inconvenient* to carry garbage around, and that's why people often dump it in the wrong places.

There is something in the American mindset that doesn't see something wrong with disposing of garbage, or anything else *inconvenient* to carry, in a beautiful forest or along a scenic highway.

2. Correct choice (D) predictable..unruly

Notice the flag word "but" in this sentence. It tells you that the first part of the sentence will be opposite in meaning to the second part. Another clue here is that the second word is paired with (and should be similar in tone to) the word "bizarre," which means odd or eccentric.

The correct choice has both the opposite meanings (*predictable* means dependable, and *unruly* means difficult to manage) and a similarity of meaning and tone (*unruly* is similar in meaning and tone to the word "bizarre").

Most chemists believe that the course of a chemical reaction is *predictable*, but some catalytic reactions in both inorganic and organic chemistry can behave in bizarre and *unruly* ways.

3. Correct choice (B) inured to..rudimentary

This sentence describes a man who lived in the desert for eight years. He eventually learns to survive in good form. These clues should help you find the right choices to fill the blanks. The first blank should describe how he adapted to his years in the desert. *Inured*, which means "habituated" (got used to), is good. The second blank should mean something like "minimal." How could you expect life in the desert to be anything else? *Rudimentary* does the trick.

After exploring the desert south of Tucson for eight years, Rimal became *inured to* the hardships of desert life and learned to subsist with the most *rudimentary* requirements for life.

4. Correct choice (D) spate..reverse

The best way to solve this problem is to read in the choices and eliminate those that don't make sense. Because of the flag word "but," you should expect that lots of angry phone calls came in and the executive changed her mind. Only (D) follows this line of reasoning. *Spate* means flood or deluge.

The TV executive canceled the popular soap opera last fall, but the *spate* of angry phone calls and letters convinced her to *reverse* her decision.

5. Correct choice (C) assault..blighted

You can't anticipate. But there's a subtle flag. " . . . transmuting what once was a pristine environment into a —— landscape . . ." So, the second blank should be the opposite of pristine. *Pristine* means "unspoiled or pure." (A), (B) and (D) can be eliminated. *Blighted* and *ravaged* are possible opposites.

Check (C) and (E) in the first blank. Both fit, but (C) makes more sense. You need an *assault* to *blight* (rapidly destroy) a pristine environment. *Operation* is too neutral to fit the imagery in the sentence.

The oil industry's *assault* on the western Siberian plain is transmuting what once was a pristine environment into a *blighted* landscape of almost unimaginable proportions.

6. Correct choice (E) outdated..incompetent

By reading the sentence, you should get a feel for the missing words. Dr. Shilling is upset about something, so it must be bad. So the first word must be a negative one. Because the sentences are connected by "furthermore," you should also look for a negative connotation in the second part of the sentence. In this instance, the second blank itself will be negative. The only choice that has two negative words is (E).

Dr. Shilling was upset that the computer center was *outdated*; furthermore, she felt that the computer support staff was *incompetent*.

7. Correct choice (B) contemporaries

The correct choice here is not likely to jump out at you. The best strategy may be to try each choice, eliminating those that don't make sense and then comparing the logic of the remaining choices. But the semicolon (;) lets you know that what comes after the semicolon *continues* the idea preceding it. Choices (C), (D), and (E) don't make sense. (A) and (B) both make sense, but (B) is more logical in the context of this sentence.

The irrevocable fact about twins and triplets is that their brothers and sisters will always be their *contemporaries*; they can't ever quite leave them.

8. Correct choice (E) patriot..mishandled

"Because" is the flag word that tells you to look for a cause-and-effect relationship between the two parts of the sentence. The first part should present Mann's motivation for bristling at the politicians. (By the way, *consummate* means "complete or thorough.") In reading through the choices, (E) should stand out clearly as the best. *Patriot* is in keeping with the main idea of the sentence: politics. And if Mann were indeed a patriot, he would understandably be upset with politicians who *mishandled* things.

Because Mann was a consummate *patriot*, he often bristled at the way politicians *mishandled* the affairs of the day.

9. Correct choice (A) loquacious

Loquacious is the best choice here because it means talkative. This describes the boy quite well—someone who talks and talks. It also does a pretty good job of describing what many politicians do.

When the young boy wouldn't stop talking, his teacher decided he would make a good politician because he was so *loquacious*.

10. Correct choice (C) bloom:spring

pulse—a regular throbbing caused by the contractions of the heart

life—the period from birth to death

A *pulse* is a sign of *life*.

Is a *bloom* a sign of *spring?* Yes, trees and flowers bloom in the spring.

11. Correct choice (E) comatose:consciousness

bankrupt—lacking resources of value; lacking something

assets—valuable business or personal resources

Bankrupt is the condition of having lost all *assets*.

Is *comatose* the condition of having lost all *consciousness?* Yes. Therefore, *bankrupt* is to *assets* as *comatose* is to *consciousness*.

12. Correct choice (E) baker:bread

vintner—someone who makes wine

wine—alcoholic beverage made from grapes

A *vintner* is someone who makes *wine.*

Does a *baker* make *bread?* Yes! Therefore, *vintner* is to *wine* as *baker* is to *bread.*

13. Correct choice (A) turbid:cloudy

raucous—harsh, grating, strident

strident—having a harsh or grating sound

Raucous means the same as *strident.*

Does *turbid* mean the same as *cloudy?* Yes. So *raucous* is to *strident* as *turbid* is to *cloudy.*

14. Correct choice (E) pastor:parish

sylvan—one who frequents groves or woods

woods—a forest or thicket of trees

A *sylvan* spends time in the *woods.*

Does a *parson* spend time in a *parish?* Yes. A *parson* is a clergyman, and a *parish* is a church community.

15. Correct choice (B) painful:agonizing

pulchritudinous—beautiful, pleasing to the senses

redoubtable—inspiring awe or reverence

Pulchritudinous describes something that can be extremely *redoubtable.*

Does *agonizing* describe something that can be extremely *painful?* Yes. Thus, *painful* is to *agonizing* in the same way that *pulchritudinous* is to *redoubtable.*

16. Correct choice (C)

The author's main point is to identify the single characteristic that is common to all great works of literature. This characteristic, according to the passage, is a work's ability to capture life in such a way that readers will identify the description (or the expression) as real or accurate. In other words, the work will resonate with something deep inside the reader's being. You may not agree with the view of great literature, but that's what the author advocates here.

17. Correct choice (D)

Although we mostly use the word *vital* today to mean "very important," another meaning of the word is "life giving." This is the meaning the author uses here. The *vital* in literature, then, will be that element that makes stories or plays or poems come alive in the readers' minds.

18. Correct choice (D)

The passage gives at least two clues that the author is using the words "creation" and "originality" as synonyms. At the end of paragraph one, the author states that the vital in literature is creation. At the beginning of paragraph two, the author says that originality is the vital in literature. Later, in paragraph two, the author further establishes these terms as synonyms by defining originality as creation.

19. Correct choice (C)

The author uses both an example about a servant and one about a child to argue that those with limited imaginations will form very strong impressions; in other words, the "type" becomes "powerful." It's not clear why—and seems unfair that—the author would characterize servants as people with limited powers of imagination.

20. Correct choice (E)

The author would agree with all the statements except (E)—that not all human beings have a moment of symbolic understanding. One of the surprising things about this passage is that it claims that each human being will indeed have at least one moment of symbolic understanding in his or her lifetime.

21. Correct choice (A)

The point the author is making at the end of the passage is that people have different levels of symbolic understanding. Some have a lot; some have very little. The fleeting moonbeam describes those with very little, while the long tropical sunset describes those with greater ability for symbolic understanding.

22. Correct choice (D)

This passage is about the influence of mental states on our behavior in the world. The very first sentence tells us that the function of thoughts and feelings is to influence actions. Clearly then, the author believes that mental states are highly correlated with action.

23. Correct choice (E)

Unlike humans and animals, acid and metal are inanimate materials that have no conscious life. Also unlike humans and animals, the reactions of acid and metal are unchangeable, uniform and predictable. The passage tells us that acid and metal "always react by forming hydrogen and salt." Animate life, however, can "adapt behavior" to suit changing circumstances and conditions.

24. Correct choice (D)

This passage discusses how our thoughts *and* our feelings guide our behavior. The very first sentence states that "the function of thoughts and feelings . . . is to influence actions." To *eradicate* means "to remove or abolish." The author of this passage sees emotions as an essential part of "conscious life," not as something to be eliminated or destroyed. Clearly then, the author would not include *the eradication of emotions* as a part of intelligent behavior.

25. Correct choice (A)

The overall purpose of this passage is to explain the connection between thought and behavior. In paragraph five, the author tells us that the aim of education should be not simply to enhance our understanding of the connection between our actions and the world, but also to help "transform the imperfect world into some better world of the future."

26. Correct choice (C)

The verb *manifest* means "to exhibit or show." If you don't know what "to manifest" means, you could probably deduce it from the context. In the sentence, the phrase *manifests useless organs* is used to illustrate the previous clause, which states that "the body does not keep pace with changes in the environment." What concept would bridge the two clauses together? The concept of "exhibiting" useless organs is a good choice.

27. Correct answer (E)

This passage deals with the relationship between our thoughts and behavior *and* how our behavior affects the external world. Throughout the passage, the author repeatedly tells us that the most important role of mental life is to adapt our behavior to suit the circumstances. For example, lines 57-61 tell us that "it would be of little advantage to have sensations of cold or knowledge of the physiological effects of low temperature if one never was moved thereby to put on a coat or build a fire." In other words, mental life guides us to adjust our actions to suit the environment.

28. Correct choice (B)

Although the passage discusses how emotions play a central role in mental life, the author also appears cautious about how emotions can sometimes cause "useless sensations such as hysterical fear or joy."

29. Correct choice (B)

This passage deals both with the relationship between our thoughts and behavior *and* how our behavior affects the external world. In other words, the passage suggests that "thought changes reality." In the first paragraph, for example, the author discusses how mental states "alter the physical world." Similarly, at the end of paragraph five the author tells us that reasoning is profitless unless it "influences the world's behavior."

30. Correct choice (E)

The passage is educational: It describes, explains, and evaluates the relationship between thought and behavior. To be erudite is to be scholarly or learned. Among the five choices provided, then, the author's tone would be best described as erudite.

Test 2, Section 5: Math and Section 6: Verbal

Questions and Answers

Assignment for Today:

Take a sample SAT Math Test and a sample SAT Verbal Test under actual test conditions. Allow yourself only 15 minutes to complete the 10-question Math Test. Then allow yourself another 15 minutes to complete the 13-question Verbal Test.

SECTION 5: MATH

Directions: *Solve each problem, and circle the letter of the appropriate answer choice, A–E.*

1. A classroom has 72 computers and 96 students. If each computer can be used by only 1 student, what percent of the students do not get to use a computer?
   (A) 24
   (B) 25
   (C) 33
   (D) 67
   (E) 75

2. The sum of the two sides of a rectangle is 18 and one side is 25 percent longer than the other side. What is the length of the *shorter* side of the rectangle?
   (A) 7.2
   (B) 8
   (C) 10
   (D) 10.28
   (E) 14.5

3. A farmer wants to harvest 250 acres of land. He harvests 20 percent of the land one day and 80 percent of the remaining unharvested land over the next two days. What is the average (arithmetic mean) acres of land harvested per day?
   (A) 50
   (B) 70
   (C) 80
   (D) $83\frac{1}{3}$
   (E) $123\frac{1}{3}$

4. In the number line shown below, the tick marks are equally spaced. What is the ratio of P to Q?

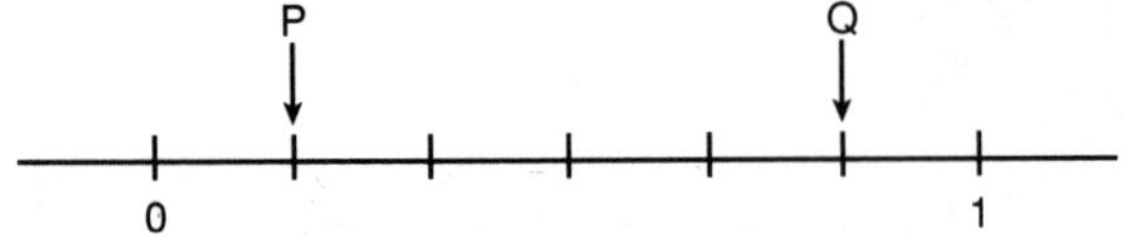

(A) $\frac{1}{9}$

(B) $\frac{5}{36}$

(C) $\frac{1}{5}$

(D) $\frac{1}{4}$

(E) 5

5. Which of the following must be true?

I. $-(8 - 3) = 8 + 3$
II. $(10 \times 3 + 10 \times 5) = 10(3 + 5)$
III. $(10 \times 5 - 10 \times 3) = 10(5 - 3)$

(A) I only
(B) II only
(C) III only
(D) II and III
(E) I, II, and III

6. Four out of every 7 apples in a basket are rotten. If it is known that 28 apples in the basket are rotten, the number of rotten apples is how many more than the number of apples that are not rotten?

(A) 4
(B) 7
(C) 12
(D) 16
(E) 21

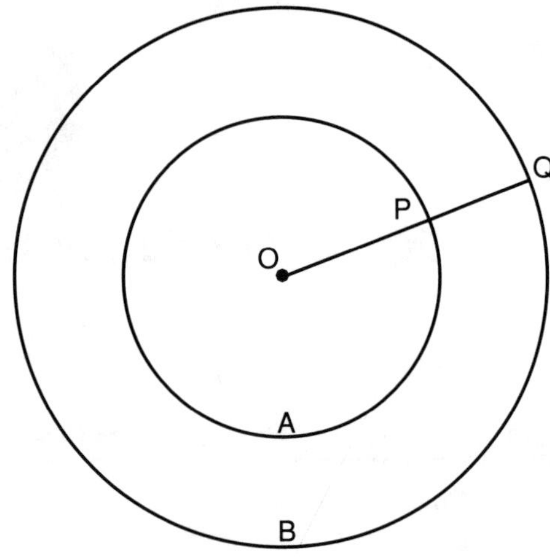

7. Circles A and B are concentric. If the area of circle A is 16π and the area of circle B is 36π, what is the distance from P to Q?

(A) $\sqrt{2}$
(B) 2
(C) 6
(D) 10
(E) 20

8. Let the operation $\lozenge$ be defined by the equation $m \lozenge n = mn + \frac{m}{n}$. If $8 \lozenge 2 = s$, then $s =$

(A) 10
(B) 14
(C) 16
(D) 20
(E) 48

9. If $15t - 6u = 12$, then $5t - 2u =$

(A) 0
(B) $\frac{4}{5}$
(C) 4
(D) 36
(E) It cannot be determined

10. A bag contains 240 gloves and 210 balls. All 450 objects are either yellow or red. If 30 percent of the objects are yellow and 60 percent of the balls are red, how many red gloves are there?
    (A) 126
    (B) 168
    (C) 189
    (D) 240
    (E) 270

SECTION 6: VERBAL

Directions: *Read the two passages below. Then answer questions 1–13, basing your answers only on what is stated or implied in the passages and any introductory material given.*

Passage 1

The Sundar School is devoted to instruction and research in the mathematical, physical, and natural sciences, with reference to the promotion and diffusion of science, and also to the preparation of young men for such pursuits as require special proficiency in English, History, Anthropology, Economics, and Political Science.

The Sundar School is one of the departments of the University, like the Law, Medical, Theological, and Art Schools, having its separate funds, buildings, teachers, and regulations, but governed by the corporation of Radnick University, which appoints the professors and confers the degrees. It is, in part, analogous to the academic department or college and, in part, to the professional schools.

Instruction is intended for two classes of students: (1) graduates of this and other universities or colleges, and other persons qualified for advanced or special scientific study, and (2) undergraduates who desire a training, chiefly mathematical and scientific, in less part linguistic and literary, for higher scientific studies, or for various other occupations to which such training is suited.

The school was started in 1847. In 1860, a convenient building and a considerable endowment were given by Lawrence O. Sundar, whose name, at the repeated request of the corporation of Radnick University, was subsequently attached to the foundation. Mr. Sundar afterwards frequently and munificently increased his original gifts.

In 1863, by an act of the state legislature, the national grant for the promotion of scientific education (under the congressional enactment of July 1862) was given to this department of Radnick University, which thus became the College of Agriculture and the Mechanic Arts. By an act of the state legislature in 1892, this was revoked and the special relations of the school to the state were terminated.

In addition to the bequests made by Mr. Sundar, numerous liberal gifts have been received for the endowment of the school and the increase of its buildings and collections, by which the facilities of the institution have been greatly enlarged. Special mention is made of some of these gifts in the descriptions of buildings, apparatus, collections, scholarships, and prizes.

Students who have completed undergraduate courses of study, here or elsewhere, also may avail themselves of the facilities of the school for more special professional training in the natural and physical sciences and their applications and, unlike the previous mentioned classes of students, may continue their purposeful study apart from either of the school's degree-granting programs.

Passage 2

In 1862, Congress donated to the several states large bodies of the public land for the endowment of colleges, giving special prominence to instruction in agriculture and mechanic arts. In 1872, this grant was accepted by the General Assembly, and the Agricultural and Mechanical College was opened to students in the fall of the same year. Congress followed up in subsequent years with other acts of almost equal importance. This was the initial legislation in the field of agricultural and industrial education. In 1890 and

1907, Congress gave to each state additional appropriations for the better support of its land grant college, or colleges. By act of the state legislature, the College was allowed two-thirds of these several appropriations.

In 1887, Congress gave to each state an annual grant for the establishment and support of an Agricultural Experiment Station, and in 1906 increased the amount of this grant. In the same year the State gave the Station a small annual appropriation. In 1888, the General Assembly made the Station a department of the College.

In 1914, the General Assembly transferred to the College the work which had been conducted by the United Agricultural Board. In May 1914, Congress passed what is commonly designated as the Smith–Lever Act, giving appropriations from the Federal Treasury, through the land grant colleges, for demonstration and extension work.

The original act of Congress (1862) providing for the creation and maintenance of a college of this type in each state sets forth the purpose of this gift as being for the "endowment, support, and maintenance of at least one college, where the leading object shall be, without excluding other scientific and classical studies, and including military tactics, to teach such branches of learning as are related to agriculture and the mechanic arts, in such manner as the legislatures of the states may respectively prescribe, in order to promote the liberal and practical education of the industrial classes in the several pursuits and professions in life."

The College is located in one of the most beautiful sections of the country, on the summit of the Allegheny Mountains, some 2,100 feet above sea level. The summers are mild, and the winters are by no means severe.

The buildings are mostly of brick. The halls and lecture rooms are large and well lighted. The grounds contain about one hundred acres, and are well set and landscaped. The walks, drives, and quadrangles are exceedingly attractive.

1. The main purpose of passage 1 is to
   - (A) promote the Sundar School to potential applicants
   - (B) praise the distribution of private and government funds for education
   - (C) explain the origins and purposes of the Sundar School
   - (D) outline the curricular development of the Sundar School
   - (E) demonstrate how government is best left out of the education process

2. According to passage 1, the Sundar School is designed to
   - (A) replace the outdated Radnick University
   - (B) prepare students for professional schools
   - (C) research issues in the social sciences
   - (D) appoint professors and confer degrees
   - (E) teach certain areas of hard science

3. According to passage 1, the Sundar School is designed to instruct
   - (A) undergraduates who seek special training of all types
   - (B) only graduates who have special proficiency in another area
   - (C) both undergraduates and graduates with interests in the Sundar philosophy of learning
   - (D) graduates and undergraduates in the hard sciences
   - (E) students equally in literary and scientific fields

4. The author of passage 1 uses the word "munificently" in line 32 to mean
   - (A) generously
   - (B) monetarily
   - (C) regularly
   - (D) freely
   - (E) sporadically

5. According to passage 1, the state legislature in 1892
   (A) rescinded an earlier legislative act
   (B) voted to change the name of the school
   (C) formed a new department of Radnick University
   (D) required all donors to pay income tax on charitable donations
   (E) withdrew its tacit support of the Sundar School but continued financial support

6. The primary purpose of passage 2 is to
   (A) discuss the formation of the college via government legislation
   (B) demonstrate the government's commitment to higher education
   (C) critique the lack of funding for land grant colleges
   (D) explain the intricacies of the Smith–Lever Act
   (E) describe the grounds and buildings of the college

7. The "Station," referred to in line 80 of passage 2,
   (A) was clearly more technologically advanced than the College
   (B) formed the foundation for the Agricultural and Mechanical College
   (C) originated as a result of a congressional grant
   (D) performed experiments in agricultural engineering to increase farm productivity levels
   (E) made it possible for the government to give the college additional appropriations

8. Passage 2 implies that the congressional appropriations of 1890 and 1907
   (A) were of greater importance than the 1862 land grant
   (B) were almost as important as the 1872 acceptance by the General Assembly
   (C) provided the College with two-thirds of its operating expenses
   (D) were divided unequally between the College and some other institution in the state
   (E) served to build brick buildings with well-lighted rooms

9. The phrase "extension work" in line 89 most likely means
   (A) work done in a longer period of time
   (B) work performed away from headquarters
   (C) work paid for by private companies
   (D) work that ranges beyond the norm
   (E) work given to graduate students for tuition waivers

10. The last two paragraphs in Passage 2 are notable because they
   (A) drastically differ from the tone and focus of the rest of the passage
   (B) represent the end result of government involvement in the land grant colleges
   (C) provide the reader with a description of the College
   (D) describe a setting much like any other college campus around the country
   (E) are written in iambic pentameter

11. One difference between the Sundar School in passage 1 and the College in passage 2 is that one institution
   (A) received government funding, while the other did not
   (B) focuses on science, while the other focuses on agriculture
   (C) began in the eighteenth century, while the other institution began in the nineteenth century
   (D) offers degrees, while the other institution does not
   (E) received state support, while the other did not

12. When compared to passage 2, passage 1 focuses more on the
    (A) requirements for graduation from the institution
    (B) role of government land grants in founding the institution
    (C) types of students who study at the institution
    (D) effects of the Smith–Lever Act
    (E) employment opportunities for graduates from the institution

13. Which of the following statements is *not* true for either passage?
    (A) A government research institution was merged into an institution of higher learning.
    (B) Government funding brought about a name change.
    (C) A private donor requested that his name be attached to the institution.
    (D) The government took away institutional funding at some point.
    (E) The institution was designed to teach the industrial classes.

Quick Answer Guide

Test 2, Section 5: Math

1. B
2. B
3. B
4. C
5. D
6. B
7. B
8. D
9. C
10. C

Test 2, Section 6: Verbal

1. C
2. E
3. D
4. A
5. A
6. A
7. C
8. D
9. B
10. A
11. B
12. C
13. C

For explanations to these questions, see Day 28.

Day 28

Test 2, Section 5: Math and Section 6: Verbal

Explanations and Strategies

Assignment for Today:

Review the explanations for the Math and Verbal Tests you just took.

SECTION 5: MATH

1. Correct choice (B) 25

Since there are only 72 computers, the number of students who don't get to use a computer = 96 – 72 = 24.

We are asked to find the percentage of students not using a computer. In other words, we need to find what percent is 24 out of 96. So, percent = $\frac{24}{96} \times 10 = 25$.

2. Correct choice (B) 8

Let's plug in answer choices. As usual, we start from answer choice (C). We want to find the length of the shorter side, so we'll plug in 10 as the length of the shorter side.

If 10 is the length of the shorter side, the length of the longer side should be 25% more than 10. Well, 25% of 10 is 2.5, and so the longer side must be 10 + 2.5 = 12.5. We know that the length of the two sides must be 18. Does 10 and 12.5 give us 18? No, they give us a sum of 22.5. This tells us that the value of 10 we plugged in is too high. So, if choice (C) is too high, choices (D) and (E) are also too high. At this point, we can zap choices (C), (D), and (E).

Let's try choice (B), 8. If 8 is the length of the shorter side, the length of the longer side is 25% more than 8, which is 2 + 8 = 10 (because 25%, or a quarter, of 8 is 2). So, one side is 8 and the other is 10. And their sum is 8 + 10 = 18. This choice works; and so the right answer is choice (B).

3. Correct choice (B) 70

Before working this problem, let's scan our choices. We know that the farmer harvested 3 days. So, if he harvests $83\frac{1}{3}$ acres per day, which is choice (D), over 3 days he will have harvested $83\frac{1}{3} \times 3 = 250$ acres. This is not possible because we know that all the land was *not* harvested. So, zap choice (D).

If choice (D) is too high, so is choice (E). Zap it, also.

We know that he harvested 20% the first day. So, land harvested on the first day is $.2 \times 250 = 50$ acres. Then, land remaining to be harvested is 250 – 50 = 200 acres. Over the next two days, he harvested 80% of this land, which is $.8 \times 200 = 160$ acres. So, the total acres harvested over 3 days is 50 + 160 = 210. Then, the average is 210/3 = 70, which is choice (B).

4. Correct choice (C) $\frac{1}{5}$

The trick here is to see that there are 6 divisions separating 0 from 1, which means each tick mark is worth $\frac{1}{6}$. We see that point P is on the first tick mark, which means its value is $\frac{1}{6}$. And, point Q is on the fifth tick mark, which means its value is $\frac{5}{6}$.

Now we need to find the ratio: $\frac{P}{Q}$. If we substitute the values of P and Q, we'll get the answer.

$$\frac{P}{Q} = \frac{\frac{1}{6}}{\frac{5}{6}}$$

Don't let the double fraction scare you. It just means one fraction is divided by the other.

In other words, think of "P over Q" as "P divided by Q."

Then, we can write $\frac{P}{Q} = P \div Q = \frac{1}{6} \div \frac{5}{6}$

To divide two fractions, we keep the first one as it is, flip the second one, and multiply. So,

$$\frac{P}{Q} = \frac{1}{6} \times \frac{6}{5}$$

The 6s cancel and we're left with:

$$\frac{P}{Q} = \frac{1}{5}$$

5. Correct choice (D) II and III only

Let's work each option to see which one is true.

Option I:

Left side: $-(8-3) = -(5) = -5$

Right side: $8 + 3 = 11$

So, option I is *not* true. Let's cross out all answer choices that have numeral I. We can zap choices (A) and (E) and we're left with choices (B), (C), and (D).

Option II:

Left side: $(10 \times 3 + 10 \times 5) = (30 + 50) = 80$

Right side: $10(3 + 5) = 10(8) = 80$

This option is true. So, the right answer has to have option II in it. Of the three choices we have left, we can knock out choice (C), which means we're left with choices (B) and (D).

Option III:

Left side: $(10 \times 5 - 10 \times 3) = (50 - 30) = 20$

Right side: $10(5 - 3) = 10(2) = 20$

This is also true. So, the right answer has to have a III in it. Between choices (B) and (D), only choice (D) has III in it and so it's the right answer.

6. Correct choice (B) 7

We know that 4 out of 7 apples are rotten. We also know that there are 28 rotten apples. This tells us that $\frac{4}{7}$ = 28. This should tell us how many apples there are, total, in the basket. Well, if $\frac{4}{7}$ is 28 then $\frac{4}{7}$ must be 28 ÷ 4, which is 7. Again, if $\frac{1}{7}$ is 7, the total number of apples in the basket is 7 times 7, which is 49.

If $\frac{4}{7}$ apples are rotten, $\frac{3}{7}$ are "not rotten." That is, $\frac{3}{7}$ of 49 are not rotten. So, the number of apples that are not rotten is $\frac{3}{7} \times 49$, which is 21.

We now know that 28 are rotten and 21 are not. So, there must be 28 – 21 = 7 more apples that are rotten than "not rotten."

7. Correct choice (B) 2

Notice that the distance from P to Q is actually the difference in the radii of circle B and circle A. So, if we can find the radius of each circle, we can find the difference.

The equation for the area of a circle is $A = \pi r^2$. For circle A,

$\pi r^2 = 16\pi$

$r = \sqrt{16}$

$r = 4$

So, the radius of circle A is 4.

For circle B,

$\pi r^2 = 36\pi$

$r = \sqrt{36}$

$r = 6$

So, the radius of circle B is 6.

Then, the difference between the two radii = $6 - 4 = 2$, which is the distance from P to Q.

8. Correct choice (D) 20

To apply the operation ◊, we simply follow the pattern described in the operator's definition.

$$m \lozenge n = mn + \frac{m}{n}$$

$$8 \lozenge 2 = 8 \times 2 + \frac{8}{2} = 16 + 4 = 20$$

9. Correct choice (C) 4

This is a tricky problem. It's tempting to say this problem can't be solved because there are two unknowns, *t* and *u*, and only one equation. But, look closely at the coefficients of *t* and *u* (that is, the numbers that go with *t* and *u*) in both equations. If you don't see what's going on, write the second equation directly below the first:

$$\begin{aligned} 15t - 6u &= 12 \\ 5t - 2u &= \end{aligned}$$

You probably noticed that the first equation is 3 times the second. That is, $15t$ in the first equation is 3 times $5t$ in the second equation and $-6u$ in the first equation is 3 times $-2u$ in the second equation. Then, what do you think is the answer?

In other words, what is $\frac{1}{3}$ of 12? Choice (C) 4 is the correct answer because 3 times 4 will give us 12.

10. Correct choice (C) 189

Before we work this problem, we can automatically zap choices (D) and (E) because they don't make sense. There are only 240 gloves. So, choice (E) is ridiculous and choice (D) is not possible because if all 240 gloves were red, there would be no red balls.

We're told that 30% of the objects are yellow. There are 450 objects. So, the number of yellow objects = .30 × 450 = 135.

Then, the number of red objects = 450 − 135 = 315.

We know that 60% of the balls are red. Total number of balls is 210. Then, the number of red balls = .60 × 210 = 126.

We found that the total number of red objects = 315. Then, if 126 of them are red balls, the number of red gloves = 315 − 126 = 189 (because red gloves + red balls must equal total red objects). So, the correct answer is choice (C).

SECTION 6: VERBAL

1. Correct choice (C)

Passage 1 explains the Sundar School's purpose, including its origins. The first three paragraphs and the last paragraph describe who typically attends the school and what programs are offered. The middle section, quite frankly, goes off track, discussing where all the money came from for the school. The author probably saw these two issues—origins and purposes—as closely related ideas.

2. Correct choice (E)

The first sentence of passage 1 makes it clear that the purpose of the Sundar School is all about teaching and researching mathematics, physical sciences, and natural sciences—in other words, the hard sciences.

3. Correct choice (D)

Finding the right answer to this question should be fairly easy. The school concentrates on teaching the hard sciences (lines 1-3); its students include both graduates and undergraduates as stated in lines 17-25. So choice (D) is clearly the best answer.

4. Correct choice (A)

"Munificent" means lavishly generous. In other words, Mr. Sundar dumped a ton of money on this school.

5. Correct choice (A)

Passage 1 states explicitly that in 1892 the legislature overturned the 1863 decision to give a grant to what was first known as the Sundar School and then became the College of Agriculture and the Mechanic Arts.

6. Correct choice (A)

Passage 2 is primarily concerned with how the government provided the land and money to begin the Agricultural and Mechanic College. Most of passage 2 discusses various grants and money given away.

7. Correct choice (C)

The third paragraph makes it clear that a congressional grant in 1887 funded the Agricultural Experiment Station. One year later, this Station became a part of the college.

8. Correct choice (D)

This answer is tricky. The passage says the college got two-thirds of these government appropriations. That means another third—an unequal amount—went to another institution in the state.

9. Correct choice (B)

Although it's not exactly clear what the author means by "extension work," the most likely answer is work performed away from headquarters. In other words, the government had specific projects it wanted done; it would farm these projects out to the various land grant schools around the country.

10. Correct choice (A)

The last two paragraphs differ drastically from the rest of the passage. The author spends several paragraphs explaining congressional funding and grants and then, all of a sudden, starts describing what the college looks like. Frankly, these last two paragraphs don't fit.

11. Correct choice (B)

It should be clear if you read both passages that the Sundar School focused its courses on the hard sciences, while the college in passage 2 was concerned with agriculture.

12. Correct choice (C)

Passage 1 specifies that the school is for both graduates and undergraduates, and gives areas of study. Passage 2 makes no such specification. In fact, passage 2 doesn't mention students at all.

13. Correct choice (C)

Neither passage states that a private donor wanted his name to be attached to the institution. Passage 1 says, in contrast, that Mr. Sundar's name was attached at the request of the university, not at Sundar's own request.

Day 29

Final Review

Assignment for Today:

Review strategies in Days 1–8. Look over the sample tests and explanations.

If you have followed this 30-Day Program, you should be in great shape to take the SAT. By now you have taken two complete tests—12 sections in all—and you have gone over all the questions and explanations. Remember, doing well on the SAT requires not only good verbal and math skills but also "test smarts."

In this book you have been introduced to lots of strategies and shortcuts designed to save you time and make you test smart. We recommend that you use whatever time you have left before your test to go back and review the test-taking, verbal, and math strategies. Then you should look over the sample tests and the explanations and make sure you understand how to tackle each question type.

Day 30

Last-Minute Preparations

Assignment for Today:

Learn what to take to the test and what to leave home. Pick up a few suggestions on sleeping, eating, and thinking positive thoughts.

Okay. You've reviewed the strategies. You've done practice problems. You've worked some, if not all, of the practice tests. You've analyzed your answers. The SAT is a few days away.

Now what?

There *are* some things you can still do, apart from studying math facts or verbal strategies, that can help you do better on the SAT. And they are easy to do.

Get Your Materials Ready

Certain items are permitted at the test center, and certain items are prohibited. What should you bring?

These Are the "Musts":

Pencils

Although the test site will probably provide pencils, bring your own. Make sure they're "number 2," sharpened, with good, clean erasers. A half-dozen should be enough, in case you break a few points, or have to lend one to a friend who forgot to bring any.

Identification

Any standard ID with your name and photograph will do, as long as the photo is fairly recent and looks like you. For example, a driver's license, a student ID, or a passport will do. You *must* have such an ID to get into the test center. If not, you'll be faced with the dilemma of trying to prove you are who you are, which is not something you want to worry about on the day of the SAT.

A watch

You'll probably have a clock in the testing room, but your desk may be in the back or off to the side, and so the room clock could be hard to read. Instead, bring your own watch—a digital is best—so that you can set it for 30 minutes and so that everything you need—test booklet, answer sheet, pencils, and watch—are within the confines of your desk. If you have a watch that beeps, turn the sound off, since proctors will confiscate any watches that cause a disturbance.

A calculator

The SAT allows the use of a calculator. Bring one you're comfortable with, and make sure it has new batteries. You may use it only occasionally, or not at all, but since it's allowed, bring one if you think you might use it. (See also our tips on using a calculator.)

Sweater or jacket

One of the most common complaints about test sites is that the room is either too hot or too cold. It may be 95 degrees and sweltering outside, and yet your test room could be air-conditioned to a brisk 62 degrees. Or on the coldest day of the year, the custodian may have pumped the heat up to a sweat-inducing 82 degrees. What can you do?

You can come prepared for the worst. Dress in "layers." That way if the room becomes too hot, you can—at a break between sections—quickly take off your sweater, or long-sleeved shirt, and work in a short-sleeved tee-shirt. If it's too cold, you can put on the extra sweater and/or jacket that you've brought with you.

But whatever you wear or bring with you, make sure it's comfortable.

These Are the "Don'ts":

Scratch paper

You are not allowed scratch paper. All scratch work must be done in your test booklet. Paper brought into the test site will be confiscated, so don't bring any.

Books

Any notebooks, notes, textbooks, dictionaries, encyclopedia, almanacs, or other educational aides will either be checked at the door, or you'll be told to place them under your desks. Since you are not permitted to consult them during the test, leave these items home.

Laptops or Powerbooks

While the computer age is upon us, the SAT does not allow computers at the test site. Leave your machine at home!

Highlighter pens

Don't bring any. Highlight by circling with your number 2 pencil.

These Are "Maybes":

Food

The administration of the SAT is supposed to be "standardized." That means that every proctor at every test site is supposed to give the same directions and follow the same rules and procedures. But we all know that in real life, people (even proctors) don't always follow the book. Some proctors may be more or less strict than others. With that in mind, here is one item you may want to consider bringing to your test site: food. Be advised, however, that it could be "confiscated" (held by the proctors until the end of the test) if it is readily apparent. So be discreet, and don't flaunt.

It's a long test. Some students get hungry. Some need a "sugar boost." If you decide to bring a candy bar, juice, or a soft drink, don't take it out to eat or drink during the test. Wait until the break. Even the most strict proctor can't prohibit you from eating during the break.

Cash

You may be taking the SAT at a university, college, or some other site that you're unfamiliar with. Parking may cost anywhere from two quarters to $5 or more. You may have an opportunity to buy a soft drink from a machine situated in the hallway during the test break. Bring some cash (bills *and* coins) with you for just these eventualities.

GET PHYSICALLY AND MENTALLY FIT

Different people have different needs. Some of us need nine hours of sleep to be sharp and clear-headed; others of us need only seven hours of sleep.

At this point in your life, you ought to know what suits you best. If you never eat breakfast, then don't eat on the day of the SAT. If you know you need eight hours of sleep to be sharp the next day, then don't feel compelled to get $9\frac{1}{2}$ hours simply because someone said it's better to get extra sleep the night before a test. Listen to your body. Only you know how *you* respond.

Perhaps what you should remember most for the day of the test is to keep positive. Of course, the SAT won't be easy. But remember you're not expected to be able to answer all the questions. So instead of focusing on what you don't know, think about how much you've learned over the past 30 days and how much better prepared you are now than you were just a month ago.

As you look around the exam room, don't worry about how other students are doing. Keep your focus on your own work, and do the best you can.

Good luck.